unequal under law

unequal under law

RACE

IN THE

WAR

ON

DRUGS

DORIS MARIE PROVINE

THE UNIVERSITY OF CHICAGO PRESS

CHICAGO AND LONDON

Doris Marie Provine is director of the School of Justice and Social Inquiry
of the College of Liberal Arts and Sciences at Arizona State University. She
is the author of *Case Selection in the United States Supreme Court* and
Judging Credentials: Nonlawyer Judges and the Politics of Professionalism.

The University of Chicago Press, Chicago 60637
The University of Chicago Press, Ltd., London
© 2007 by The University of Chicago
All rights reserved. Published 2007
Printed in the United States of America
16 15 14 13 12 11 10 09 08 07 1 2 3 4 5
ISBN-13: 978-0-226-68460-4 (cloth)
ISBN-13: 978-0-226-68462-8 (paper)
ISBN-10: 0-226-68460-1 (cloth)
ISBN-10: 0-226-68462-8 (paper)

Library of Congress Cataloging-in-Publication Data

Provine, Doris Marie.
Unequal under the law : race in the war on drugs / Doris Marie Provine.
p. cm.
Includes bibliographical references and index.
ISBN-13: 978-0-266-68460-4 (cloth : alk. paper)
ISBN-10: 0-266-68460-1 (cloth : alk. paper)
ISBN-13: 978-0-266-68462-8 (pbk. : alk. paper)
ISBN-10: 0-266-68462-8 (pbk. : alk. paper)
1. Race discrimination—Law and legislation—United States.
2. Discrimination in criminal justice administraton—United States.
3. Equality before the law—United States. 4. Drug control—United States.
5. United States—Race relations. I. Title.
KF4755 .P76 2007
345.73'0277—dc22

                                                2007006546

contents

acknowledgements and dedication

Many people have been involved in the creation of this small book, in part because it took such a long time to write! Along the way, I benefited from the insights of people who have been close to the struggle for more equitable and humane U.S. drug policy. I am grateful for the help of Rodney Cahill, Judge Richard Conaboy, Michael Gelacak, Gary Goldberg, Paul Hofer, Keenan Keller, Marc Mauer, Barbara Meirhoefer, Andrea Smith, and Nkechi Taifa.

Generous colleagues who read and commented upon all or portions of this manuscript include: Kitty Calavita, Ellen Cohn, Josefina Figueira-McDonough, Roy Flemming, David Greenberg, Julie Horney, Mary and Peter Katzenstein, Richard Lempert, Lynn Mather, Elizabeth Mertz, Suzanne Mettler, Kristen Monroe, Ruth Peterson, Helen Quan (HQ), Carroll Seron, Rogers Smith, and Marjorie Zatz.

Arizona State University School of Justice & Social Inquiry provided an ideal venue to complete this research, not just because of the encouragement my colleagues offered, but because of their inspiring commitment to the study of justice. They will recognize their influence by some of the arguments I make in this book, and by my frequent citations to their work. Various graduate students were very helpful in digging out obscure sources and making suggestions. I am grateful to Francine Banner, Gregory Broberg, Michael Coyle, Amy Gay, Rosalie Gonzales, and William Parkin.

I also want to thank John Tryneski, Rodney Powell, and two anonymous reviewers for all their help in getting this manuscript to become a book. For John and me, this is our third book. The University of Chicago Press has been a terrific organization with which to be associated during my entire academic career.

❖ ❖ ❖

I owe a very special debt to my sons, Charles and Stuart Provine, and to my husband, Michael Shelton. Charlie was always willing to read a draft, fix a problem with my computer, or help me resolve any difficulty I faced in turning ideas into prose. Without his help, another year might have passed before this book appeared. Stuart offered regular and welcome encouragement every step of the way, as well as many good ideas and suggestions; I am grateful for the unwavering confidence he had in me. Mike's many contributions included ideas, research help, proof reading, and encouragement. He also contributed another essential ingredient: time to work. He has done much more than his share of dishes, errands, and cooking in the interests of getting this book into shape. No one could have asked for a more supportive home team. I am delighted to dedicate this book to these three wonderful men: Charles Provine, Stuart Provine, and Mike Shelton.

introduction

Eighteen-year-old Edward James Clary was up for sentencing in federal court.[1] He had been convicted of possession of crack cocaine with intent to distribute. Clary's demographics were typical of the drug defendants who came through the federal District Court for the Eastern District of Missouri: young, Black, male, of limited education, and without regular employment. His home was the inner city of East St. Louis, which was over 97 percent African American and an economic disaster area in which drug dealing and prostitution were significant sources of income. Clary was younger than some East St. Louis drug defendants—seventeen when he was caught carrying crack cocaine on the plane trip home after visiting his older brother in California. The small packet he carried contained 4 grams of crack, a form of cocaine base derived from powder cocaine, mixed in with 16 grams of an inert substance. The mixture had melted into an unsalable blob by the time of Clary's arrest.

With no previous convictions, Clary might have seemed an unlikely candidate for a long sentence. The public defender described him as "a goofy kid." But neither youth nor inexperience could save him. Federal legislation prescribed mandatory sentences for offenses involving crack cocaine. The law required a ten-year minimum term of imprisonment for anyone caught with 50 or more grams of a material containing cocaine base, whatever its purity. It was February 1994, and Clary was about to become another depressing statistic in the nation's seemingly permanent war on drugs.

The anti-crack initiative that prescribed ten years of imprisonment for young Clary is part of a broader policy of imprisonment that emerged in the 1970s and 1980s. This imprisonment initiative has since expanded and become entrenched in the American polity. In 2005, the United States reached a new high of 2.1 million inmates, with six times as many Americans locked up as thirty years ago (Mauer 2006, 20). Striking racial differences are evident in this movement toward increasing imprisonment. In 2003, nearly 8 percent of all adult African American males in the United States were incarcerated on any given day; for young men in their late twenties, the rate is now over 12 percent. Mauer projects that an African American male born in 2001 has a 32 percent chance of imprisonment at some point in his life, compared to a 17 percent chance for a Hispanic boy and a 6 percent chance for a white boy (2006, 137).

These are remarkable statistics. How did the United States come to rely so heavily on imprisonment, and why has the burden of punishment fallen so heavily on African Americans and, to a lesser extent, on Hispanics? Sociologist Darnell Hawkins describes a "best of times/worst of times" situation for African Americans: "Confronting the nation is the irony and seeming inconsistency of a large and growing racial disparity in the administration of justice amid evidence of black socioeconomic progress and reductions in many of the more blatant forms of interracial conflict that have historically characterized American race and ethnic relations" (2003, 433, 434). For Hawkins, these questions are related to others about the stubborn persistence of racial inequality in educational attainment, labor-force participation, earnings, family structure, home ownership, health, and other aspects of social well-being.

There is no dearth of scholarship and speculation about why racial inequality is proving so durable decades after a major civil rights struggle that has been widely hailed as successful. This book is part of that broad-based quest. The fundamental question is whether the United States has developed a fully functioning democracy, based on equal respect for all members, or whether it remains, in important respects, a racial state where opportunities are hierarchically organized to benefit some groups at the expense of others (Bonilla-Silva 1996; Brown et al. 2003; Smith 1997). More precisely, this book asks whether the law that Congress produced to control one particular crime, abuse of crack cocaine, reflects what Eduardo Bonilla-Silva calls "a racialized social system" in which the racial categories to which people are assigned partially determine their placement in the economic, political, and social order (1996, 469). Beliefs and practices that create racial disadvantage are particularly important with respect to crime and punishment, where the stakes are sometimes literally life and death.

By focusing on a law that has had an undeniable and serious racial impact, it may be possible to understand how race matters. The case of crack cocaine is important not just because African Americans (and, increasingly, Latinos) have been so affected, but because it has engaged all three branches of our legal system, and because it has endured for over two decades despite its racial impact. But in looking at the relationship between race and illicit drugs in historical context, it becomes obvious that this is not so unusual. Racial minorities have always been the target of the harshest drug laws. Those who have actively promoted these laws, the moral entrepreneurs of drug legislation, have relied on racial slurs and allusions to bolster their arguments for criminal controls. The history of the debate over illicit drugs thus provides relevant context and a plausible explanation for the current legislative assault on crack cocaine.

Whether or not one is prepared to believe that law in this post–civil rights era could be designed to incorporate and perpetuate racial oppression, it cannot be denied that race has been relevant in the federal government's war on crack. Since its "discovery" in the 1980s, crack has been associated with African Americans in poor, inner-city neighborhoods. Fear that crack use would spread beyond the ghetto was a key motivator for criminal sanctions (Reeves and Campbell 1994; Gordon 1994; Beckett and Sasson 1998).

The public image of crack as an inner-city drug has been strengthened by the way police and prosecutors have enforced the law. Police resources have been overwhelmingly concentrated on poor minority neighborhoods like East St. Louis, where Clary lived (Mauer 2006, 165; Beckett et al. 2006; Blumstein 1993; Davis 2005; Miller 1996; Tonry 1995; cf. Blakeslee 2005). In most other respects, these neighborhoods remain an isolated "other America" where the expanding economy of the 1990s had virtually no impact.[2] In areas like East St. Louis, recent surveys indicate, over half of the young people drop out of high school and are unable to find legitimate employment. The rate of joblessness among young Black men rose from 65 percent to 72 percent between 2000 and 2004. By their mid-thirties, over 60 percent of them have served time in prison.[3]

It might seem surprising that a drug so associated with the urban underclass would draw lawmakers into a frenzy of legislative activity. Crack was somehow threatening enough that both the states and the federal government have deployed their most powerful weapons against it: felony status for all offenses, onerous sentences for even minor violations, broad federal jurisdiction usually reserved for serious criminal activity, and a well-funded enforcement apparatus with incentives for vigorous investigation and arrest. Penalties are much more severe than for any other drug. Crack, in fact, is punished more severely in the federal system, with an average term of 103.5 months, almost nine years, than most violent offenses (U.S. Sentencing

Commission 2002). The mandatory sentences minimize any discretion judges might otherwise exercise in light of extenuating circumstances like youth and poverty. Anti-crack legislation, as the Clary case illustrates, is intentionally sweeping in its reach. Even a seventeen-year-old youngster involved in a minor drug deal is subject to severe mandatory punishment.

The contrast with crack's pharmacological twin, powder cocaine, is noteworthy. Crack is made by dissolving powder cocaine in a solution of sodium bicarbonate and water and boiling it, which creates a solid substance that can easily be sold in small quantities to be smoked for a rapid, euphoric high. The Drug Enforcement Administration estimates that crack rocks are between 75 percent and 90 percent pure cocaine. Yet under federal law, it takes one hundred times more powder cocaine to elicit the same prison term as would a mixture containing crack.

It is important to understand how crack came to be punished with such severity, and why such a policy has survived, virtually undisturbed, for over two decades in the face of unprecedented levels of racially unbalanced imprisonment. As policy analyst Ryan King notes: "In 2003, 81 percent of those sentenced for crack cocaine offenses were African American, despite the fact that the greatest number of documented crack users are white" (2006, 5).[4] In the estimation of the U.S. Sentencing Commission: "This one sentencing rule contributes more to the differences in average sentences between African-American and White offenders than any possible effect of discrimination. Revising the crack cocaine thresholds would better reduce the gap than any other single policy change, and it would dramatically improve the fairness of the federal sentencing system" (2003, 132).

These facts are part of the public record and are well known. Crack laws have been the subject of strong criticism from some respected quarters, including international human rights organizations. Considerable scholarly effort has been devoted to documenting the failure of drug prohibition and the consequences associated with continuing the current approach (see, e.g., Lusane 1991; Musto 1999; Donziger 1996; Miller 1996; Tonry 1995; Chambliss 2003). Increasingly, investigators are also studying how race matters in enforcement of the drug laws (see, e.g., Beckett et al. 2006; Davis 2005).

Imprisonment continues as the favored solution to the war on drugs, not because it has been effective in reducing drug abuse, but because it supports other political goals. As Patricia Erickson and Jennifer Butters observe: "As a social policy directed at reducing the harms of drugs, prohibition is a failure. As an ideology, it must be regarded as one of the great success stories of the twentieth century" (1998, 177). William Chambliss is more explicit in his indictment of the war on drugs:

> The war on drugs is a failure by any objective measure. It has not reduced drug consumption, the prevalence of drug-selling gangs, the production of new products for consumers, or the volume of drugs flowing into the United States. It has been successful, however, in legitimating the creation of a virtual police state in the ghettoes of our cities. (2003, 315)

Yet the laws endure, and those who permit them to endure are not castigated as racist. Racial impact is treated legally and politically as an irrelevancy, a collateral effect of the war on drugs. Nor is the origin of these harsh laws considered suspect, even though they were quite obviously a panicky reaction to a drug scare with strong racial overtones. How can this be so in a nation that guarantees equal protection of its laws?

Explaining the Persistence of the War on Drugs

The most striking aspect of this policy, and arguably the one most worthy of study, has become clear only with the passage of time: its persistence. It is clear now that the lack of positive results, harshness, and very disproportionate impact on vulnerable communities count for little. Why does public opinion continue to support tough drug laws, even in the face of general awareness that a highly punitive approach is expensive and has failed to stem the drug trade? Why do lawmakers refuse to consider a change of direction? Why is it no longer news that poor minorities pay the largest price for this approach to drug control in their roles as residents of drug-plagued neighborhoods and as the persons most at risk for arrest, prosecution, and harsh punishment?

The normalization of a policy that works such disadvantages on minority populations is particularly striking in the context of the nation's much-touted commitment to equal opportunity. The paradox is that federal, state, and local governments claim to be, and to some extent are, actively committed to racial equality, while at the same time supporting policies that condemn a young man like Clary to a ten-year prison term for a relatively minor offense. Increasing racial diversity is public policy in every institution except the prisons, where crack laws have helped to Blacken the population to unprecedented levels.[5] The growing racial skew in imprisonment also has had pernicious effects on minority voting power. Nearly every state temporarily or permanently disenfranchises persons convicted of serious crimes, including selling and using illicit drugs. Current anti-drug initiatives are thus undermining a central plank of the civil rights movement and a fundamental tenet of American government (Manza and Uggen 2006).

The nation's faltering war on drugs suggests at least three areas for critical inquiry:

- The appropriate role of punishment in combating dangerous drugs. Why has the United States invested so heavily in this approach?
- Racial differences in punishment. Do they reflect racial difference in involvement with dangerous drugs? If not, why not?
- Effectiveness in reducing drug abuse. Harsh punishments, particularly when they fall on the shoulders of disadvantaged minorities, must be effective if they can be justified at all. Has this standard been met?

It is sometimes argued, incorrectly, that the racial impact of the drug laws is simply an artifact of racial differences in offending, an argument that overlooks racially skewed patterns of law enforcement that target some minority communities for greater surveillance and aggressive arrest policies (Beckett et al. 2006). Also overlooked is the relative insulation from police surveillance enjoyed by student drug dealers, who are generally white and from relatively privileged backgrounds (see, e.g., Mohamed and Fritsvold 2006). Their activities escape notice because they occur out of sight of law enforcement; Troy Duster observes: "Police police the streets" (1997, 265).

Nevertheless, many people believe that whatever differences there might be in police practices, the primary problem is that African Americans are "the cultural architects of their own disadvantage" (Bobo and Smith 1998, 212). Brown et al. (2003) describe a profound racial divide in the United States over the meaning of race: "'Racial realists' like Abigail and Stephen Thernstrom believe that the economic divide is over-rated and that racism is, for the most part, a thing of the past. From the perspective of 'racial realists,' those who insist on calling attention to racism and who push racially conscious programs like affirmative action are whipping up racial consciousness and slowing progress toward a society in which race is completely irrelevant" (Brown et al. 2003, 6–9).

But even those who believe racism is fading into insignificance should question why officials have allowed the current failed policy to continue in the face of its manifest shortcomings. Somehow the people at risk for drastic penalties—the Edward James Clarys of our society—have become so marginalized that they have ceased to be objects of public concern. If all citizens were valued, the war on drugs would have to be considered a deeply problematic approach to satisfying the important goal of effective drug control. As Mauer observes in comparing Scandinavian with American approaches to crime policy: "Communities that feel a sense of commitment to their members are able to see the humanity of offenders despite their criminal behaviors and to see the potential for positive change in their lives" (2006, 151).

Perhaps the answer to this puzzle is that the nation's historic and much-celebrated break with racial oppression has not been as profound as commonly thought. Racism in criminal law, a bitter reality during most of the nation's history, may have morphed in the 1970s rather than disappeared. The contemporary war on drugs followed suspiciously close on the heels of the civil rights movement of the 1960s and early 1970s, and, in a certain sense, grew out of it. Fear of urban disorder and rising crime rates were part of the backlash to the civil rights movement that fueled get-tough, "law and order" policies designed to increase incarceration rates for street crime and drugs (see, e.g., Beckett and Sasson 2000, chap. 4). Rogers Smith suggests that this is the way racial reform always works: "Every period of racial legal reform has been followed by a period of resistance, producing stagnation and partial reverses on the road to greater racial equality" (1999, 7).

To investigate the possibility that racism and fear of a restive underclass explain the persistence of the American war on drugs requires a critical attitude toward much of the criminal justice research on race and crime. As David Greenberg notes:

> [A] truly remarkable volume of research has been undertaken to identify and explain racial and ethnic differences in American criminal justice outcomes. On the basis of many published studies, it has become the conventional wisdom that the overrepresentation of blacks and other minorities in the criminal justice system is not *primarily* due to discrimination in law enforcement, but rather to high levels of minority involvement in those crimes that the criminal justice system regularly prosecutes." (2003, 325–26)

As important as it is to explore why racial minorities tend to be so overrepresented in U.S. prisons and jails, keeping the spotlight trained only on discrimination in law enforcement may, in the case of drug crimes at least, be too narrow a focus. Police practices like racial profiling, focusing surveillance on poor minority neighborhoods, and consensual, no-cause searches certainly deserve critical attention, but law enforcement is not the only relevant issue in exploring racial discrimination in law. Criminal statutes and those who write them also deserve critical scrutiny.

Theoretical Starting Points

Crimes do not arise out of the earth as products of nature. Crimes are defined by statutes, which are designed for particular purposes. Legislation prohibiting drug abuse should particularly draw our interest. Drug taking is a generally private activity whose destructiveness is mostly confined to individual users and their friends and families. Perhaps this is why during most of the nineteenth century, as the dangers associated with hallucinatory and habit-forming drugs began to be understood, they were considered to be medical problems. How did this private, pleasure-seeking activity become such a favorite of the criminal law? The answer, some observers suggest, implicates racism. As Musto observes: "The most passionate support for legal prohibition of narcotics has been associated with fear of a given drug's effect on a specific minority. Certain drugs were dreaded because they seemed to undermine essential social restrictions which kept these groups under control" (1999, 294).

The issue of race in drug policy, as Musto suggests, should be pursued historically and from its legislative roots. The investigation should start from the proposition that society "constructs" its own problems. That construction process is very selective, as Kevin Ryan observes: "The constructive process involves the selection of certain sets of circumstances and the treatment of them as problematic, while other sets of circumstances are ignored. A large body of research explores the dimensions of this 'picking out' process" (1998, 141). The people who do the "picking out" are moral entrepreneurs—activists who claim to represent public values as they push a specific policy agenda. Sometimes, as in the case of the war on drugs, they help to create a "moral panic" that speeds up, and may overwhelm, democratic deliberation (Cohen 1972, 2002; Goode and Ben-Yehuda 1994a). Punitive policies like the contemporary war on drugs (and its predecessor drug wars) are the typical result of moral panics. Racial minorities and those perceived to be socially deviant are typical targets for such policies and the negative media attention that accompanies them (Duster 1970; Reinarman and Levine 1997; Schneider and Ingram 1993; Neubeck and Cazenave 2001; Gilens 1999).

The constructionist approach to crime is compatible with scholarship that focuses attention on how racial and ethnic differences are made manifest and given social meaning. Race, after all, is an invented category maintained in politics and culture, not in nature: "Entire races have disappeared from view, from public discussion and from modern memory, though their flesh-and-blood members still walk the earth. What has become of the nineteenth century's Celts and Slavs, for instance? Its Hebrews, Iberics, Mediterraneans, Teutons, and Anglo-Saxons?" (Jacobson 1998, 2). Mai Ngai notes the social and legal construction of races through restrictive immigration laws: "Race is always historically specific. At times, a confluence of economic, social, cultural, and political factors has impelled major shifts in society's understanding (and construction) of race and its constitutive role in national identity formation. The Civil War was obviously one of those times; the present multicultural moment is another" (2004, 7; and see Bonilla-Silva 1996, 472).

If race is more about maintaining social hierarchy than biology, then the crucial question is whether current understandings of race retard progress toward a post-racial democracy, or whether instead they tend to obscure structural inequities. Derrick Bell, a law professor who has devoted his career to understanding U.S. race policy, is pessimistic:

> The very visible social and economic progress made by some African Americans can no longer obscure the increasingly dismal demographics that reflect the status of most of those whose forebears in this county were slaves. Statistics on poverty, unemployment, and income support the growing concern that the slow racial advances of the 1960s and 1970s have ended, and retrogression is well under way. (1995, 2)

We are in what Kevin Brown (2005) has dubbed a "post-desegregation era" marked by increasing racial separation in some arenas, like public education, and a growing disinclination to promote equality (see Guinier and Torres 2002).

A government that venerates equality under law has a weighty responsibility to avoid creating racial and class disadvantage in the criminal justice process. The fundamental goal of crime policy, after all, is social justice, not simply efficient control of designated pathologies (Chambliss 2003, 295). Justice must be a foundational concern in research on crime. I agree with John Braithwaite's admonition to avoid both a moral relativism indifferent to social harms and a legal positivism that ignores social consequences. The goal should be explanatory theory built around the normative concerns that justify criminal law: increasing individual freedom and equality, and enhancing the quality of deliberation, procedural justice, and institutional checks and balances that preserve political institutions against corruption (Braithwaite 2000, 88).

An important question in this analysis is why appellate courts have avoided critically examining the racial implications of the war on drugs. Trial judges have urged another course, sometimes in dramatic terms. Troy

Duster, for example, describes how a San Francisco judge wept at imposing a ten-year term on a shipyard worker who carried drugs to help out a friend (1997, 261). Part of the answer lies in the concerted effort of Republican presidents, beginning with Richard Nixon, to appoint Supreme Court justices who are conservative on crime and criminal justice. In the 1970s, this effort moved to the lower federal courts, politicizing and slowing down the process of lower-court appointments (Hartley and Holmes 2002; Scherer 2005). The way cases go up on appeal also plays a role in insulating appellate judges from the day-to-day realities of drug-law enforcement, including the racial and class dimensions of a harsh sentencing law. Judicial respect for the separation of powers also tends to deter judges from interfering with legislative authority to set sentencing standards.

The issue of why courts refuse to intervene, however, runs deeper, to a judicial commitment to the idea that racism is a personal failing, what Bonilla-Silva calls "an expression of 'original sin'—as a remnant of past historical racial situations" (1996, 468). This conception of racism focuses judges on intentional acts of discrimination, as evidence of the actor's racist mental state. It leaves little room for the play of racialized fears and misunderstandings that can lead to severe sanctions in legislation. Ignoring such psychological complexities, constitutional law treats racial discrimination as a clear, conscious choice between color blindness and intended action. Racial disproportion, even when extreme, is considered irrelevant unless there is direct evidence that bad motives were at work in producing it.

There is no acknowledgment that institutions might embed racial stereotypes and disadvantage in their day-to-day operations, despite an enormous volume of social science scholarship that suggests the importance of institutionalized racism (see, e.g., Bonilla-Silva 1996; Brown et al. 2003; Frymer 2005; Mendelberg 2001; Ngai 2004; Williams 2003). Institutions provide incentives that make racism rational, as Frymer points out: "We need to examine the ways in which institutions encourage racist acts by providing rules and procedures that motivate people to behave in a racist manner or behave in a manner that motivates others to do so" (2005, 374). Those rules and procedures are powerful motivators, and at the same time, they offer an exit strategy from racism because institutions can be redesigned to make racial equity rational.

By maintaining that racism is always intentional, irrational, and personal in the face of much evidence that it is not, courts play an important role in perpetuating the war on drugs, both in the obvious practical sense of permitting it to continue and, more broadly, in supporting an ideology of color blindness that takes little note of the evidence of structural disadvantage and institutional pathology in contemporary race and class relations.

The judicial response to challenges to the contemporary war on drugs has helped to set the public agenda on race. Courts legitimize government action (or inaction) in the United States. They have this power in part because of our constitutional structure, but also because of the determined efforts of judges over two centuries to hear and respond to the political sentiments of the day and to make their power manifest. Courts draw their power partly from their sensitivity to their own limits in the political order, but also because judges absorb the prevailing opinions of the day and act on them. They work in a symbiotic relationship with popular opinion, reinforcing it, and at the same time are reinforced in their own power by not being too distant from the mainstream.

Such institutional priorities are central to the story of how racial disadvantage has come to be inscribed in the criminal law and how large racial differences in criminal outcomes can persist without much public fanfare. Courts do not act alone. Also influential are the institutional priorities of police, prosecutors, legislators, interest groups, and administrative agencies. This is not the first study, of course, to focus attention on the capacity of institutions to maintain and promote racial inequity, despite their claims of neutrality and beneficial racial motives. But this study is unusual in paying close attention to how the relevant institutions have developed and maintained their positions over time and how, through their incentives and rules, they make racism rational. As Frymer notes, "even studies of 'institutional racism' emphasize less how institutions motivate individuals than simply making the important point that racism is located within places of power" (2005, 374).

Race in America, of course, is a much more complicated process than the contrasting opportunities between white and African American citizens. While references to other racial conflicts and dilemmas are helpful to this analysis, the focus in this study remains on the struggle over the place that African Americans will hold in the American political experiment. This issue is central in all racial conflict in this nation. Nicholas De Genova reports, for example, that the Mexican immigrants that he studied in Chicago define themselves in terms of their place in relation to African Americans and whites:

> The book's ethnographic research reveals how Mexican migrants in Chicago tended to systematically infer and consistently recapitulate a

socially ubiquitous equation of "American"-ness with racial whiteness, to the exclusion of African Americans as well as U.S.-citizen Latinos (including Mexicans born in the United States). Mexican migrants thus negotiated their own re-racialization as Mexican, always in relation to both a dominant whiteness and its polar opposite, a subjugated and denigrated Blackness. (2005, 8)

The Organization of This Book

The set of theoretical starting points just discussed lays the foundation for the analysis that follows. Chapter 1 returns to the story of Clary and his encounter with the federal drug laws; in so doing, it illustrates all the central themes of this book. Taken to its conclusion, and buttressed with the facts of historic and contemporary drug wars, Clary's experience is a good "teaching case" for how law perpetuates racial inequality. The case and the reaction it produced at the appellate level also provide a useful framework for examining the basic elements of contemporary drug policy and a helpful context for the more institutionally focused chapters that follow. The trial judge assigned to Clary's case, Judge Clyde Cahill, did something unusual. He refused to treat the ten-year sentence prescribed for this youth as an acceptable consequence of the nation's determined effort to stamp out crack abuse. Instead, he framed Clary's predicament on the broad canvas of racist reactions to threats posed by drugs and other urban dangers. He saw the routinization of extreme punishment like Clary's as a problem in civic membership with roots in slavery and two centuries of continuing racial oppression through law.

The remainder of this book falls into three parts. The three chapters following the denouement of the Clary case trace the American experience with drug legislation, beginning with the campaign against alcohol that ended in a national Prohibition amendment. Racism and fear of a restive underclass, these chapters show, has been salient in every one of these antidrug initiatives. Without this backdrop of racism, it is hard to imagine how the United States would have settled so quickly, and so definitively, on a highly punitive, expensive approach to drug abuse, particularly as more humane, less costly alternatives have become available. Our history of embedded racism also helps to explain the public's otherwise surprising tolerance for failed policies, even in the face of the tremendous human suffering associated with incarceration.

The campaign to prohibit alcohol consumption, one might think, was an exception to the entanglement of race and drugs. In fact, it was not, as chapter 2 shows. Although its racial underpinnings are not commonly acknowledged, racism was a key to the success of the Prohibition campaign. It is a particularly good example because it grew out of a nineteenth-century temperance movement that was initially quite egalitarian in its aspirations. The goal was education and voluntary desistance from alcoholic drinks. All comers were welcome. The campaign turned racist when it morphed into an effort to create a punitive law. In the end, what defeated Prohibition was not a wakening sense of racial justice, but the changing demographics of drinking and the Great Depression.

Race played a better-known role in the campaigns for criminal controls on opium, marijuana, cocaine, and heroin. This effort began at about the same time that Congress was considering anti-alcohol legislation, and it drew on some of the same scare-mongering images that had begun to circulate about alcohol. The lawmaking process of this earlier era, guided by self-serving policy entrepreneurs and an uncritical news media eager for frightening stories, presaged the anti-crack campaign, but in more racially lurid terms. Opium was the drug of the seductive, secretive Chinese who spread their addiction to unsuspecting whites. Marijuana was something Mexican laborers brought with them to the United States that threatened America's young and promoted fighting among impoverished agricultural workers. Cocaine was a drug the Black underclass used that made them brazen and reckless and sometimes even invulnerable to the bullets of police officers. Chapter 3 considers these early anti-drug campaigns to show how the nation became accustomed to the paradigm of drug abuse as a crime deserving significant punishment.

The civil rights movement of the 1960s briefly drew the criminalization approach into question. Race and class disadvantage became a reason for *not* punishing drug use harshly. This moment passed in the Nixon years. Chapter 4 shows how the racial upheavals of the time affected drug policy. This chapter goes on to examine the congressional debates that led to the 1986 and 1988 federal crack laws. The old tendencies to associate dangerous drugs with dangerous minorities bent on corrupting white, law-abiding youth were much in evidence in this debate. Those who disagreed with the take-no-prisoners approach were ignored in the rush to legislate. As Michael Tonry (1995) has suggested, Congress knew, but apparently did not care, that the brunt of its harsh new laws would fall on poor, urban Blacks. Lack of concern for this fact can be laid to racial insensitivity, but also to a historically circumscribed lack of imagination.

The remaining two chapters assess the government's reaction to its own growing awareness that the war on drugs is, in effect, a war on poor, mostly urban minorities (cf. Blakeslee 2005). The matter was debated, briefly, when the U.S. Sentencing Commission confronted Congress with the racial results of its mandatory minimum penalties. Chapter 5 covers this debate and shows how Congress deflected the Commission's proposal to lower sentences for crack offenses to the level of those for powder cocaine. The Sentencing Commission, as this chapter shows, was repeatedly rebuffed in its effort to lower penalties. These episodes reveal a Congress confident in its convictions and unconcerned about the constitutionality of its differential penalties, even when they resulted in unprecedented rates of Black imprisonment.

Chapter 6 indicates why Congress paid so little attention to constitutional strictures against racially discriminatory legislation. Appellate courts have repelled every challenge, using rules of decision that allow them to avoid looking broadly at allegations of racial bias. The issue has been joined only in trial courts, where sentencing judges come face to face with the realities of the crack cocaine policy as they sentence young offenders like Clary to long terms of imprisonment.

This analysis, taken as a whole, reveals a disturbing lack of realism about race in criminal justice policymaking and practice, and an equally disturbing disengagement in the judiciary and in the public. The need for more robust appreciation of racial disadvantage is clear, not just for the marginalized, but also for the marginalizers:

> Those who are racially marginalized are like the miner's canary: their distress is the first sign of a danger that threatens us all. It is easy enough to think that when we sacrifice this canary, the only harm is to communities of color. Yet others ignore problems that converge around racial minorities at their own peril, for these problems are symptoms warning us that we are all at risk. (Guinier and Torres 2002, 11)

one	# Racial Discrimination in the Eyes of the Law

The federal legislation that decreed Edward James Clary's fate dates from 1986, a period of intense concern about the rise of crack cocaine. Congress, transfixed by frightening images of a "ghetto drug" spreading addiction throughout the nation, adopted legislation requiring five- and ten-year sentences for offenses involving sales of crack cocaine; in 1988 it added a five-year penalty for simple possession. The mandatory-minimum legislation sent a message not just to drug sellers and users, but also to law enforcement and the courts. The high penalties were a signal to police forces that they should make enforcement of these laws a priority. For judges, the signal was rejection. Mandatory-minimum penalties drastically reduced the traditional power of judges to fashion sentences individually to the circumstances of the offender and the priorities of the judge. When the legislature prescribed a mandatory-minimum sentence, it reduced the factors at stake to those chosen by the legislatures, for example, the weight of the substance seized. The idea was to get tough, and also to make sentences more certain and more uniform from case to case.

In the Clary case, however, the mandatory-minimum sentencing structure did not work as planned. Judge Cahill was not willing to passively impose the ten-year sentence prescribed for Clary. The prospect brought the severity of the drug war into sharp relief for Judge Cahill, creating a dilemma that would not easily be resolved. So he postponed the case, and postponed it again. For Judge Cahill, the issue was not just the harshness of the mandatory sentence, but also the inherent racial bias in focusing a massive, very punitive drug-control effort on crack cocaine.

This chapter follows *United States v. Clary*[1] through to its conclusion. The importance of this case for our consideration lies in Clary's ordinariness as a drug felon and Judge Cahill's extraordinariness as a trial judge.

The case forced Judge Cahill to choose between what the law prescribed for Clary and a more fully elaborated moral reality that suggested a more compassionate outcome. Clary was Judge Cahill's Billy Budd, pitting the regularity of law against a backdrop of injustice—and demanding a choice between them.

Judge Cahill's resolution of his dilemma in this case reflected his own roots in the civil rights struggle and his awareness of the issues that face African Americans less successful than himself. The story does not end with Judge Cahill, however. The trial court decision went up on appeal and was reversed. The Eighth Circuit, which reviewed the case on appeal, reaffirmed prevailing constitutional values and restored Clary's original sentence. This case nevertheless lives on. Although it is no longer "good law" in legal terms, Judge Cahill's opinion continues to be cited because it resonates with concerns on and off the courts about the constitutionality and fairness of the war on drugs.

Casualties in the War on Drugs

The drug war in Judge Cahill's federal district had been waged almost entirely against the undereducated minority youth in East St. Louis, an area that lies on the Illinois side of the border between Missouri and Illinois. Cases like Clary's crowded the docket, reminding the court staff of the racial and class dimension of an imprisonment-oriented drug-control policy. Of the fifty-seven people in this court charged with crack cocaine offenses during the three years preceding the Clary case, fifty-five were Black, one was Hispanic, and one was white. From the court's perspective, the constant lineup of crack prosecutions had made the whole staff complicit in a system of mass incarceration for poor, mostly minority, youth.

The irony was that the harsh criminal sanctions for this drug and the flow of convictions seemed to have no effect on the market for crack cocaine in East St. Louis. When Clary's case came before the court in 1994, the effort to stamp out crack use had been going on for nearly a decade, with no sign that it had reduced the flow of illicit drugs into East St. Louis. Nationally, the pattern was the same: Rates of use had hardly changed, and drug prices had fallen (King and Mauer 2002). Illicit drugs had become a significant element—estimated at $64 billion—in the underground economy. At the same time, the number of inmates incarcerated for drug offenses was growing exponentially.

In 1993, when Clary committed his crime, the federal prisons already contained 234,600 convicted drug offenders, a nearly tenfold increase from

1980 (Schaffer Library of Drug Policy 1995). As the number of drug arrests had increased, the proportion of Blacks and Hispanics under arrest and in prison had grown accordingly. Between 1976 and 1996, the rate of white drug arrests climbed by 86 percent, while the rate of Black arrests increased 400 percent. The pattern was particularly stark in urban areas like East St. Louis. In 1994, Blacks and Hispanics constituted over 75 percent of those charged with felony drug offenses in the nation's seventy-five largest cities. The racial pattern was the same in the federal courts, but it was even more dramatic in cases involving crack cocaine, where 85 percent of those sentenced were African American, 9 percent were Hispanic, and 6 percent were white (Spohn and Spears 2003, 197–98).

In many respects the law-enforcement picture has not changed appreciably. Remarkably, drug offenders now make up nearly 60 percent of the federal prison population. Nearly three-fourths of these 325,000 offenders have no history of violence; many are addicts (Sentencing Project 2004). Only 11 percent of them could possibly be classified as high-level dealers, according to a study conducted by the Federal Sentencing Commission (U.S. Sentencing Commission 2002). Over 90 percent of those convicted of crack cocaine offenses are minorities, and half of those offenders are thirty years old or younger. The average sentence for distribution of crack cocaine is 123 months, or over ten years (U.S. Sentencing Commission 2002).

Meanwhile, crack cocaine has been slowly declining in popularity among drug users. By the mid 1990s, the rate of use was down in many parts of the nation, though not in St. Louis (Golub and Johnson 1997). Informal means of social control, primarily stigmatization of crack users, may be responsible, according to sociologist Bruce Jacobs, who studied the social world of crack selling: "Powerful anti-crack norms have taken root in urban areas across the country that make 'crack' a dirty word and vilify those who use it. . . . The epidemic is essentially over: demand for the substance has been siphoned off by stigma" (1999, 128). The most recent data come from the National Survey on Drug Use and Health, which reports reductions in use within the past year and over a lifetime in 2002, 2003, and 2004 (U.S. Department of Health and Human Services 2006).

Still, the rate of use remains impressive. According to the Office of National Drug Control Policy, users spent $35.3 billion on cocaine in 2000, a decrease from $69.9 billion spent in 1990. Americans consumed 259 metric tons of cocaine in 2000, a decrease from 447 metric tons in 1990 (Office of National Drug Control Policy 2003). Arrests for crack cocaine are down only slightly, and the penalty structure remains the same, so rates of imprisonment have not been noticeably affected. The most notable trend has been toward lower-level arrests and, partly as a result, the imprisonment of more women.

The declining significance of crack, centerpiece of the federal war on drugs, nevertheless illustrates an important aspect of the drug war: its capacity to continue, and even expand, without any clear agenda. The drug war has been institutionalized and will continue even in the face of declining interest in dangerous drugs. Drug arrests increased by 41 percent between 1990 and 2002, largely because of greater law-enforcement attention to marijuana, a drug innocuous enough that it has been a perennial candidate for legalization. Marijuana arrests now constitute 45 percent of the 1.5 million drug arrests that occur annually, and 79 percent of those arrests are for possession alone (King and Mauer 2005, 9). This aggressive arrest policy, which takes an inordinate amount of police time, in the estimate of many state and local officials, costs the nation an estimated $4 billion annually. There appears to have been no effect on the availability of marijuana, or the tendency for young people to experiment with it, or its potency (which has increased in the past decade). African Americans, an estimated 14 percent of marijuana users, make up 30 percent of marijuana arrests.

The Racial Impact of the War on Drugs

The war on drugs has sent unprecedented numbers of poor, minority citizens to prison. Most of those imprisoned are either African American (56 percent) or Hispanic (23 percent). Law-enforcement agencies have helped to create this racial skew by focusing their attention on nonwhites. "Those communities that are subject to police surveillance," Angela Davis observes, "are much more likely to produce more bodies for the punishment industry" (Davis 2005, 41). Racial profiling that leads to pretextual traffic stops and "consent" searches, anti-gang initiatives that target minority youth for police scrutiny, and drug-free zones that automatically enhance penalties have also helped to create racial disparity in arrests, creating a misleading impression of racial differences in offending (see, e.g., Zatz and Krecker 2003).

Two recent studies of drug-enforcement policies and practices in Seattle provide insight into how race factors into the drug-enforcement process. The first found that African Americans and Latinos were overrepresented among those arrested for drug possession, as compared with the overall drug-using population in Seattle. The reason was that law enforcement had focused almost all of its efforts on crack users, rather than drug users more generally (Beckett et al. 2005). A second study, relying on needle exchange survey data, ethnographic observations, and incident reports, found that crack arrests were nearly twice as frequent as the combined total for all of the drugs preferred by whites (methamphetamine, ecstasy, and powder cocaine), yielding an overall arrestee pool that was nearly two-thirds Black. The authors, who accompanied police and observed many drug deals, also noted that police tended to focus their attention on mixed-race neighborhoods and outdoor venues, which tended to increase the rate of nonwhite arrests. The authors also observed that police displayed a pervasive tendency to overlook whites making drug deals: "Police officers and officials are simply less likely to perceive whites who are involved in illicit drug activity as drug offenders" (Beckett et al. 2006, 130).

Arrests of poor, uneducated minority defendants tend to become convictions for a variety of reasons that scholars have explored (see, e.g., Miller 1996; Cole 2000; Kennedy 1997; Tonry 1995; Walker, Spohn, and DeLone 2004; Belenko 1993; Zatz 2000). This means that the social disadvantages associated with convictions and imprisonment will be visited particularly on impoverished minority populations. Long prison terms, as has been well documented, tend to exacerbate social inequalities, to create dysfunctional personal relationships, and to produce more imprisonment. State and federal legislatures have created additional penalties that make those convicted of crimes ineligible for public assistance, education loans, driving privileges, public housing, and food stamps. Most states restrict rights to vote, and many make it easier to terminate parental rights. Some felons are required to register with the police for the remainder of their lives, and some can be deported (Travis 2005, 63; and see Mauer and Chesney-Lind 2002).

Poverty is a key factor, not just in creating disproportionate rates of punishment for African Americans, but also in creating incentives for illegal activities such as drug selling, prostitution, and gambling (Reiman 1995, chap. 3; and see Mirandé 1987). Economically deprived groups engage in illegal industries because it makes economic sense, despite the risks. "Ethnic vice industries," sociologist John Hagan observes, provide a much-needed route to economic mobility in poor, racially segregated neighborhoods. The attractiveness of vice industries is particularly high in periods like our own, characterized by disinvestment in the urban core (Hagan 1995).

Economic and social marginality are the keys to this pattern. Immigrant groups that are now in the economic and cultural mainstream—Irish, Germans, and Italians, for instance—were once on "the crooked ladder" to economic survival in many urban areas, as James O'Kane (1992) notes in his analysis of ethnic vice industries and gangsterism in American history. Daniel Bell calls vice the "queer ladder of social mobility" and notes "the specific role of various immigrant groups as they, one after another, become involved in marginal business and crime" (1960, 115, 117). The dilemma is that poor, minority communities in which vice is important economically are not moving toward assimilation in the general economy. Heavy-handed laws to suppress the drug trade have increased its violence. Meares and Kahan (1999) describe the paradox of attitudes in depressed areas, where police are simultaneously resented for their rough and aggressive tactics, but sought after to enhance public safety. Meanwhile, groups that were once in similar positions do not generally acknowledge their pasts, which tends to obliterate the difficulties that isolated groups of all kinds face in gaining acceptance and to mask the actual historical changeability of "whiteness" (see, e.g., Jacobson 1998).

The cycle of impoverishment, illicit industry, arrest, punishment, and further marginalization is particularly vicious with respect to illicit drugs like crack cocaine. Federal initiatives have significantly extended the reach of law enforcement, providing many inducements for arrests, including budgetary incentives and broad power to confiscate and auction off the property of drug dealers. Federal agents are supposed to assist local police in their drug-fighting efforts, taking cases to federal court only when they involve big-time drug dealing. The incentive structure, however, works the other way, encouraging law-enforcement agents at all levels to concentrate on the low, exposed end of the drug-selling network, where minorities predominate and arrests are easiest to make.

The extent to which the federal government has become involved in the bottom-most end of drug distribution was evident in Judge Cahill's docket, which was full of minor cases like Clary's. In three years of federal prosecutions in Judge Cahill's court, none of the fifty-seven defendants charged under the federal law could have been called kingpins. Eight of them had less than 10 grams of crack when arrested, and five had less than a gram, barely enough to detect or to use. The largest drug bust in the three-year period was 944 grams involving three defendants. The average arrest involved less than 25 grams of crack.

The consequences for African American and mixed-race communities are well known. Drug cases have changed the demographics of the poor, mostly urban areas where African Americans and Latinos predominate. Prison has become almost a rite of passage for young men growing up in these areas, and the ability of citizens in these communities to raise families and participate in civic life has been severely compromised (see, e.g., Miller 1996; Bourgois 1995; Western 2006). Some of these impacts are more obvious than others. Approximately 13 percent of African American males in the United States, for example, are ineligible to vote under state felony disenfranchisement laws; approximately 30 percent of Black males in Alabama and Florida have lost the right to vote permanently (National Association for the Advancement of Colored People 2005).

Challenging the Incarceration Approach

Judge Cahill had to confront—face to face—the racial impact of the war on drugs in carrying out his responsibilities as a federal district judge. The requirement that sentences be fixed without regard to the broader context in which drug policy is being pursued has caused many complaints from judges and some resignations and retirements. The federal crack penalties have also, from their inception, precipitated many legal challenges on a variety of constitutional grounds. Some were successful at the trial level, but at the time Judge Cahill was considering Clary's case, most of these cases had been taken up on appeal and reversed. Federal courts of appeal around the nation were reasserting congressional authority to control the sentencing process and to select crack for particularly harsh punishment.[2] In light of these decisions, most trial judges in the federal courts were doing as they had been told to do by Congress and by the federal Sentencing Commission, which assisted Congress in this process. Judges were, sometimes complainingly, sentencing offenders to long terms in prison for crack offenses. Judge Cahill decided that he could not go that route in Clary's case.

What is a judge's responsibility in a situation like this? Does a trial judge, before imposing sentence, have a duty to determine whether the law is just? Perhaps a moral duty, but not a legal duty. American judges are expected to be "priests, not prophets," Thomas Ross observes. "Their job is to serve and maintain the state's law and not to 'make law'" out of moral or philosophical conviction (1996, 137). The rule-of-law approach finesses the question of whether a law is just by offering constitutionality as a substitute. Judges can act against the will of the legislature or executive, but only if they do so in the name of upholding the higher authority of the federal or relevant state constitution.

The American system discourages judges from taking up constitutional issues unless counsel for one of the parties puts them before the court. This prescribed passivity stands in contrast to the European civil law tradition of investing some judges with investigative authority. The appropriate metaphor for an American judge is the umpire in a contest between litigants over the truth (see, e.g., Fletcher, 1988). Judges maintain the fiction of their own absence from the process in the way they write opinions, referring to *the court* as the source of decision, and avoiding *I* and *me* at all costs.

Judge Cahill decided against passivity in Clary's case, perhaps seeing an opportunity to move the law toward a more realistic fit with the demands of justice, or perhaps out of despair at the job he was expected to do. He asked Clary's lawyer, federal public defender Andrea Smith, to invite experts to testify on the law's sharp distinction between crack cocaine and powder cocaine. Judge Cahill was particularly struck by the fact that the penalties for crack are triggered by drug quantities just one-hundredth of that for powder cocaine, even though they are pharmacologically identical. He noted a racial aspect to the distinction between crack and powder cocaine that might create an opportunity for a constitutional challenge. The grossly higher penalties for crack, which the media had portrayed as a "Black" drug, suggest the possibility that racial bias might have been operating when Congress adopted the 1986 and 1988 anti-crack initiatives. Judge Cahill prepared to call into question the *bone fides* of the war on drugs.

Judge Cahill's willingness to engage this issue can perhaps be explained by his experience as an activist and child of the civil rights era. He was no stranger to racial discrimination. Clyde Cahill had attended segregated schools as a child. He had been a high school student when Missouri's last lynching had occurred; a Black man had been accused of molesting a white woman. Cahill joined the air force during World War II, when integration of the armed forces was still a largely untested and unrealized ideal. Cahill had felt racial discrimination personally on many occasions. As a young officer, he formally protested his exclusion from the whites-only officer's club. Racial segregation in the World War II era was common in the American military. Suzanne Mettler, in her study of this generation of soldiers, describes how conflicted African American enlisted men and officers felt about the complicated mission of "proving themselves as a group even as they were treated as inferior to white soldiers" (2005, 30; and see Katznelson 2005).

Cahill was one of the first African Americans to graduate from St. Louis University Law School. He was an activist public interest lawyer from that point on, serving as the chief legal advisor to the Missouri NAACP from 1958–65, a time of major activity in the civil rights struggle in the state. Under his leadership, the local NAACP filed the first suit in Missouri to implement school desegregation under the mandate of the Supreme Court's decision in *Brown v. Board of Education*. He also became involved in other civil rights litigation in the region. After this distinguished career of advocacy for the poor and for legal aid, Cahill had become a judge, first at the state and then at the federal level. Even this last appointment broke new civil rights ground. He was the first African American to be appointed to the U.S. District Court for the Eastern District of Missouri.

Experience and inclination thus prepared Judge Cahill to see the injustice of the law that applied to Clary, and to push for reform. Judge Cahill was certainly not the only trial judge willing to express skepticism about the mandatory minimum sentences that Congress had prescribed for crack cases, however. There were critics of the one-size-fits-all mandatory-minimum approach, even in Cahill's own Eighth Circuit, not a particularly liberal appellate bench. In *United States v. Marshall*, a panel of the Eighth Circuit had noted the "extraordinary disparity in punishment between possession of cocaine powder and cocaine base" and suggested that the issues surrounding these punishments might possibly deserve exploration.[3] As Judge Pasco Bowman wrote for the panel: "With so much at stake ... in this and other cases, we are reluctant to say that full exploration of the issues is unwarranted ... in connection with crack cocaine punishments, which continue to perplex many sentencing judges." He was cautious in suggesting concern, however: "We do not invite mere repetition of prior rejected arguments, without new facts or legal analysis."[4] Judge Cahill may have read these rather tepid words of encouragement as an invitation to break new ground. And the timing was right. Judge Cahill was seventy years old and on senior status. He had plans to retire. Perhaps he saw this case as a capstone in his lifelong fight against racism. Public defender Andrea Smith described the Clary case as Cahill's "swan song."

The Constitutional Challenge

As Judge Cahill saw it, the case against crack cocaine rested on the Fourteenth Amendment to the U.S. Constitution, which promises that no state shall deny "equal protection of the laws" to any citizen. Assuming that crack and powder cocaine are basically the same drug, the drastically different penalty structure looks suspicious because the subjects of prosecution for crack offenses are overwhelmingly African Americans, while those prosecuted for powder are mostly white. How can it be reasonable for poor African Americans, who buy and sell crack on the streets because it is cheap and plentiful, to receive the same penalty that a seller of powder cocaine would receive for one hundred times as much of the drug? And why are the courts seeing such an overwhelming number of drug prosecutions of young, uneducated African American men when the user communities and the big-dollar business world of drugs are more often than not white?

The whole case in Judge Cahill's court would turn on what Congress intended when it drafted the legislation, not on what actually came to pass as police officers applied it. The Rehnquist era Supreme Court declared that intent to discriminate must be shown in challenges under the Fourteenth Amendment's equal protection clause, a requirement that is difficult to satisfy. The federal courts tend to be very cautious in criticizing Congress, in deference to the separation of powers among the three branches and their own fragile legitimacy as an unelected branch of government. Previous cases provided Judge Cahill only a narrow basis for judicial critique. The task would be to show convincingly that Congress meant to do Blacks harm in adopting crack penalties. Nothing less would do. Flawed, negligent, or even reckless judgment is beyond constitutional reproach under prevailing constitutional jurisprudence.

Even by this constricted standard, however, Judge Cahill saw possibilities. What if the crack penalties could be shown to have arisen from a panicky reaction to an exaggerated, racially tinged threat? What if racism could be shown to underlie the whole criminalization approach to dangerous drugs? There were difficulties with this argument. The adversary system does not lend itself easily to complex analysis of legislative intent under conditions of strain and uncertainty. To begin with, Congress is not an easy institution to analyze; its large membership and complicated rules of political engagement pose daunting problems for anyone trying to determine the body's state of mind. Courts must also be aware of the limits of their own investigative capacities. Congress had expressed itself in nonracial terms in proposing and adopting this legislation. Danger to the whole society, and especially to young people of all races, had been the theme in the minimal legislative debate that had occurred. How could Judge Cahill show that there was a racial subtext lying below the surface?

Public defender Andrea Smith was aware of the obstacles to a decision in her client's favor. She knew that the prosecution would appeal any deviation from Clary's prescribed sentence. Her goal was to give the judge a good record on appeal. She asked for, and was given, extra time and resources to prepare the case. She chose eleven expert witnesses to testify over a four-day period. The witness list included doctors, academics recognized for their expertise in the history of drug law, and people knowledgeable about the circumstances of sentencing law because of their own participation in the legislative process. The witnesses brought with them a wide variety of documents to back up their arguments, including scholarly articles, books, and newspaper articles.

Much of this material found its way into Judge Cahill's fifty-eight-page opinion, which boldly declared the mandatory minimum penalty unconstitutional as applied to Clary. Judge Cahill set the story of the crack/powder distinction against a backdrop of historical racism in the criminal law, beginning with slavery. He argued that what had once been explicit racism in law and policy had become an implicit racial bias in legislating against crime associated with African Americans. The prejudicial attitudes were not necessarily conscious, but they were no less powerful because of that. Judge Cahill determined that an unconscious racial bias must have been at work in the rush to punish crack much more severely than other drugs. There could be no other explanation for the crack/powder disparity when the punishment assessed for crack possession was "100 times greater than the punishment for the same crime but involving powder cocaine."[5]

This conclusion deviated significantly from the traditionally cautious judicial approach to Fourteenth Amendment claims. Judge Cahill essentially was playing the role a unanimous Supreme Court did in 1954 in *Brown v. Board of Education*, drawing on scientific evidence to challenge received doctrine about race. In this instance, though, the issue was the motivation of the legislature rather than the impact of the legislation. The suggestion that courts could recognize unconscious, as well as conscious, motives as part of legislative decision making was perhaps the most significant innovation. How would a judge be able to determine if unconscious motivation had a role in creating a statute? Judge Cahill suggested that the court make a realistic assessment of the context in which the legislation was adopted and act with sensitivity to the history of racial bias in the criminal law. Cahill also suggested that racial impact can be a sign of legislative bias in enacting legislation. This principle of examining impact to determine motivation is used in employment discrimination cases arising under federal civil rights legislation. In those cases, evidence of adverse impact shifts the burden of proof to the defendant employer to explain racial discrepancies. Constitutional cases, Judge Cahill reasoned, should be decided the same way because outcomes deeply disadvantageous to minorities always suggest the possibility of bias—conscious or unconscious—in policy design.

Judge Cahill believed that he had located racial bias in the congressional discussions of appropriate penalties for offenses involving crack cocaine. Prior to enacting the mandatory minimums, members of Congress had been deluged with "[l]egions of newspaper and magazine articles regarding the crack cocaine epidemic" that "depicted racial imagery of heavy involvement by blacks in crack cocaine."[6] Many of these articles characterized crack cocaine use as a "black problem" that needed to be prevented from spreading to the white suburbs.[7] This evidence was enough, Cahill argued, to make unintended racism the central issue in the case. Rejecting intentional racism as unlikely, he suggested that "unconscious feelings of difference and superiority still live on even in well-intentioned minds. There is a realization that most Americans have grown beyond the evils of overt racial malice, but still have not completely shed the deeply rooted cultural bias that differentiates between 'them' and 'us.'"[8] This constituted a violation of the constitutional right to equal protection, rendering the crack statute unconstitutional as it applied to Clary.

Having declared the harsh penalties for crack invalid as applied in this case, Judge Cahill sentenced Clary as if the substance he had carried home had been powder cocaine. Following standard practice under the federal Sentencing Guidelines, Cahill enhanced the penalty slightly because Clary had made a significant effort to transport the drug from California. This behavior indicated forethought and planning that arguably merited additional punishment. The sentence was four years in the federal prison at Springfield, Missouri. Clary served his four-year term and was released. At this point he married and started a family.

Meanwhile, the prosecution decided to take the matter to the Eighth Circuit Court of Appeals. Judge Cahill's opinion was clearly at variance with the prevailing law of the circuit, and indeed, with all of the relevant federal appellate case law. The prosecution anticipated a reversal at that level, and quickly got one.[9] The court of appeals rejected Judge Cahill's reasoning and followed the other circuits that had examined the issue. It found no constitutional defects in the crack legislation. It rejected the finding of unintentional racism, noting that although the trial record in the Clary case "undoubtedly present[ed] the most complete record" on the issue of the crack/powder disparity to come before the court, Judge Cahill's findings nonetheless fell short of establishing that Congress had exercised discriminatory intent in enacting the Sentencing Guidelines.[10] From the appellate court's point of view, the case was not even close. The appellate review panel had no questions for Clary's attorney, and the panel's opinion was unanimous. Judge Cahill had erred, and Clary must be resentenced. So the case went back to the district court for resentencing, and Edward James Clary—now married and a father—went back to prison to complete his ten-year term.

Judge Cahill may not have expected to persuade the higher courts to support his decision. His approach challenged long-accepted rules of interpretation in constitutional law. He was attempting to create a new standard in racial discrimination claims. Legally speaking, the judge was tilting at windmills. But in the realm of science and experience, Judge Cahill's critique was on much firmer ground. There is little doubt that white prejudice has played a significant role in the development of criminal law. The South during the pre–civil rights era, for example, openly used police, courts, and law to enforce white superiority (see, e.g., Sutherland and Cressey 1974;

Tonry 1995; Hawkins 1995; Miller 1996; Higginbotham 1996). That white prejudice continues to influence thinking about crime is also well established (see, e.g., Zatz 2000; Kansal and Mauer 2005; Reiman 1995, chap. 3). The idea that prejudice operates subtly to influence decisions and that its influence is not necessarily consciously felt is also broadly accepted (see, e.g., Banaji and Greenwald 1995; Fiske and Taylor 1991). Judge Cahill's opinion can thus be seen as one judge's crusade to bring jurisprudence into line with reality. Perhaps he thought of himself as the miner's canary that Guinier and Torres describe (2002, 11–12), signaling concern about a crime-control system that cannot persuasively claim to be achieving racial justice in American society (see Chambliss 2003, 315).

Punitive Prohibitionism

Craig Reinarman and Harry Levine (1997), who have written widely on drug policy in America, coined the term *punitive prohibition* to describe the harsh system of arrest, prosecution, and imprisonment that began in the 1920s and has since become the dominant U.S. approach to crime. An important milestone was the adoption in the 1970s of harsh drug laws in New York State at Governor Nelson Rockefeller's urging. The Rockefeller drug laws imposed mandatory-minimum sentences for even minor drug crimes, including possession of small amounts of marijuana. The New York law also increased penalties for repeated offenses and placed restrictions on sentence mitigation, probation, and parole for drug crimes (Reinarman and Levine 1997, 321–22). This extreme form of drug legislation, Reinarman and Levine suggest, should be distinguished from "more tolerant and humane forms of drug prohibition that do not rely so heavily on arresting and imprisoning men and women for possessing and using illicit drugs or for small-scale dealing," an approach these authors dub "regulatory prohibition" (1997, 322). While the United States remains firmly committed to the extreme punitive approach, the nations of Europe tend to more regulatory and are moving increasingly in that direction (Reinarman and Levine 1997, 322).

The struggle over penalties for crack cocaine, in short, is part of a much broader conflict over the means and, in some minds, the ends of the criminal law in the United States. The outcome of this conflict, William Chambliss argues, has implications not just for the poor and racial minorities, but also for the welfare of the nation as a whole:

> Not since the early days of the Civil Rights Movement has there been such a gap between the views of minority and white communities on the

legitimacy of the criminal law. We face a crisis unprecedented in our history with the creation of a crime control industry and a criminal justice
system that is out of control. Reconciling the contradiction between social justice and crime control will require a massive effort, one that is
certain to be resisted by those with a vested interest in the status quo.
(2003, 315)

Those with an interest in the status quo include most of the political establishment and, apparently, much of the law-abiding public. William Brad-
ford Reynolds, attorney general during the first Bush presidency, describes
the approach the federal government took to the control of illicit drugs:
"Overall, we should send the message that there are two ways to approach
drugs: the soft, easy way that emphasizes drug treatment and rehabilitation
versus the hard, tough, approach that emphasizes strong law enforcement
measures and drug testing. Naturally, we favor the latter" (quoted in Chambliss 1999, 94–95).

A decade later, that approach has not changed, despite its apparent ineffectiveness in reducing the demand for illicit drugs and its hefty price tag
(about $40 billion per year when foreign anti-drug efforts are included).
There has been some movement toward drug courts and rehabilitative sentencing, but the punitive framework remains basically intact and not significantly contested at a political level. It is important to ask, as Roland Chilton
did in his presidential address to the American Society of Criminology, how
the current approach to nonviolent crimes like Clary's gained such primacy:

We need to know more about why so many Americans are willing to accept the staggering social, political, and economic costs of creating a vast
set of prisons and filling them beyond capacity not only with people who
are dangerous, but with hundreds of thousands of people who are not
dangerous and never have been. We need to know more about why so
many people accept the drug war as a fact of life—as something that has
always been there and that will always be there. (2001, 4)

Part of the answer may be that harsh criminal controls satisfy a widely
felt yearning for simple, clear-cut standards that put moral responsibility
squarely on the individual's shoulders. This view, historian Michael Willrich
notes, has "ideological roots running deep into the soil of Anglo-American
culture: in the classical Christian doctrine of free will, in the common law,
and, most recently, in liberal political thought" (2003, 68–69). The prevalence of crime news in the media and entertainment tends to make Americans more pessimistic than they might otherwise be about disorder and

disorderly persons. Times of stress, historians observe, tend to bring out the Hobbsian view that justifies drastic, unequivocal state action to preserve social order (see, e.g., Stone 2004). Cost is quite appropriately a secondary issue if the problem is conceived to be preservation of the social fabric of civilized life.

Still, it is remarkable how much the public's fear of crime and its devotion to punishment have increased in the past thirty years, even as victimization rates have been stable or declining (Altheide 2002). Current attitudes stand in sharp contrast to periods of more rehabilitation-oriented thinking. In the Progressive era around the turn of the twentieth century, for example, some cities and states committed themselves to social-control policies that emphasized the potential for rehabilitation. Progressives in Chicago and other cities invented new specialized courts for juvenile, domestic relations, and morals offenses. Judges invited social workers into their courts to work with defendants and fashioned penalties to facilitate rehabilitation. States changed their laws and constitutions to facilitate these developments. There was even talk about the possibility of wiping out crime (see, e.g., Willrich 2003). While these reforms arose out of a somewhat patronizing conviction that immigrants and Blacks newly arrived from the South needed to learn the norms of white, middle-class society, they nevertheless represented a sense of social responsibility and humane concern. Edward James Clary, a youth of disadvantaged background and limited opportunities, would have been an excellent candidate for the soul-saving efforts of Progressive-era reformers.

The Construction of a Social Problem

Clearly, the American public's long-term fascination with law as the basis of effective social control can be shaped in more or less punitive directions. Politicians and the media have a hand in focusing public opinion on punishment. The case of drug control suggests, in addition, a particular interest at the federal level in making the case for law and order in a way that aggrandizes federal power over states and localities. This is a role not envisioned by the drafters of the Constitution, which left crime control to the states.

The federal government first inserted itself aggressively into local law enforcement in the 1920s in the campaign to prohibit alcohol consumption. Mandatory minimums for drug crimes were tried in the 1950s in the Boggs Act and not abandoned until the 1970s, only to return a decade later. The trend toward federal control gathered momentum in the 1970s when Congress began duplicating the jurisdiction of state and local codes. Prohibition of illicit drugs once again provided a rationale for expanding federal authority. Lisa Miller and James Eisenstein observe (2005, 240), "nearly every state felony can now be pursued through federal criminal statutes, and ... cooperative relations between federal and local prosecutors (formal and informal) are increasingly promoted as a solution to urban crime problems." Federal spending on crime control has followed the same pattern, playing a greater and greater role in government's response to perceived crime threats. Federal spending on law enforcement grew from $15 billion in 1991 to $34 billion in fiscal year 2002 (U.S. General Accounting Office 2002).

The problem for democracy is that dissenting voices have tended to get drowned out in the march toward greater and greater reliance on imprisonment as a solution to persistent social problems. The crime-control industry has become a powerful lobbyist in behalf of its own interests. It has been aided by a corporate mass media eager for crime news, which is cheap to produce and offers mass appeal. For political leaders, punitive policies offer a path of least resistance that wins votes. This current instantiation of the traditional American reliance on legal controls, bolstered by strong economic and political forces, feeds a broader shift in public policy away from concern for society's underclass and a new pessimism about its potential for successful integration into the social fabric. More and more, the underclass is something to be feared and protected against, a target for surveillance, blame, and incapacitation.

Political scientists Anne Schneider and Helen Ingram describe this process of targeting groups for ostracism and punishment an example of "degenerative pluralism," to suggest its deviation from a more desirable healthy pluralism in democratic society. Degenerative pluralism occurs when

> [p]luralism no longer reflects reasoned analysis and a balance among competing interests, but degenerates into ill-founded characterizations that set one group against another. Policy arenas dominated by this type of divisive social constructions and the political opportunism of officials do not serve justice, do not create arenas for public discourse, and are not held accountable in terms of effectiveness or efficiency. Without the participation of reasonable interest groups and an informed, alert public to create a balanced dialogue, the discourse about punishment policy is one-sided. (2003, 13; and see Schneider and Ingram 1993)

John Pratt (2007) locates the drift toward punitiveness in a decline of deference for law-enforcement professionals among politicians and in the public at large. Politicians and the media have tended to dismiss the opinions of penal professionals and research on the complexities of crime. It is easier to blame high recidivism rates on lack of punishment. These sentiments have been channeled through the tabloid press, crime-saturated local news, and talk-back radio. The trend is evident not just in the United States, but in many Western nations, where rates of imprisonment have risen steadily during the last decade.

Other analysts speak more pessimistically of the manipulation of public sentiment and cultivation of mass emotionalism as standard fare in politics (see, e.g., Edelman 1988; Burke 1989; Goffman 1974). Sentencing has grown more severe, in this view, because the public finally took notice of the sentencing process. Whatever variant of the pathologies of the democratic process one finds most persuasive, it is clear that the subtleties of modern racism are easily exploited. Policies that target racial minorities play to longstanding racial and economic divisions in American society that are barely acknowledged to exist. The most effective target for these public anxieties is disadvantaged minority youth. Politicians and special interests can exploit this racial divide, playing up the dangers of drug and street crime, and laying the groundwork for a moral panic about crime by drugged teenagers in order to perpetuate their own terms in office as guardians of public safety (see Chambliss 1995, 256).

To analyze the current situation in this way, it should be noted, turns traditional approaches to public policy analysis on their head. The suggestion here is that at least some policies begin not with a broad sense of social need, but with determined manipulation of public sentiment by public elites. Borrowing on deviance theory in sociology, the idea is that powerful moral entrepreneurs, seeking particular policy outcomes, create their own support by successfully labeling some behavior as needing strong social controls (see, e.g., Becker 1973). They do this perhaps out of conviction, but always with the goal of consolidating and extending their power and control.

While there is no denying that illicit drugs pose dangers to society, it must be acknowledged that the contemporary war on drugs represents an extraordinary response to the problem, and that the payoffs have been significant for politicians and powerful law-enforcement interests in our society. The considerable damage this approach has produced—from harassment and profiling of law-abiding minority citizens, to the ruined lives of minor players in drug enterprise—has been largely ignored.

The panicky reaction to crack cocaine in the 1980s and the general hardening of attitudes toward drugs and crime that began in the 1970s,

however, are only the latest manifestations of a much longer-running relationship among race, prohibitionism, and drugs. Punitive prohibitionism has been the predominant approach in dealing with drugs favored by
minority populations throughout U.S. history, even before the nation was
founded. What changed in the 1970s and 1980s was the degree of effort devoted to drug-law enforcement, and the targeting of that effort with hyper-
harsh penalties for sale and possession of crack cocaine. The dramatic outcome—a huge increase in Black imprisonment—should not obscure the
fact that racial prejudice has always been used to promote harsh punishment for drug use.

What demands explanation, then, is not only the recent acceleration of
punitive prohibitionism, but also the long-term resonance of drug-control
policy that targets African Americans and other racial minorities for punishment. The United States has demonstrated remarkable zeal in its effort to
stop the ingestion of mind-altering drugs associated with feared minorities
and the underclass. Dangerous drugs and dangerous minorities, particularly
in combination, are what Murray Edelman (1988) labels "condensation
symbols," providing images that powerfully concentrate public anxieties.
Condensation symbols can evoke positive feelings, as the American flag
does, or negative ones. Most significantly, they discourage pragmatic thinking: "Where condensation symbols are involved, the constant check of the
immediate environment is lacking" (Edelman 1988, 6.)

The association of minorities with drug abuse also feeds the convenient
fiction that racial minorities are responsible for their own victimization.
Harsh, uncompromising penalties for drug abuse suggest the resurgence of
a Victorian sensibility in which the collectivity bears no responsibility for
the unassimilated "others" in American society. The individualistic ethos is
evident not just in the emphasis on punishment, but also in the rules determining what mitigating factors can be considered in imposing it. Federal
sentencing guidelines then in effect specifically discouraged judges from
considering poverty, lack of education, family responsibilities, and social
disadvantage in sentencing.

Judge Cahill was right to see the struggle over Clary's sentence in terms
of the long struggle for civil rights in American society. With the institutional support punitive prohibitionism enjoys and the ideological purposes
it serves, drug policy is unlikely to change unless it becomes a civil rights issue. The most significant obstacles to change may not be a prison-industrial
complex that favors high rates of imprisonment, as is commonly thought, but
American society's unwillingness or inability to confront the legacy of race
in the war on drugs. Racial fears were key to the original criminalization of

drug use, and they played a significant role in the harsh penalties Congress established for crack.

Racism in Law

Racism has been widely recognized as a problem in the criminal justice system. Racial profiling, for example, was a topic in the second presidential debate between Al Gore and George W. Bush (Second Presidential Debate 2000). Both vowed to root out the "bad apples" in the system who perpetuate this practice.[11] Social scientists demonstrate their concern about racism when they design studies to find racial difference in the administration of justice. The working assumption is that racism is a cultural or social force that affects law when its agents are prejudiced. The source of racism, in other words, is outside of law, in society. Law itself is color-blind. This view is widespread, as political scientist Rogers Smith observes: "Through most of modern intellectual history, most American writers have treated race either as essentially a biological category, a cultural/sociological category, or as both" (2004, 43). Political scientists, for example, have generally tended to focus on race as an explanatory variable in the behavior of officials, not as an inherent characteristic of American political institutions.

American political experience, however, is open to another, possibly more persuasive, interpretation. What if race has a more intimate relationship with law and politics than the nation's (recent) commitment to color blindness admits? Critical race theorists reject the assumption that law and the political processes that support it are fundamentally race neutral. They highlight the role that law has played in creating and maintaining racial categories throughout our history. Rogers Smith criticizes political science for not being more aware of the role governing institutions have played in maintaining racial separation in American society: "American racial identities have gained much of their practical reality from their institutionalization by political elites in laws, public policies, and governmental programs" (2004, 43). The consequences of these rules have been enormous for oppressed populations. As Michael Omi and Howard Winant remind us:

> For most of its existence, both as a European colony and as an independent nation, the U.S. was a *racial dictatorship*. From 1607 to 1865—258 years—most non-whites were firmly eliminated from the sphere of politics. After the Civil War there was the brief egalitarian experiment of Reconstruction, which terminated ignominiously in 1877. In its wake followed almost a century of legally sanctioned segregation and denial of

the vote, nearly absolute in the South and much of the Southwest....
These barriers fell only in the mid-1960s. (1994, 65–66)

The pre–civil rights period is not ancient history. Many Americans remember when racial apartheid prevailed by law and social convention. In
the North, as in the South, part of the experience of growing up was learn-
ing how to recognize racial and class differences and to treat them as social
barriers. Failure to do so was grounds for social ostracism, or worse. Law
organized the separation of the races with race-based school districting,
restrictive covenants, redlining, membership rules, and other technical de-
vices. Law also sanctioned the obvious racial markers: segregated restaurants, hotels, drinking fountains, restrooms, and waiting rooms. At every
turn, the promise of violence reinforced the norm of separation (see, e.g.,
Smith 1997; Higginbotham 1996; Katznelson 2005).

The elimination of this system of racial rules was an important first step
in changing American racial policy, but it was only a first step. Institutions
do not operate by rules alone. They have their own internal systems of control and their own priorities that help them maintain their power and place
in society (see, e.g., Becker 1973, chap. 8). Change is difficult because institutions—not individuals or the community as a whole—have the staying
power and commitment to set norms, establish social priorities, and determine what people remember and take for granted, including what seems
fair in society. Institutions set priorities for individuals to act in racist or
nonracist ways (Frymer 2005). Institutions, in the words of anthropologist
Mary Douglas, "secure the social edifice by sacralizing the principles of justice" (1986, 112; and see Orrin and Skowronek 1994, 320). Criminal justice
will change only when these internal mechanisms are revamped to make racial categorization and racial hierarchies irrational for the individuals who
enforce the norms. Changing institutions at this level is fundamental to the
success of the struggle for racial equality.

The persistence of the contemporary war on drugs is a clear indication
that the criminal justice system has not rejected the negative racial stereotypes and prejudice that serve its institutional interests. The problem is not
only the much-discussed racial differences in surveillance, arrest, and prosecution associated with the implementation of the laws on crack, as serious
as these are. These practices derive their support and rationale from the
legislation that authorizes prosecutions. The United States has not come
to grips with the fact that Congress knew that poor minorities, principally
African American, would bear the brunt of its policy (see, e.g., Tonry 1995;
and see chapters 4–6). In a fundamental sense, Congress got exactly what

it intended, which helps to explain its imperviousness to appeals based on racial impact.

Conclusion

Some scholars speculate that our system of criminal justice, reflecting America's deep ambivalence about race and ethnicity, is firmly committed to maintaining a two-tier moral order (Reiman 1995; Beckett and Sasson 2000; Scully 2002). But even if one is less pessimistic, the failure of the system to police itself is, at the very least, part of the unfinished civil rights revolution of the 1960s. The Clary case is a particularly apt illustration of the problems discussed here because Judge Cahill laid the problem bare in his lengthy opinion, and his analysis was summarily rejected on appeal.

The current legal approach, by conceiving of racism only in terms of evil intent and treating it as an anomaly, allows "innocent" whites to escape responsibility for the conditions they help to create (Reiman 1995; Romero 2005). The "intentionalist" approach favored by the courts can usefully be contrasted with how corporations, the military, universities, and other organizations approach lack of racial and gender diversity in their ranks. When the goal is increasing diversity, the emphasis is not on exposing subversive racist behavior within the organization but on adjusting procedures to attract and retain a more varied clientele or workforce. The working assumption is that institutional norms can exclude people on the basis of race or gender without anyone in particular desiring that effect. This outcomes-oriented approach rests on a more complex version of racial motivation than courts have used in discrimination cases, and demonstrates more determination to change institutional priorities. While courts do not have the freedom to ignore intentions, as these organizations do, they could embrace a more nuanced appreciation for race in decision making.

The silence of the Supreme Court on the role of unconscious racism is unfortunate because jurisprudence can sometimes provide Americans with a helpful vocabulary for talking about fundamental governing values, offering concepts that take issues to another level of consideration. But the Supreme Court has done nothing to discourage Americans from continuing to treat words like *racism* and *racist* as moral insults, rather than conditions based in social structures and institutional norms. *Racism* and *racist* are personalized and decontextualized, and so become fighting words, much too strong to be used dispassionately in an effort to create change. As Randall Kennedy describes this tendency:

Allegations of racism put into question more than a person's judgment; they put into question a person's basic moral fitness. Once the racism charge is voiced, considerations of personal honor and public reputation elevate the stakes and polarize the antagonists. Moreover, once a charge of racism is alleged, it tends to dominate all other concerns. Instead of determining on a broad basis the relative merits of a policy, discussion is channeled toward the narrow question of whether the policy at issue is "racist." (1997, 384)

Efforts to define a more useful set of terms are also frustrated by the changing face of race and ethnicity in the United States. As popular and scientific beliefs about race and ethnicity have changed, so has the politics of race.[12] As expressed in law, for example, contemporary racial prejudice is quite sharply at odds with the racism expressed in the laws of the Jim Crow South in the post-Reconstruction, pre–civil rights period. Racism, in other words, is socially constructed and historically contingent. It is hard to create an encompassing approach that takes account of the full range of historical practice. The difficulty is evident in this rather abstract definition: "A racial project can be defined as *racist* if and only if it *creates or reproduces structures of domination based on essentialist categories of race*" (Omi and Winant 1994, 71).

Lawrence Bobo has dubbed our contemporary period one of "laissez faire" racism, which he describes as a "persistent negative stereotyping of African Americans, a tendency to blame blacks themselves for the black-white gap in socioeconomic status, and resistance to meaningful policy efforts to ameliorate U.S. racist social conditions and institutions" (2004, 16–17; and see Kinder and Sanders 1996). Public opinion research and years of experimental research in social psychology support this analysis. Social psychologists have identified prevalent negative habits of mind about African Americans in whites that combine easily with the current ascendancy of free-market individualism and the comforting presence of color-blind policy (Sears et al. 2000).

The ostensibly color-blind philosophy of our day, as Bobo and others suggest, bears a certain family resemblance to this nation's overtly racist past. Nowhere is this more evident, this book argues, than in the evolution of drug policy. The next step, then, is to turn back the clock to the nation's first well-organized national war on drugs: the effort to deter and eventually stamp out alcohol as a social beverage. This ancestor drug policy contains important lessons for anyone concerned about the contemporary war on drugs and its pernicious racial impacts.

two

Race in America's First
War on Drugs

The campaign against alcohol that resulted in the Eighteenth Amendment to the U.S. Constitution is America's best-known war on drugs, but it was not without precedent. The consumption of drugs was an issue even in the colonial period, when alcohol use by Indians, slaves, servants, and other social inferiors was considered a problem serious enough to merit legislation. The irony is that whites in this period were very heavy drinkers by contemporary standards. They consumed rum, beer, wine, hard cider, and whisky, all in large amounts. While some Puritan congregations considered alcoholism within their own community a problem, drinking per se was not particularly frowned on. What the colonials feared was the inebriation of their social inferiors, who might become dangerously out of control. Colonial laws restricting alcohol sales to Indians and other subordinated groups were not particularly effective, but they show how drugs, laws, and concerns about maintaining social hierarchies are connected (see, e.g., McWilliams, in press).

The nationwide Prohibition campaign and the contemporary war on drugs offer further evidence that anxieties about race and class hierarchies underlie the criminalization of drug use. Drinking and drug use became issues when immigration, urbanization, and the growth of industrial society shook up old hierarchies and began to transform American society. This chapter shows how racism and ethnic prejudices bolstered the case for criminalization in the Prohibition era. Although not always acknowledged in histories of the Prohibition movement, the role of racism is easy to see in the evolution of the anti-alcohol campaign. The moral entrepreneurs who led the criminalization campaign against alcohol, like those who led the campaign against crack and other drugs, found race a powerful tool in justifying drastic action.

In standard accounts of Prohibition, the emphasis is on the failure of the new law to change ingrained behavior and the consequences of that failure. This chapter looks in the opposite direction, at the creative effort that led to Prohibition. How did people convince themselves that alcohol use should be made a crime? The coming-to-be of Prohibition was a grass-roots movement of monumental proportions, the largest anti-drug campaign in U.S. history to arise out of popular sentiment, rather than from the government's own manipulation of public opinion. Government's role in the Prohibition movement was to respond, somewhat reluctantly at first, to pressure from the Anti-Saloon League and other activist organizations, rather than to promote its own agenda. Most public officials had not yet realized the potential for self-aggrandizement offered by a war on drugs.

The effort to control alcohol spanned a century and dominated local, state, and national campaigns for four decades. It was a decisive factor in three presidential elections, engaging every sector of society in debate about the dangers of alcohol. Prohibition changed American drinking habits. Prohibition also changed the relationship between states and the federal government, revealing the potential for a national drug policy and marking the beginning of federal encroachment into local law-enforcement concerns. The enactment of a federal Prohibition amendment was a huge victory for Progressives and for religious and other organizations determined to play a role in politics. Prohibition is also an object lesson in the power of moralistic argument in American politics.

Racial stereotypes figured prominently in this national effort, as it had in the Puritan-era anti-alcohol campaigns. In the South, the image was the menacing drunken Negro male and his inherent propensity to alcoholic excess. In the West, it was the drunken Indian. In the North, the racialized rallying point was the working-class immigrant who had no desire to assimilate. The use of race to push Prohibition was obvious and fundamental to the entire effort. The practical ramifications were devastating for Black citizens in the South. Blacks were falsely charged with being uniformly "wet"; this misrepresentation provided momentum to forces determined to take away the right of southern Blacks to vote. By the turn of the century, southern whites had changed their state constitutions to disenfranchise Blacks and poor whites. Northern Prohibitionists generally accepted this development without complaint in order to get the South to join their anti-alcohol campaign.

In the way it portrayed race, Prohibition was clearly a movement of a different age. The racial and ethnic images were flamboyant in publications of all types, including national circulation magazines, scholarly journals, and the *New York Times*. There was no compunction about drawing on the crudest stereotypes of degeneracy in subordinated populations. Significant physical and mental differences were taken for granted. Blacks were assumed to be both mentally and morally inferior. The separatist proclivities of immigrants were assumed from their failure to speak English. Patronizing assumptions about white superiority and fears of "infection" by nonwhite elements were openly deployed to justify criminal controls. Native-born whites of the middling classes were encouraged to see themselves as bearers of the burden of alcohol prohibition for the sake of weaker souls in their midst.

This chapter begins with an overview of the movement from temperance to Prohibition. Subsequent sections look at how the effort developed, first in the North and then in the southern states. There were obvious changes in the racial tenor of the campaign as it progressed. Anti-alcohol advocates were at first eager to recruit members, and therefore welcomed everyone. Toward the end of the nineteenth century, as the movement focused less on volunteerism and more on punitive legal measures, activists more frequently deployed racist arguments. Racism and ethnic stereotyping gave energy to the campaign for criminal controls.

The Remarkable Fact of Prohibition

Temperance—the idea that the drinking of alcoholic beverages damages individuals, families, and society—was a matter of conviction among many people nearly a century before Prohibition took effect. In the 1820s and 1830s, Protestant ministers around the nation were actively promoting temperance in their sermons. The Woman's Christian Temperance Union (WCTU), founded in 1874 in the Reconstruction South by Christian evangelicals, helped to organize already existing temperance sentiment among women. There were also secular groups dedicated to reforming American drinking habits. The dominant spirit of the early movement was benevolent reformism, which concentrated on persuading drinkers to embrace abstinence, or at least moderation, in order to lift themselves and their families out of poverty.

Reform efforts nevertheless had a coercive element, and this side of the movement grew as many drinkers proved resistant to the call for abstinence. The message was both moralistic and perfectionistic, appealing to some of the same sentiments that grounded the anti-slavery movement, with which temperance became associated in the 1850s. By 1856, eight states had passed some form of legislation to limit the sale of alcohol. Most of these laws left the liquor question to localities. Some towns and small cities opted for stringent regulation of dram shops, rather than an outright ban on the sale of liquor. Experimentation and debate were the rule in this period, with some towns prohibiting all sales of alcoholic beverages for a few years, and then repealing the most onerous restrictions a few years later.

In the North, the movement became more coercive near the end of the nineteenth century, fueled partly by dissemination of scientific findings suggesting that alcohol was quite harmful to the human body, and partly by fear of the burgeoning immigrant classes then crowding into the slums of American cities and showing an interest in unionization. The new immigrants tended to be of peasant stock from eastern and central Europe, and they were growing in number, to nearly 1 million per year in 1900. In addition, uneducated Blacks were arriving from the rural South.

Some Prohibition advocates brought these two concerns together, suggesting that the industrializing environment was growing too competitive to tolerate alcohol use by the flood of new immigrants (Patton 1891, 706). Social workers focused on the corrupting power of the liquor industry and on the saloon as the breeder of poverty, prostitution, vice, and crime. Embedded in this critique was discomfort about the impact of the Irish, Germans, Italians, and other newcomers on American political traditions:

> The saloon fosters an un-American spirit among the foreign-born population of our country. The influx of foreigners into our urban centers, many of whom have liquor habits, is a menace to good government. . . . [T]he foreign-born population is largely under the social and political control of the saloon. If the cities keep up their rapid growth, they will soon have the balance of political power in the nation and become the storm centers of political life. The hope of perpetuating our liberties is to help the foreigners correct any demoralizing custom, and through self-restraint assimilate American ideals. (Barker, *The Saloon Problem*, quoted in Timberlake 1963, 118)

Bars and saloons became a rallying point for reform in 1895 with the formation of the Anti-Saloon League, one of the nation's first single-interest groups. Refusing to align itself with any party, the League focused on individual candidates, supporting anyone who was anti-alcohol, including reformed alcoholics. At first, it concentrated on state-level Prohibition, but soon the League began to press for an amendment to the Constitution that would prohibit the manufacture, sale, and consumption of alcoholic beverages.

The Temperance Movement in the South

The fear of immigrants that animated the anti-alcohol campaign in the North was largely absent in the South. There the perceived menace was drinking by the indigenous poor, especially Blacks. The images were often lurid:

> The primitive Negro field hand, a web of strong, sudden impulses, good and bad, comes into town or settlement on Saturday afternoon and pays his fifty cents for a pint of Mr. Levy's gin. He absorbs not only its toxic heat, but absorbs also the suggestions, subtly conveyed, that it contains aphrodisiacs. He sits in the road or in the alley at the height of his debauch, looking at that obscene picture of a white woman on the label, drinking in the invitation which it carries. And then comes—opportunity. There follows the hideous episode of the rope or the stake. (Irwin 1908, 28)

As in the North, the political effort began with pressure for local option legislation, but eventuated in strong southern support for a national amendment. In the short period between the summer of 1907 and early 1909, for example, six southern states adopted Prohibitionist legislation, outlawing the sale of alcohol and its manufacture for sale. Historian Dewey Grantham estimates that "the movement to prohibit the manufacture and sale of alcoholic beverages may well have been the most dynamic and passionately supported 'reform' in the South during the Progressive era" (1983, 160). Supporters preached that Prohibition would help end political corruption and would bring the South into the modern era through government's reassertion of traditional values of respect for family and community. The argument was that alcohol "retards the highest development of the individual, and the prosperity of the community. The ablest and most far-sighted leaders of Southern opinion have come to the realization of this truth. . . . The South needs for its development capital and intelligent and diversified labor. It cannot attract either if industry is made irregular and life and property insecure through the multiplication of doggeries and dives" (Foxcraft 1908, 632). The movement gained support from the fact that it did not seek to end home brewing or personal consumption of alcohol, traditions that were long established among wealthy and rural classes in the South. It was commerce in alcohol and drinking in public that was under attack.

Evangelicals, numerous in the South, were an important part of this movement. They had long disdained alcohol as the root of many social problems, and they were becoming more willing to advocate for legislation that would advance their views. Their advocacy of morals legislation, Ted Ownby suggests, "showed that evangelicals were coming to terms with a larger world by trying to conquer it. No longer satisfied to separate themselves from the sinful excesses of non-evangelical behavior, they now tried to stamp out many sins altogether" (1990, 208). As the movement developed, those attracted were not just the religiously devout, but also social justice advocates and business interests (Grantham 1983, 161). The legal reform agenda was broader than alcohol. It included proposals to eliminate gambling, prostitution, prizefights, and even spitting and swearing. The regulation of business and public services was also part of this reformist effort (Pegram 1997, 59). As Reverend John White wrote in 1908:

> The intelligent people of the South are looking upon Prohibition, not as a temperance reform, but as statesmanship—a public policy, favorable to religion, favorable to education, favorable to industry, favorable to the coming generation, and as a necessity of Southern conditions in particular, and as an ideal of social obligation to the broad general good. (135)

America's emergence into World War I spurred the national Prohibition movement in both the North and South. Anti-German sentiment was high, and it was noted that a large proportion of the breweries and saloons in the United States were owned and operated by Germans or German Americans. It also seemed unpatriotic to make alcohol when the nation was rationing itself to send grain shipments to Europe (Slosson 1935, 106). The adoption of Prohibition began to be regarded as part of the war effort (Warburton 1932, 42). The determined efforts of Protestant clergymen and women's groups were paying off. The availability of alcohol was beginning to seem like a serious social problem that demanded a national response. But the idea of national Prohibition also tapped the growing confidence in the reform capacities of government that was characteristic of the Progressive era. Not all Progressives favored Prohibition, but most of them did.

The Coming of Prohibition

These forces created a confluence of circumstances favorable to Prohibition. A new wave of state laws took effect around 1906, just before the Anti-Saloon League began campaigning for a national amendment. At that point, the momentum began to swing toward national Prohibition. By 1914, fourteen states had approved Prohibition, and many others had allowed localities to go dry by local option. Three-fourths of the area of the United States had outlawed saloons, and the South had almost entirely gone dry. In many areas, only the large cities and mill towns remained wet. Chicago, for example, had more saloons than all the states in the South combined (Slosson 1935, 105).

Advocates of national Prohibition confronted scattered opposition. Clarence Darrow argued in a 1909 speech that working people needed protection from industrial machinery and mining hazards a lot more than they needed Prohibition (quoted in Monahan 1909, 89–91). Labor leaders described the movement in hostile terms: "All this temperance legislation proceeds on the theory that those who patronize saloons or who take a drink are weak or irresponsible or need a guardian" (Monahan 1909, 87–88). But most politicians, including Al Smith, who later made repeal a central plank in his 1928 bid for president, did not oppose the Eighteenth Amendment at this time. Those who provided the ethnic grist for the Prohibition campaign and those offended by it had no effective avenues for complaint:

> Only brewers, distillers, and other commercial interests made strenuous efforts to block the reform. Individuals and groups offended by the challenge to their ethnic cultural traditions or by the limitation of their right to choose what to drink objected to the national liquor ban, but they lacked the channels and agents to give their protest focus and strength. (Kyvig 2000, 5)

At this point, the campaign for the Eighteenth Amendment was moving "like a whirlwind" (Kyvig 2000, 5). The Senate and the House of Representatives approved the constitutional proposal in 1917, and within five years, forty-four states had ratified the amendment, which prohibited "the manufacture, sale, or transportation of intoxicating liquors within, the importation thereof into, or the exportation thereof from the United States, and all territory subject to the jurisdiction thereof for beverage purposes...." This was arguably the most important legislation the Progressive era produced.

Enforcing Prohibition

Once adopted, Prohibition seemed impregnable, regardless of the opposition it aroused (Pegram 1998, 166). Most observers, Kyvig notes, assumed that liquor would quickly disappear from the American scene: "The possibility that a constitutional mandate would be ignored simply did not occur to them" (2000, 20; and see 53–54). Prohibition had strong bipartisan support in the House and Senate. The amendment had been adopted by large majorities in most states, and history itself seemed to suggest its invincibility: No amendment to the Constitution had ever been rescinded.

Both political parties were deferential to the single-issue Prohibitionists, although the Republicans, as the party in power, became associated with the law's enforcement. Democrats in Congress were of somewhat mixed minds about their support because many of them had ties to unions and ethnic groups opposed to the policy. But the strong public sentiment in favor of Prohibition made them reluctant to push for repeal.

From the outset, however, there was resistance to Prohibition at the local level, particularly in places where immigrant populations were large and politically organized. New York, New Jersey, and Massachusetts responded to the federal government's first enforcement statute, the 1919 Volstead Act, with state laws permitting the production and sale of low-alcohol beer and light wines (Pegram 1998, 151). Although these laws were later overturned by the U.S. Supreme Court, a consistent supporter of national Prohibition legislation, state-level defiance was a sign of problems to come. Many immigrants continued to make beer and wine as they had in the past. Constantine Panunzio, a sociologist who studied the reaction to Prohibition among immigrants, observed that ethnic and working-class groups remained steadfast in their opposition to Prohibition:

> The first broad fact to be recorded is that the foreign born of all European nationalities at no time conformed to Prohibition. There were groups, consisting mainly of Protestants and some reformers, who conformed. . . . But generally speaking, the foreign born of European extraction or culture, as well as many of their American-born children, did not adhere to the movement. (1934, 120)

Support for Prohibition soon began to wane among urban professionals, a traditionally abstemious sector of the population. Spurred on by the prosperous 1920s, a secular consumer culture was emerging: "Whereas saloons had offended middle-class sensibilities before Prohibition, Prohibition-era speakeasies furnished enjoyment and a hint of illegal adventure to the self-indulgent new middle class of the 1920s" (Pegram 1998, 168, 177). Women, to the chagrin of Prohibitionists, were among those participating. In the past, women had been the mainstay of the movement, both in the churches and in somewhat more secular organizations, most famously, the WCTU.

Despite these defections, the political commitment to the idea of national Prohibition remained strong throughout the 1920s. Members of Congress spoke eloquently in favor of Prohibition, and those who opposed the policy lost elections. It became increasingly obvious, however, that the political commitment was more rhetorical than pragmatic. Congress appropriated only $6 to $10 million per year between 1921 and 1926 for enforcement (Pegram 1998, 159). The actual need, one federal official estimated, was closer to $300 million per year (Warburton 1932, 44–45).

Prohibitionists complained that the funds committed to enforcement were inadequate at every level. Most of the states passed "baby Volstead" acts, some of which were very severe, but they spent little money to enforce them. The states had spent a total of only $550,000 by 1923; in 1927, twenty-eight states allocated no funds at all for the purpose (Pegram 1998, 159). Convictions under the Volstead Act never exceeded 60,000 per year, and acquittals were frequent, reaching 20,000 in 1928, for example (Pegram 1998, 159). As Warburton notes: "It was truthfully remarked that the drys had the law and the wets had the liquor" (1932, 45).[1]

The consumption of alcohol probably did decline during Prohibition, though it is difficult to know because the practice went underground. It is clear, for example, that the market for illegal drink was huge and growing during the 1920s. Home brewing and distilling had become major sources of alcohol for consumers in cities. Weak and corrupt enforcement efforts ensured that there were plenty of people in the business of selling alcohol to Americans determined to drink it. In urban areas, they tended to be young, white, ethnic entrepreneurs willing to run and sell liquor with the support of criminal gangs. Prohibition had spawned an ethnic vice industry.[2]

Temperance as a Symbolic Crusade

The real prize in the struggle over Prohibition, sociologist Joseph Gusfield suggests, was the amendment itself, not an actual revolution in drinking habits. Effective enforcement was never the point. The consumption of alcohol—like gambling, political corruption, and illicit sex—can be expected to continue because people enjoy doing it. The tendency toward nonenforcement does not make these laws unimportant or insignificant, however. Prohibition served the important purpose of differentiating groups and assigning status. It marked the supremacy of small-town and rural middle-class, white Protestant morality over the norms of the foreign-born, the Catholics, the Jews, and the Blacks—groups who were believed to have another approach to alcohol. Most important, these groups threatened the old order by their growing numbers and their growing economic significance in industrial society (1986, 6).

Conflicts over status and rank are real conflicts, even though we do not always recognize them as such, Gusfield argues:

A political model that ignores symbolic action in politics would exclude an important category of governmental action. It is a major way in which conflicts in the social order are institutionalized as political issues. Groups form around such issues, symbols are given specific meaning, and opposing forces have some arena in which to test their power and bring about compromise and accommodation, if possible. This is precisely what the issues of Prohibition and Temperance have enabled the status groups involved as Wets and Drys to accomplish. (1986, 182)

Temperance, Gusfield concludes, was about which status group would be dominant in the new century, with alcohol consumption marking the difference among the groups: "Drinking (and abstinence) has been one of the significant consumption habits distinguishing one subculture from another. It has been one of the major characteristics through which Americans have defined their own cultural commitments" (Gusfield 1986, 3; and see 5–6, 23, 29–30). This point was also evident to some critical observers of the time:

How many Roman Catholics are Prohibitionists? How many Jews, the most temperate race on earth, are to be found in the ranks of Prohibition? Or Lutherans? Or German Protestants generally? What is the proportion of Episcopalians to that of Methodists, Baptists and Presbyterians, and the like, in the active Prohibition army? The answer to these questions will, I venture to say, prove conclusively the assertion that the fight for Prohibition is synonymous with the fight of a certain religious sect, or group of religious sects, for the supremacy of its ideas. (Andreae 1915, 12)

Prohibitionists were also unself-conscious about using racial rhetoric to argue for the cause. The Anti-Saloon League, a leader in the drive for Prohibition, was clear in its white supremacist stance: "The Anglo-Saxon stock is the best improved, hardiest and fittest—if we are to preserve this nation and the Anglo-Saxon type, we must abolish saloons" (quoted in Gusfield 1986, 100). The rhetoric grew even more extreme later as it became clear that Prohibition was a failing campaign:

The political influence which appoints grafting agents, protects bootleggers, and corrupts courts, finds a powerful support in our alien population. Our experience during the war disclosed conditions that otherwise we might not have realized for another generation. We discovered among us what are practically colonies of foreign peoples who are not assimilated and have no desire to become assimilated. We found five millions of foreign birth who cannot read, write, nor speak the English language.

If naturalized ... they will call themselves, not Americans, but German-Americans, Irish-Americans, Italian-Americans, Greek-Americans, Polish-Americans, or whatever other prefix may denote the nationality to which they cling.... These insoluble lumps of unassimilated and unassimilable peoples are "wet" by heredity and habit. They come from wine-drinking nations and, ignorant of our language and laws, they see no reason why as citizens of what they understand is a "free country" they should not manufacture, sell, and use the liquor to which they are accustomed. They vote as racial groups and seek to impose their racial views on Congress and state legislatures. (Oakley 1923, 127–28)

This vengeful analysis came not from a fringe element in the movement, but from a mainstream figure, Imogen Oakley, an officer in the General Federation of Women's Clubs. The WCTU, an organization of upper-class, educated women, was similar in deeming liquor as alien and un-American, a despicable "foreign influence." Along with other organizations in the movement, the WCTU became a supporter of legislation to drastically limit immigration. It was joined by the Ku Klux Klan, a strong advocate of Prohibition and immigration control.

Even members of the clergy promoted Prohibition by cultivating fear of foreigners and prejudice against Jews and Catholics. The most prominent and notorious among them, Methodist Bishop James Cannon, was an activist in the Anti-Saloon League and influential figure in Washington. Cannon campaigned tirelessly against the presidential bid of Catholic Al Smith, a supporter of repeal, and he did not hesitate to reveal his anti-Catholic and anti-Semitic views: "Governor Smith wants the Italians, the Sicilians, the Poles and the Russian Jews. That kind has given us a stomachache. We have been unable to assimilate such people in our national life, so we shut the door to them. But Smith says, 'give me that kind of people.' He wants the kind of dirty people that you find today on the sidewalks of New York" (quoted in Dabney 1949, 188).

The tendency to draw on anti-Catholic and anti-Semitic epithets to characterize the opposition continued, even after repeal of Prohibition. For example, Ernest Gordon, in his pro-Prohibition book, *The Wrecking of the Eighteenth Amendment*, describes "the debacle" of repeal with reference to "Mr. Celler, a Jewish representative from Brooklyn" and "his Russian Jewish colleague, Mr. Dickstein" (1943, 202).

Anti-Catholic and anti-Semitic rhetoric also played well in the southern states. But whites there were much more preoccupied with maintaining the system of white supremacy than with conflicts over immigrant influence.

Lacking large industrial cities, the South was not a magnet for foreign immigration in this period. Maintaining white control in states with large populations of citizens who had once been slaves, however, was a major challenge. It should not be surprising that racism played an important role in the Prohibition movement in the former Confederacy and, less directly, in the North as well.

Anti-Black Racism: Unacknowledged Bulwark of the Prohibitionist Cause

Alcohol, many Prohibition-era whites assumed, demoralized and debauched Black men, reducing their efficiency as workers and fueling the secret lust they allegedly harbored for white women. Barrooms were thought to create the potential for serious racial conflict because they encouraged uninhibited behavior among the poorer classes of both racial groups. To some extent, the concern was paternalistic. Many dry leaders were convinced that Prohibition would prove morally and economically beneficial to Blacks. Reverend John White, for example, pronounced Prohibition "the opportunity to emphasize our recognition of the South's responsibility for the negro's moral welfare. Anglo-Saxon supremacy should thus be exercised in consideration of our kindly concern about his development in our midst" (1908, 141). This idea attracted even some Black leaders, most notably Booker T. Washington, who characterized Prohibition as a "moral movement" that would benefit both races (Walton and Taylor 1971, 247; Grantham 1983, 176). Washington's position suggests the complexity of the issue for African Americans, who sought to participate in the national dialogue, but who were handicapped by the limitations of white racism and by their marginalized status. Ultimately, they were unable to resist the tendency for whites to objectify them in the rush to legislate.

Preston Slosson describes the overwhelming support that eventually developed in favor of Prohibition in the southern states and its connection with racial issues:

> The attitude of the South is unmistakable. Nearly the whole section was dry by state law before the federal amendment was proposed, and the Southern states, in spite of traditional state-rights scruples, were among the first to approve the Eighteenth Amendment and the staunchest in supporting it against later attack. In part this may be explained by the predominantly rural character of the South, as the great cities were always the centers of opposition to prohibitory laws; in part also by the absence of European immigrant colonies to whom wine and beer were as

much a matter of course, as milk and water. But undoubtedly the major factor was the widespread conviction that to the Negro, as to the Indian, alcohol was a perilous incitement to crimes of violence. (1935, 108; see also 253)

The struggle over Prohibition in the South thus involved the kinds of middle-class concerns over competing visions of the coming era that Gusfield found in the North, but also a race and social control element that tended to unite southern whites of all walks in life against their nonwhite fellow citizens. Racial antagonism energized Prohibitionism in the South, as ethnic and class antagonism fueled Prohibitionist fervor in the North.

The question of how to develop a unified Prohibition movement was complicated by the Civil War and postwar strains in the relationship between the North and South. White southerners firmly rejected the postwar effort of northern Prohibitionists, many with roots in the anti-slavery movement, to develop a racially integrated anti-alcohol movement. The ultimate solution to the "problem" of Black participation in the political debate over Prohibition was disenfranchisement in the South and passive acceptance of this development in the North.

Alcohol as a "Negro Problem"

In the 1700s, even before the temperance movement had a name, there were concerns among whites about drinking by Blacks (see, e.g., Walton and Taylor 1971). Liquor was widely available because the South's agricultural economy made it easy to produce brandy and other forms of alcohol. In Alabama, James Sellers notes, "nearly every well-regulated plantation and farm had its own distillery and a considerable quantity must have been produced" (1943, 27). Plantations and farms sold what they did not drink. Alcohol was also part of the slavery system, used by masters to reward their slaves and to increase output. The habit of consuming alcohol had been part of the African societies from which the slaves came, so it was easy to assimilate it into the system (Lusane 1991, 28–29). Slaves were also part of the alcohol distribution network. They were often sent to buy alcohol for their masters, but they were also allowed to buy it to drink themselves and for resale to other slaves (Pearson and Hendricks 1967, 26–27).

Many whites were uncomfortable with this arrangement, regarding Blacks as too irresponsible to be trusted with regulating their own alcohol consumption. A subtext in the elaborate chivalry of the period was the fear that white women would be violated by Black men. Alcohol was believed to elevate the risk, a perspective that was reflected in early state liquor laws. Virginia's regulations date from 1705, when all liquor traffic with slaves was forbidden without the master's consent (Pearson and Hendricks 1967, 25–26). The Alabama territory began regulating alcohol sales to slaves and to Indians in the 1760s (Sellers 1943, 3–4, 11–12). Tennessee passed a similar law in 1779 (Walton 1970).

Free Blacks were also considered a problem because they sometimes sold liquor to slaves. An 1822 Alabama law made it illegal for "any free Negro or mulatto, either directly or indirectly, to retail any kind of spirituous liquors within this state" (quoted in Sellers 1943, 29). These concerns grew stronger after the Nat Turner rebellion in 1831, when fear of slave uprisings led to a new round of liquor legislation covering both slaves and free Blacks. An 1832 Alabama law forbid liquor sales at any public meeting and fined masters who allowed these purchases knowing that their slaves would resell (Sellers 1943, 29; Pearson and Hendricks 1967, 27). During this period Tennessee first regulated, then eventually forbad, liquor sales to free Blacks (Walton 1970). But prosecutions were rare before the Civil War. Pearson and Hendricks sum up the public mood, which regarded alcohol consumption by Blacks as regrettable, but common, despite the law: "Even more objectionable than permitting on-premise drinking was selling to slaves. This was done extensively, as is shown by numerous petitions, laws, newspaper reports, proposals in lodges, and private correspondence which speak against the practice" (1967, 116–17).

Yet increasingly alcohol was also beginning to be seen by some southerners as a menace in its own right. The temperance movement was making inroads on the region's traditional tolerance for heavy drinking. A temperance society in Northern Neck, Virginia, for example, described drunkenness as a "prevalent, loathsome, and pernicious vice" that "brings thousands prematurely to the grave; fills the land with widows, and orphans; reduces multitudes of amiable families to poverty and wretchedness; populates our poor-houses, prisons, and penitentiaries; and tends to the subversion of all order, and the universal prostration of morals in society" (reprinted in Pearson and Hendricks 1967, 308).

Racial Separatism and the Temperance Movement in the South

The prewar temperance movement in the South, as in the North, focused more on amelioration than on coercion through legislation. The appeal was mostly to the religiously observant middle classes, who joined in significant numbers. The movement directed itself to both races. Records indicate that slaves and free Blacks undertook abstinence in significant numbers. In Petersburg, Virginia, for example, approximately three hundred African Americans were among the one thousand people who reportedly took the pledge in 1843 (Pearson and Hendricks 1967, 93). Temperance societies also focused on children and students, many of whom signed pledges.

There was no inclination, however, to reconsider the fundamental relationship between the races. White southerners had no patience for arguments linking the condition of alcohol addiction to the institution of slavery. This put northern organizations in a difficult position. They were under pressure from abolitionists to take more account of the interest of Blacks in temperance and to include the abolition of slavery as part of their platform. Frederick Douglass and William Lloyd Garrison excoriated the temperance movement for its failure to argue for abolition of slavery and for cooperating with slaveholders in promoting abstinence (Walton and Taylor 1971). But when northern-based temperance societies did include an abolitionist plank in their campaigns, their southern supporters protested bitterly and then dropped their association with the national movement (Pearson and Hendricks 1967, 88–89).

After the Civil War freed the slaves and Reconstruction provided Black males with the franchise, the alcohol issue became more complex. Restrictions on Black purchases and consumption of alcohol were repealed in the wave of Reconstruction-era reforms. Alcohol became more generally available in most states. In Virginia, for example, tippling houses once again became legal. Restrictions on licenses to sell alcohol were removed. Pearson and Hendricks describe a trend toward democracy in drinking that permitted alcohol consumption by the South's newly enfranchised Black citizens:

> In the cities one's opportunity to select resulted in Negro barrooms. But in the country, where three-fourths of these institutions were, the Negro came in perhaps by a separate door but drank from an end of the same counter as the whites. If he was impolite or failed to "know his place" the bartender threw him out. Whether from lack of inclination or of time or of money the numerous plantation Negroes were apt to come only on Saturdays when they would loll around and perhaps take home a bottle.... Ladies sometimes complained that the stores and the streets were unpleasant for them and later there was widespread terror of drunken Negroes in rural areas. These things were incidental—the customers did not object. The barroom was a man's institution in a man's world. (1967, 164–65)

Yet the temperance issue remained controversial and divisive, both among Blacks and whites. Both Prohibitionists and anti-Prohibitionists campaigned for the Black vote (Walton 1970, 730). Although whites often claimed that Blacks always voted wet, organizational records show that many Blacks had joined temperance societies and taken the abstinence pledge. Records show that at least one African American man was a speaker at a state temperance convention in Tennessee, and there were mixed rallies and committees on both sides of the issue in other border states (Walton 1970, 731). Booker T. Washington encouraged Blacks to create their own temperance societies, which they did in significant numbers (Walton and Taylor 1971, 247).

Outside the South, the temperance movement in the Reconstruction period began more openly to acknowledge Black interest in the cause. When northern lodges in the United Order of True Reformers were established in 1874, some of them admitted African Americans. In the South, however, white members of the organization segregated themselves in separate lodges and dominated the local movement (Walton and Taylor 1971, 160–61). The same happened with the Good Templars, whose national headquarters decided in 1866 that skin color should not determine membership. Southern whites first attempted to set up separate lodges, but when the national organization ordered racial integration, the southern units quit and founded their own society, resolving that "we will submit to no action by any parties, whether individuals or Lodges, which interferes with, or disturbs the social relations of the white and colored races" (Sellers 1943, 46–49).

Temperance-minded southern whites had little confidence in the capacity of even temperance-oriented Blacks to manage liquor or in their organizational skills and dependability. Most significantly, they feared that Black participation in the crusade would dissuade whites from joining the movement. Black volunteers were often turned away by white temperance organizations, including churches (Sellers 1943, 240, 282). Disagreement with the prevailing policy of racial apartheid was risky. When Baptist minister John R. Moffett, a lifelong temperance advocate, gave a sermon in his Danville, Virginia, church condemning white supremacy as contrary to God's plan in 1891, whites were outraged. Political leaders declared he should be hanged. Soon afterwards he was shot dead in the street by a bartender who was never prosecuted (Pearson and Hendricks 1967, 217–18).

Racial Scapegoating to Promote Prohibition

Anti-Black attitudes were hardening in this period, and media images of drunken Blacks helped to fuel the growing racist sentiment. The press and politicians circulated stories of Blacks freely indulging in alcohol and of racial mixing in saloons, creating a sense of urgency among whites to make drastic changes. The Progressive movement, with its emphasis on government as the route to social betterment, was part of this development. Sellers describes the connection between southern white uneasiness about Reconstruction, Progressivism, and the anti-alcohol movement:

> Men glimpsed new possibilities of government action and control. And in the social upheaval caused by the sudden freeing of the Negroes a greater urgency than ever before was added to the cause. Fear of the drunken black man spurred the temperance people to take more vigorous measures to promote Prohibition. Here was a problem which must be solved for public safety as well as for public morality. The saloon, where blacks and whites mingled and where crime was bred, must go. (1943, 51; see also 96)

Race riots in Wilmington, North Carolina, in 1898 and in Atlanta in 1906 also frightened the white political establishment. The riots were blamed, in part, on excessive drinking in saloons, which had allegedly caused the mobs to lose control, setting Blacks and poor whites against each other. More fundamentally, the riots were seen as evidence of a breakdown in social order brought about by the North's ill-founded theory of racial equality. Some politicians called for the reassertion of white supremacy and for repeal of the Civil War amendments. Historian Charles Crowe draws on the political discourse of the day to describe the frenzied 1905–6 campaign for the governorship of Georgia in which images of Black sexual license and white chivalry dominated the debate:

> If the black man as sexual criminal illustrated ultimate evil, "the most precious flower of Southern womanhood" before "defilement" represented the highest good. Leaders reminded Georgians that society existed, first of all, to protect "the imperious beauty, the immaculate virtue of Caucasian women," the "most beautiful and purest women . . . in all of history." (1968, 249)

The Prohibition movement was similar in drawing on racist imagery about Black sexual predation in order to gain support. Consider, for example, the way Prohibition advocate John Temple Graves described the coming of Prohibition to Georgia:

> No one thing outside of religion, however, has had so telling an influence upon this movement as the effect of bad liquor upon lawless Negroes. The rural South has passed, within the last five years, through a reign of

terror from this source. Upon the Southern farms every man has left his home for work with apprehension in the morning and thanked God when he returned from his fields at the evening to find all well with the women of his home. The Atlanta riot, terrible and lamentable as it was, was an abnormal outburst of apprehension over the appalling increase of the crime of crimes that was casting a shadow over every Southern home in suburb and small city and on the farms. And the idea became lodged in the Southern mind that the brutal impulse behind these fiendish assaults was fired and inspired by the rotten whiskey and the viler cocaine and other drugs which were dispensed to the Negro race. (1908, 88–89)

Many southern whites became convinced that the route to racial calm and general improvement of conditions was through strong restrictions on the consumption of alcoholic beverages (Pegram 1998, 126–27). The biggest impediment to this reform, they believed, was the Black vote. Whites who favored temperance complained that they were forced to choose between racial solidarity, which usually required voting Democratic and wet, and voting their views. In the words of an observer sympathetic to the white southern position:

The smallest split in the ranks of the party might mean the end of white control. To permit the discussion and division so essential to democracy and progress and to bring an end to the necessity for fraud, many leaders of the Democratic party in Virginia as elsewhere in the South decided that disfranchisement of the Negro was necessary." (Pearson and Hendricks 1967, 227n; see also 230; Grantham 1983, 164)

Temperance Becomes an Argument for Disenfranchisement of Black Citizens

The most respectable segments of white southern society began to argue for disenfranchisement of Black voters in the post-Reconstruction period. Protestant churches preached the necessity for "the purification" of suffrage, while political candidates criticized each other for any softness on the issue of white supremacy. Politicians who had once courted the Black vote were at pains to distance themselves from their previous position, advocating complete political disenfranchisement and strict segregation of the races in all social situations "to "improve race relations" (Crowe 1968, 245). The racial undertone was threatening, with threats of retaliatory violence and talk of colonization and deportation coming from respected spokespersons, such as Prohibitionist John Temple Graves (Crowe 1968, 253). Temperance was an important part of this discussion. Whites saw the Black vote as a serious threat to their best reformist impulses: "When it became evident that white factions would compete with one another for the Negro vote, and thus frequently give the Negro the balance of power, it was time for the complete disenfranchisement of the Negro, the Fifteenth Amendment to the contrary notwithstanding" (Franklin and Moss 1988, 235).

The legal changes the southern states adopted to effectuate disenfranchisement were carefully crafted in apparently race-neutral terms to avoid critical review by the Supreme Court. Typical features were poll taxes, exclusion of voters convicted of certain crimes, and exclusion of the illiterate and those who could not interpret constitutional provisions. Mississippi was the first state to write these changes into its constitution in 1890. The handful of Black delegates at the state constitutional convention objected strongly, but they were outvoted, with only two whites joining them in opposition to disenfranchisement (see generally Dittmer 1977). The movement to take away the Black vote soon became a stampede, despite some objections from organizations like the National Association for the Advancement of Colored People (NAACP) and from scholars and journalists sympathetic to the suffering of southern Blacks (e.g., Baker 1904/1973). By 1910 Black men and some poor, landless whites had been disenfranchised, not just in Mississippi, but also in North and South Carolina, Louisiana, Alabama, Virginia, Georgia, and Oklahoma (Baker 1904/1973, 237). White southerners were, in general, proud of this accomplishment, regarding it as a "purification" of the electoral system (Crowe 1968).

The Prohibitionist cause had given the disenfranchisement movement a principle on which to stand. As Reverend John White explained, Blacks are "child-people" requiring protection from "the perils of liberty." Disenfranchisement allowed whites to act responsibly, shaping law to protect Blacks from their own animal instincts: "This idea of the negro is more pronounced in the Prohibition movement. It stands out more nobly. The saloon was the ravager of the negro people. It plundered them at all points, robbed them of their wages, fed their animalism, and was, as everyone knows, a debauching agent let loose by law upon them" (1908, 136; and see Pegram 1997, 75). A. J. McKelway, famous for his campaigns against child labor, described the coming of Prohibition to Georgia in these terms:

> The United States Government has protected that other weaker race, the Indian, from the operations of the liquor traffic. The United States and Great Britain have combined to protect the Pacific Islanders. It will hardly be disputed that the Negro needs the same protection. And the

white people of the South have resolved to protect him.... The disenfranchisement of Negroes is the heart of the movement in Georgia and
throughout the South for the Prohibition of the liquor traffic. (1907, 949)

The southern press uniformly treated disenfranchisement as a Progressive reform, based on the need to control the easy availability of alcohol. In
the words of an editorial in the *Alabama Baptist* in 1908: "The stronghold
of the whiskey power in the state has been eliminated by the disfranchisement of the Negro, and others like him" (quoted in Sellers 1943, 101). The
press also conceptualized the problem in terms of the morally stronger
(white) protecting the morally weaker (Black, Indian, and foreign-born)
races from the evils of alcohol and the menace and violence of the "liquor-
crazed Black." A sense of the mood of the times can be gained by noting
the popularity of D. W. Griffith's incendiary white supremacist film, *Birth of
a Nation*, which mined the theme of dependent Negroes made crazy, irresponsible, and dangerous by drink. The 1915 film drew large audiences and
a presidential endorsement of its accuracy, as well as published denuncia-
tions from the NAACP and W. E. B. Du Bois for its racism.

The White South Embraces Prohibition and Disenfranchisement

With a few years, the South had generally gone dry. The law was relatively
successful in some states. In Virginia, regulators set up rules for enforcement and an inspection system. Prosecutions and convictions were frequent, particularly against Blacks (Pearson and Hendricks 1967, 296–97).
Wealthy whites avoided prosecution by using private stocks and by relying
on a legal exemption permitting property owners to consume one quart of
alcohol per month.

As the bootlegging industry gained ground and speakeasies began to
attract a middle-class white clientele in the 1920s, however, the pattern of
enforcement changed somewhat, and more whites were charged with li-
quor-law violations. In Alabama, the number of white women arrested for
drunkenness and driving while drunk became a cause for comment in the
newspapers, which noted that about half of those arrested were middle-aged
females, and that "the entire group was not confined to the lower class of
women by any means" (Sellers 1943, 255). The arrest and conviction of whites
eventually weakened the South's resolve and spurred calls for repeal.

As this brief history suggests, Prohibitionists in the North and the South
differed in the precise fears they cultivated to promote their cause, but
moral entrepreneurs on both sides of the Mason-Dixon Line were alike in

giving urgency to the movement by cultivating contemporary fears of social disorder, particularly along racial and ethnic lines. This logic, as Ted Ownby points out, applied equally well to immigrants and southern Blacks:

> Prohibitionists always associated drinking with a loss of self-control, a concern that was becoming ever stronger in the post-bellum South. Just as many Prohibitionists outside the region were concerned with the drinking behavior of the great numbers of recent non-Anglo-Saxon immigrants, white Southern Prohibitionists were troubled and often frightened by the drinking behavior of Blacks. (1990, 172; and see 193, 208–9)

Similarly, where Indians were numerous, as in Oklahoma, the specter of their drunkenness provided a rallying point for reform (Franklin 1971, 13).

The willingness of northern Prohibitionists to accept the South's disenfranchisement of its Black voters is a significant part of this story. Activists were aware that white southerners were using their cause to justify disenfranchisement. The northern press was critical as it covered the issue. Yet there was no strong white constituency supporting the political cause of southern Blacks in this period. Many whites at least passively supported racial segregation, viewing Blacks as social and intellectual inferiors. Black votes were courted pragmatically, but there was little support for the important causes, like a federal anti-lynching bill, despite the obvious need for one. It should not be surprising that the response of the northern-based Anti-Saloon League to the disenfranchisement movement in the South was to go along, shaping its message to white southern values. The organization worked with political machines and reformist southern churches, "crafting racist arguments that dovetailed with the formal resurgence of white supremacy in the early twentieth century" (Pegram 1997, 60). A few leaders were uncomfortable with "the local practice of race relations," but they were criticized by others, who urged the necessity of adapting to the local political environment (Pegram 1997, 63).

The solution of the WCTU was to stay on message about alcohol as a women's issue, but to give the organization's white southerners implicit license to discriminate against their African American colleagues. The stance is striking in light of the otherwise forward-looking character of this organization, one of the first to engage women in political reform. The WCTU was determined to include both Black and white members—it did not want to be categorized as racist domestically or abroad (Tyrrell 1991, 101; Mattingly 1998, 75). But it nevertheless took note of the color line. Chapters tended to be segregated by race, and the organization shied away from attacking white supremacy. Ida B. Wells, for example, sharply criticized the leadership for its failure to take a strong stand on lynching (Bordin 1990, 82–83; Tyrell 1991, 185; see especially Mattingly 1998, chap. 4). Toward the end of the century, the WCTU began to support a platform that favored women's vote at the expense of the voting rights of Black and immigrant men. Alison Parker reports that in 1895, "the national WCTU officially supported educational requirements for voting, a plan explicitly aimed at restricting voting by immigrants and, in the post-Reconstruction South, Blacks" (1997, 187). The organization also tolerated virulent racism in its literature. Parker describes a featured story in the *Crusader* in 1913 in which a corrupt Black politician protected a Black bootlegger; the two were in league to ruin the town until an honest young white man testified against them (1997, 183–85).

The End of Prohibition

The nationalization of Prohibition may have been the key to its ultimate demise. Prohibitionists believed that they had won such a sweeping victory that compromises with adversaries were unnecessary. They refused, for example, to consider low-alcohol beverages as an exception to the Volstead Act or an end to dual federal/state prosecution, even as enforcement became more and more problematic. Resistance to Prohibition seemed to make national leaders more firmly committed to Prohibition than ever (see, e.g., Asbury 1950, 318). The drys were also encouraged by their success in the 1928 congressional elections. Congress raised the maximum punishment for first-time offenders of the Volstead Act to five years in prison and $10,000 in fines. Critics complained that the law would punish small-time offenders with the same severity as major bootleggers (Pegram 1998, 180).

Herbert Hoover also considered his sweeping 1928 election victory as a mandate in favor of Prohibition. He embraced it as "a great social and economic experiment, noble in motive and far-reaching in purpose," authorizing the construction of six additional federal prisons, including Alcatraz, to hold those convicted of alcohol offenses. By 1930, Pegram reports, more than one-third of federal inmates, 12,332 people, were Volstead Act offenders (1998, 168–69). Prohibition was taking on some of the characteristics of the contemporary war on drugs, with the most active and determined effort flowing from the nation's capital, rather than from any particular region or state. There seemed no limit to what the federal government was willing to invest to enforce the ban on alcohol.

The number of dissenting voices was growing, however. Widespread disregard for Prohibition laws gave an indication of public attitudes and, just as importantly, created alarm that mobilized some civic leaders to begin to fight for repeal. Economic concerns also influenced this campaign. Business interests were anxious to have the liquor industry share in the national tax burden (Warburton 1932, 46). Single-issue groups emerged to push for repeal, much as an earlier generation of groups had pushed for Prohibition. The leadership of these new pro-legalization groups tended to be prosperous and well educated, suggesting that a significant reconfiguration of those for and against Prohibition had occurred in the period between adoption of the Eighteenth Amendment and the period just before its repeal. Some of the prominent figures who had once been associated with Prohibition actually switched sides as they realized the social costs.

By the late 1920s, many major organizations were going on record as favoring repeal. In 1927, the American Legion voted for repeal, and in 1930, the American Bar Association adopted a repeal resolution by an overwhelming margin. The Women's Organization for National Prohibition Reform, founded by Pauline Sabin, the socially prominent and politically well-connected wife of a New York banker, was formed in this period. In 1929, it had 17 members; by 1932, there were 1,326,862. The activism of so many women in favor of repeal shocked the drys, who had taken female support for Prohibition for granted (Asbury 1950, 313–15).

With the advent of the Depression, the argument for taxing revenue from liquor gained ground, and so did concern about the widespread disregard of the law and the violence associated with bootlegging. Americans were spending about $5 billion per year on alcohol (around $54 billion in contemporary dollars), 5 percent of the gross national product (Schlosser 2003, 5). Even die-hard Prohibitionists were becoming discouraged. Pegram describes this shift in mood:

> From its origins in the nineteenth century, temperance reform had developed as a forward-looking optimistic social movement. Its proponents had been modernizers, those who look forward to social, economic, and moral improvement. That image became badly tarnished in the 1920s as Prohibition came to be labeled the creaky obsession of puritanical moralists, rural busybodies, and religious bigots. (1998, 169–70)

As David Kyvig, a leading analyst of the repeal period, concludes: "Progressive hopes for social uplift through banishment of intoxicants were dashed, leaving national Prohibition with too few advocates to fend off attack" (2000, xvii).

What finally defeated Prohibition was not the success of the bootlegging industry in evading the law, however, but the economic depression that gripped the nation in the 1930s. The economic crisis forced America to abandon for a time its focus on status issues in order to concentrate on economic concerns. Franklin Roosevelt, somewhat reluctantly at first, ran on the platform of repeal in 1932. By that time, the Republican Party, over Herbert Hoover's objections, had drastically softened its position, but it still came short of recommending repeal. The issue, even on the eve of the Depression, dominated the 1932 elections. A few wet Republicans were elected, despite the 1932 Democratic landslide. Eleven states held referendums on Prohibition issues, and the wets won all of them, many by decisive margins.

Politicians treated the 1932 election as a mandate, so repeal, in the end, was easy. The congressional resolution to void the Eighteenth Amendment took three days, and the states required less than a year to ratify the Twenty-first Amendment. Twenty-one million Americans voted on the issue in statewide referenda, with 72.9 percent favoring repeal (Kyvig 2000, 178). This huge proportion of the electorate was much larger than the proportion that used alcoholic beverages either before or after Prohibition, suggesting that many voted out of concern that outlawing alcohol had done more harm than good (see Kyvig 2000, 197). The control of alcoholic beverages, which had for so long been a national obsession, quickly faded from public concern.

Conclusion

Those who advocate an end to the current war on drugs often cite Prohibition as an example of how the high costs and ultimate futility of criminalizing drug use can lead to policy change. This chapter argues that the advent of Prohibition also deserves critical attention. Native-born prejudice against immigrants and African Americans constituted an important, perhaps essential, feature of the campaign to criminalize alcohol. The ugliness of anti-immigrant prejudice has virtually been forgotten with the assimilation of once-marginalized groups—Italian Americans, Irish Americans, German Americans, Russian Americans, Greek Americans, Catholics, and Jews. This cultural amnesia is unfortunate because the racialized arguments to punish "problem drinkers" have their parallel in the contemporary campaign against crack cocaine and other drugs. Keeping the parallels in mind might encourage Americans to recognize the economic basis of drug use and drug selling, which could help to defuse the emotionalism, negativism, and fear-mongering that animates current arguments for a punitive approach to drug control.

Then, as now, advocates of criminalization have found it useful to portray drug users as dangerous and contemptible, a threat to the implicitly white, middle-class social fabric. The underlying messages of both campaigns are remarkably similar in suggesting that already marginalized groups are extremely dangerous under the influence of drugs. Then, as now, the mainstream press uncritically amplified these ideas, even when disenfranchisement of Black citizens was clearly at stake. Then, as now, the argument was that criminal controls are necessary to protect the nation's essential virtues against undesirable outsiders and to steer the drug user toward a more righteous path. Both the contemporary war on drugs and Prohibition targeted African Americans. In both cases Blacks lost precious rights of citizenship.

There are also parallels in how race and ethnicity, as markers of social and economic marginalization, have figured into the enforcement of these laws. Corruption and a tendency to concentrate enforcement efforts on the most vulnerable citizens were hallmarks of Prohibition, as they are of the contemporary war on drugs. Criminalization of alcohol, as of more contemporary drugs, focused on production, distribution, and sales of the drug, not on consumption, a pattern that tends to protect middle- and upper-class users from arrest. Those who took the risks to sell illicit drugs during Prohibition were often young, white ethnics shut out of other employment opportunities, a pattern that has its parallel in today's drug market, where African Americans and Latinos often play this role. The street-level sellers, runners, and mules who take the biggest risks, are, of course, the easiest and most frequent targets for arrest and prosecution.

These patterns are clear in a study that historian Edward Behr undertook of court records from 1920 to 1933. His analysis shows that enforcement of Prohibition was directed toward the poor, the barely literate, and recent immigrants. With few exceptions, the wealthy were virtually immune from prosecution; some benefited from their own involvement in bootlegging contracts (1997, 241). Businesses frequently paid off the police to stay open. Violence and death were also part of Prohibition, as they are of today's war on drugs. Behr estimates that by 1927, alcohol poisoning had been responsible for at least 50,000 deaths (1997, 221).[3]

Another connection is in the images that Prohibition advocates deployed, which have staying power. The negative stereotypes about African Americans that propelled Prohibition in the South and facilitated disenfranchisement are still in circulation today. William Unrau suggests that the same is true of the stigmatization of American Indians that once justified alcohol control on reservations: "It is worth remembering that national Prohibition applied only to Indians in the nineteenth century, and here, perhaps, may be found a key for understanding the origins and full flowering of the 'drunken Indian/sober white' stereotype that continues to this day" (1996, 122–23).

The Prohibition story also taught politicians important lessons about staying in office with tough, racially coded, words about intoxicating substances. Drug users could be blamed for society's fundamental social problems, and the federal government could use public anxieties to become more important in people's lives. This lesson, current experience suggests, has been well learned. All three branches of the federal government support the war on drugs, as they did Prohibition in an earlier day. The institutional legacy is that the federal presence in local drug-control efforts has become a permanent part of our political economy. Government has learned not just to harvest public anxieties about drugs, but also to manufacture them.

three — Negro Cocaine Fiends, Mexican Marijuana Smokers, and Chinese Opium Addicts

The Drug Menace in Racial Relief

It is no coincidence that the movement to prohibit alcohol overlapped the movement to control opium, marijuana, and cocaine. The pervasive Progressive ideology of the time exhibited an almost unbounded passion for social and individual reform. The Progressive-era mix—of optimistic, scientifically oriented reformism; evangelical fervor; and primal, racialized fears of a growing underclass—were all at work in the movement to control narcotics and other mind-altering drugs. Reformers faced less opposition than they had with alcohol, which has a long pedigree in American culture and powerful support in legitimate business. While narcotics were accepted and valued by middle-class Americans as medicines, they were not broadly accepted as recreational drugs. Escapist drug taking seemed dangerous to a society that had become obsessed with hard work and social improvement. Medical opinion also shifted, as it had with alcohol in an earlier generation, to focus more on the dangers of an unregulated drug industry. Doctors were pushed in this direction by legislation that made them vulnerable to arrest for maintaining addicts, even those they had created with their own prescriptions.

The nation's experience with Prohibition suggests that drugs are criminalized in two steps. First, the substance must be reconceptualized as dangerous, debilitating, and of no legitimate value. Second, the user must be reconfigured as socially marginal and ignorant, or contemptuous, of community standards and moral decency—the kind who responds only to the stern intervention of the criminal law. The reconceptualization of recreational drug use, from a personal matter to a cause for social alarm, can occur as part of a broad-based movement over time, as exemplified by Prohibition, or in a more centralized way, through the active efforts of a few moral entrepreneurs, as happened with drugs considered illicit today. In both cases, change agents play off of society's prevailing racial and ethnic prejudices, including attitudes hostile to immigrants and foreigners. These prejudices, and a characteristically American combination of fear and fascination with intoxicating substances, reinforce each other in a dialectical way, each giving force to the other.

This chapter brings the drug war to the modern era, highlighting the racial/ethnic dimension of the episodic outbursts against particular drugs that occurred along the way. Contemporary readers may be surprised by the virulence and pervasiveness of the racial scapegoating in mainstream, mass-circulation publications and government documents in the period that began in the 1870s with the end of Reconstruction and extended until the civil rights revolution of the 1960s. The anti-drug rhetoric of this era rests on the taken-for-granted conviction that whites from England and western Europe were more advanced in their social, and perhaps even physical, evolution than other races and ethnic groups. This preoccupation with whiteness was unself-conscious and unapologetic, reflecting what Charles Mills (1997) describes as a racial contract that gives whites, in exchange for their privileges, a special burden to maintain order and to help others achieve higher levels of development.

There is a global dimension to this racial contract. White Americans must use their laws and institutions to steer the rest of the world in a more abstemious direction, by force if necessary. Drug-criminalization advocates built on this foundation. As Kevin Ryan notes, "American drug problem 'entrepreneurs' have regularly asserted that much of the problem lies outside our borders, in those other areas of the world (always less developed nations that have been viewed as 'less civilized') where these 'evil' substances are cultivated, manufactured, and shipped into the United States" (1998, 142). Sometimes awkward facts—for example, the tradition of opium use among northern Europeans—must be ignored to maintain the fiction of white innocence about drug use (Ryan 1998).

The racial signals could be confusing, however. In much of the period considered in this chapter, the federal government was simultaneously courting foreign cooperation to control drugs and tolerating nativist and racist extremism in the name of domestic drug control. The courts were attempting to judiciously sort out who was and who was not "white" in order to determine eligibility for citizenship. The unquestioned premise behind the laws they interpreted was that whites had more capacity for republican government and for cultural development than nonwhites. Race, as Ian López observes, was "an implacable" idea that had real value (1996, 169).

The movement toward punitive prohibitionism[1] as the nation's preferred approach to drug control emerged over time, solidifying with each racialized drug crisis. This chapter considers these episodes, drug by drug, in order to show how criminalization became the starting point for thinking about the control of illicit drugs. The demonization of these drugs, my analysis suggests, could not have occurred without a sustained effort to cultivate white anxieties about specific racial and ethnic groups.

Drug Use Becomes a Social Problem

The contrast between current drug policy and what prevailed during the eighteenth and most of the nineteenth century could not be greater. Opium was a home remedy in some parts of the nation, with recipes passed on through families. Even marijuana was best known at first for its medicinal qualities. These drugs were attractive to doctors and to patients mainly because they offered pain relief, a perennial concern, and were readily available. There were few other medical options for chronic diseases such as tuberculosis or surgical procedures. During the Civil War, morphine, which had been synthesized from opium in 1803, provided pain relief for injured soldiers on both sides of the conflict. Over-the-counter narcotic-based remedies were available for toothaches, colds, and other minor ailments. Many habit-forming drugs were advertised in magazines. Toward the end of the nineteenth century, new, more powerful drugs such as heroin were appearing, competing with opium, laudanum, and morphine, which were already widely used. Doctors prescribed these drugs and not infrequently were addicted themselves.

Opium was the first narcotic drug to find favor with the medical and pharmaceutical industries.[2] Babies were fed opium to keep them quiet. The elderly took it for rheumatic pains (Berridge 1977). Some physicians regarded opium as less harmful than alcohol, "which, when taken in anything like excess, ruins the health and fills our jails and workhouses. We should be inclined rather to class opium with tobacco in its ill-effect (in excess) as regards the body" (Elliot 1881, 29). Famous works such as Samuel Coleridge's poem, "Kubla Khan," were written under the influence of opium, and some writers extolled its virtues as a mind-clarifying, mood-brightening drug. Thomas de Quincey, for example, wrote *Confessions of an English Opium-Eater* in 1821, arguing that "whereas wine disorders the mental faculties, opium, on the contrary (if taken in the proper manner), introduces amongst them the most exquisite order, legislation and harmony. Wine robs a man of self-possession; opium greatly invigorates it" (1898, 63). Morphine was thought to have these qualities in even higher degree. With the development of the hypodermic syringe in the middle of the nineteenth century, it became possible to inject pure morphine, which attracted members of the professional classes, writers, and wealthy people in Europe and the United States.

Opiate addiction began to be recognized as a problem in the 1830s, but it was not until the 1870s that doctors turned serious attention to the extent of opiate addiction and its etiology. By this time, addiction to opium and its derivatives was widespread. Addiction had become known as "the soldier's disease," in recognition of the number of morphine-dependent soldiers emerging from the Civil War. People of all ages were complaining to their doctors about an "opium appetite" induced by their prescriptions and by commercial products like Mrs. Winslow's Soothing Syrup. In this period the addicts were, in the words of one historian, "an irregular lot, cutting across social and occupational lines" (Morgan 1981, 8).

No federal agency existed to safeguard the purity of drugs or to warn of their dangers. Doctors had no national organization to give voice to their concerns or to regulate their practices. The well-organized pharmaceutical industry resisted any attempt at legal controls. Each new narcotic drug was touted as a "wonder drug" and sometimes, ironically, pressed into service as an antidote for addiction to its predecessor. Thus heroin was at first recommended as a cure for opium addiction. In this laissez-faire atmosphere, it became known only gradually that all of the powerful new pain relievers were addictive.

The introduction of cocaine in 1884, of heroin in 1898, and of barbital in 1900 added to the addiction problem. All were regarded as "wonder drugs," despite scattered warnings of their potential for abuse. When cocaine became available, for example, Sigmund Freud and other European experts praised it in medical journals as an anesthetic and stimulant; major drug companies offered it for sale. Vin Mariani, a tonic containing Bordeaux wine treated with coca leaves, became very popular throughout Europe and the United States in the latter part of the century. Queen Victoria, Pope Leo XIII, and Pope Saint Pius X were Vin Mariani drinkers; Pope Leo gave the drink a Vatican gold medal and appeared on a poster endorsing it (Morgan 1984, 16, 18; Wikipedia, http://en.wikipedia.org/wiki/Vin_Mariani).

Morphine and heroin were also popular and accepted remedies. The 1897 edition of the Sears Roebuck catalog carried hypodermic kits designed for morphine users, complete with vials and carrying cases (Inciardi 1992, 5). The Bayer Pharmaceutical Company began to market heroin in 1898 as a nonaddictive alternative to opium and morphine, and the philanthropic St. James Society supplied free samples through the mail to morphine addicts who were trying to give up the habit ("Opium throughout History" 1998). David Musto (1973) estimates that there were approximately 250,000 opium addicts at this time, a higher rate of addiction than at any time in the nation's history.[3]

At the same time, some doctors were becoming disenchanted with narcotics and members of the public were beginning to be aware of the dangers of addiction. By the turn of the century, many doctors had discontinued prescribing opium because of the risk of addiction and druggists were expressing concerns about the new wonder drugs (e.g., *Practical Druggist* 1897, 36). Popular magazines were warning consumers about opium in patent medicines and calling for labeling of all patent drugs. Samuel Hopkins Adams, for example, wrote a long series of articles in *Collier's* magazine describing the dangers of patent and prescription drugs. Muckraking journalists like Adams helped to change the climate of opinion about the drug industry (Inciardi 1992, 13).

Congress heeded the rising sentiment against uncontrolled availability of habit-forming drugs and called for a uniform approach when it passed the Pure Food and Drug Act in 1906. The new law required labeling of all ingredients in medicines. Knowledge about the addictive potential of narcotics may have been the most important factor in reducing the rate of addiction. When World War I broke out, military recruiters found relatively little addiction among their enlistees. Of the 3.5 million men inducted into the armed services, only 3,284 were rejected because of addiction to opiates. The data on drug use in this period are unreliable, however. There were no national surveys of drug use and no centralized records on medical treatment of addiction. James Hawdon estimates that there was a significant reduction in the use of narcotics, but it is difficult to be sure (1996, 192–95).

At this time, the addict population was shifting. Initially, native-born whites with the resources to seek medical attention had been overrepresented, while minorities and the poor were underrepresented. Doctors constituted the greatest proportion of male addicts; women at home under a doctor's prescription accounted for most female addicts. As doctors shifted their patients away from narcotics and this initial addicted population died off, the addict pool became younger, darker, poorer, and predominately male (Duster 1970; Musto 1973). More people were becoming addicted through pleasure-seeking activities. Workers and unemployed young people were moving into big cities and turning to marijuana, cocaine, and heroin to replace alcohol made scarce by the advent of Prohibition. Historian David Cortwright argues that the change in the composition of the addict population was "the crucial precondition for the criminalization of American narcotic policy" (2001, xi). Opium offers a good case in point.

Opium and the Yellow Peril

Toward the end of the nineteenth century, the public image of opium began to change. While still prevalent in medicine as an analgesic, it was also beginning to be associated with what was regarded as a peculiarly Chinese vice: opium smoking. In fact, Europeans, not the Chinese, started the practice of smoking opium. The Chinese learned it from Dutch sailors in the 1600s (Booth 1996, 105–6). But for Americans upset by the presence of so many Chinese in the western states, the white ancestry of opium smoking was irrelevant.

Large numbers of Chinese men had arrived in California during the 1850s seeking work building the railroads and mining for gold and other minerals. The laborers were welcomed at first because they were willing to take hard, dangerous jobs at low pay. Ten thousand Chinese men were on the payroll of the Central Pacific Railroad, for example, and the Southern Pacific was built almost entirely with Chinese labor (Sandmeyer 1939). An estimated eighteen thousand worked in San Francisco factories in the 1870s. Relatively few moved to eastern cities or the South.

The presence of so many foreign workers willing to accept very low wages and dangerous working conditions raised the same economic and social concerns that low-paid, illegal immigrant labor does today. Employers enjoyed the availability of low-wage labor, while the laboring classes resented this flexible, cheap, submissive source of competition. As the *Sacramento Record-Union* editorialized in its January 10, 1879, issue:

> The Chinaman is here because his presence pays, and he will remain and continue to increase so long as there is money in him. When the time comes that he is no longer profitable, *that* generation will take care of him and will send him back. We will not do it so long as the pockets into which the profit of his labor flows continue to be those appertaining to our pantaloons.... The people of California, while protesting against their presence, continue to utilize their labor in a hundred ways. In this matter private interest dominates public interest.

The subordination of Chinese immigrants through law began almost immediately. The newcomers were restricted to small areas of West Coast cities. Foreign miners were taxed, and in 1852 Congress levied a tax on all remaining Chinese, providing for seizure and sale of their property upon failure to pay. Although this law was later declared unconstitutional, many local laws survived. By the 1870s, San Francisco ordinances prohibited Chinese from taking public employment, buying real estate, and securing business licenses. Many jailors cut off the long, knotted pigtails of Chinese men, brought in for minor crimes, on the grounds that the pigtails violated health regulations.

Anti-Chinese sentiment took many forms. In 1871, a Los Angeles mob attacked the Chinese quarter, appropriating all moveable property and killing eighteen people (Sandmeyer 1939, 48). Anti-Chinese clubs organized and then combined as the Anti-Chinese Union "to unite, centralize, and direct the anti-Chinese strength of our Country." Members pledged not to employ Chinese or to purchase the goods of anyone who employed Chinese. U.S. senators, congressmen, and prominent state politicians were members (Sandmeyer 1939, 57). In 1877, San Francisco's representative before the Joint Special Committee of Congress expressed the sentiment of these popular groups:

> The burden of our accusation against them is that they come in conflict with our labor interests; that they can never assimilate with us; that they are a perpetual, unchanging, and unchangeable alien element that can never become homogeneous; that their civilization is demoralizing and degrading to our people; that they degrade and dishonor labor. (quoted in Sandmeyer 1939, 25)

The movement succeeded in creating a California state constitution that restricted the employment of aliens, prevented them from owning land and from voting, discouraged their immigration, and facilitated their deportation. There was only scattered opposition from churches with missionary activities in China. One delegate at the California state constitutional convention expressed the prevailing sentiment in unequivocal terms:

> The State should be a State for white men, without any respect to the treaty, or misinterpretation of any treaty. The State has the right of self-preservation. It is the same right that a man of family has to protect his house and home. . . . We want no other race here. The future of this republic demands that it shall be a white man's government, and that all other races shall be excluded. (Wills and Stockton 1881, 704, quoted in Sandmeyer 1939, 70)

This movement ran into obstacles at the national level. Trade with China was becoming ever more important to U.S. shipping interests, and many churches had missionaries in China. With the backing of commercial shippers, the U.S. government had negotiated a trade treaty in 1868 that gave

Chinese immigrants some protection against discrimination by Americans. While this treaty was unpopular in California, it had the support of shipping and manufacturing interests and, of course, the federal government. But the tide in Congress turned against Chinese Americans in 1882, when the votes of the Pacific coast states became a crucial leveraging factor in national elections.

Anti-Chinese sentiment was also rising around the nation. In 1885 a riot broke out in Rock Springs, Wyoming, in which more than twenty Chinese were killed. In Tacoma, Washington, citizens burned the city's Chinese quarter, and locals in other northwestern cities—Olympia and Seattle in Washington and Portland in Oregon, for instance—almost did. Samuel Gompers, founder of the American Federation of Labor, forcefully expressed the antipathy that these mobs demonstrated through their actions in his February 1902 testimony before the U.S. Senate Committee on Immigration:

> The presence in our country of a people entirely out of harmony and training with American comprehension of liberty and citizenship, who are alien to our customs and habits, as different from us in political and moral ideas as it is possible for two peoples to be, who are so thoroughly grounded in race characteristics that even the generations born and reared among us still retain them, can not but exercise a most demoralizing effect upon the body politic, the social life, and the civilization of the people of our nation. (Kaufman, Albert, and Palladino 1996, 471)

Gompers attributed to the Chinese an almost superhuman ability to survive deprivation: "He lives upon less than any other man in the world can live, and seems to thrive and prosper. He can live inhaling the miasmatic fumes of open cisterns and open sewerage with every disease around him and contaminating everyone, and yet remain himself immune from its effects and influence" (Kaufman, Albert, and Palladino 1996, 472–73). In 1882, Congress, after rather exhaustive hearings, prohibited all immigration by Chinese laborers; it later restricted the movement in and out of the country of those already in the United States, and created strict regulations for all other forms of Chinese immigration (see Ngai 2004; Calavita 2000, 2006).

The Criminalization of Opium

Opium smoking became a significant element in the anti-Chinese movement. The practice initially was portrayed as a sign of Chinese degeneracy with no attraction for whites. As Alfred Stillé, a well-regarded nineteenth-century medical expert concluded: "It is true that opium is not likely to become popular among an active and industrious race like the Anglo-Saxon,

whose preference must always be for the more potent, though less permanent, stimulus of ardent spirits" (quoted in Terry and Pellens 1928/1970,
95). Local ordinances restricted opium dens to the Chinese quarter or the
poorer parts of town, where they formed tight-knit cultural centers for the
Chinese. Opium could be purchased and smoked there, providing a respite
from the harsh existence of poorly paid, rough employment far away from
families and familiar institutions.

But even at this time, opium smoking was beginning to attract a different clientele, and to cross racial boundaries as it did. Chinatowns, at once
symbols of exclusion, were also major sources of attraction for tourists and
locals curious about things foreign. Legitimate Chinese businesses, such as
laundries and restaurants, drew many white customers. Beginning in the
1870s, opium dens began to attract petty criminals, prostitutes, and street
people, as well as young whites from comfortable circumstances seeking a
taste of the exotic. G. Pichon, a French physician who had studied fifty-five
cases of opium addiction, divided these users into two groups: the first, those
addicted through therapeutic treatments and the second, those "drawn toward the unknown and mysterious, to licentiousness if they do not belong
to that great class of unstables, abnormals, degenerates, etc. . . ." (quoted in
Terry and Pellens 1928/1970, 103). The beautiful aristocrat enchanted by the
opium pipe became a stock character in popular entertainment (Cortwright
2001, chap. 2). By the late 1870s, opium smoking was moving east to a variety
of locales, including flophouses and luxurious retreats (Morgan 1981, 35).

Opium smoking became a focus for more vigorous police action during
this period. For the most part, the dens the police raided were the ones
frequented by whites (Cortwright 2001, chap. 2; Lauderdale and Inverarity 1984). Local politicians cited concerns that children might be attracted
to this indolent vice, which was thought to enslave its users. Advocates of
vigorous enforcement also routinely exploited white fears of racial mixing.
The Hearst newspapers, for example, portrayed opium as a drug that Chinese men used to seduce and enslave white women.

Jacob Riis takes a similar tack in *How the Other Half Lives*, a muckraking classic framed as an exposé of the lives of the poor in New York City
first published in 1890. The book was an instant hit. President Theodore
Roosevelt praised it as "an enlightenment and an inspiration."[4] Riis describes tenements in Chinatown teeming with white women who had prostituted themselves to Chinese men to satisfy their addiction to opium:

> The women, all white, girls hardly yet grown to womanhood, worshipping
> nothing save the pipe that has enslaved them body and soul. Easily tempted

from homes that have no claim upon the name, they rarely or never return.... Of the depth of their fall, no one is more thoroughly aware than
these girls themselves; no one is less concerned about it. The calmness with
which they discuss it, while insisting illogically upon the fiction of a mar-
riage that deceives no one, is disheartening. (1890/1957, 70–71)

Riis, who saw no value in the continued presence of the Chinese in the
United States, opined that these women had been seduced by the "cruel
cunning" and "crafty submissiveness" of the Chinese (1890/1957, 72).

Courts supported laws against the opium trade, even when they sus-
pected that legislatures were acting out of racial fear or malice. An 1886
Oregon case exemplifies the reasoning that allowed convictions to stand.
Yung Jon brought a habeas corpus action challenging his imprisonment for
opium selling and the confiscation of his supplies. Judge Deady rejected
his petition, explaining that the drug was unfamiliar to Americans, "save
among a few aliens," which gave the legislature a broad mandate to impose
its own moral vision:

> Smoking opium is not our vice, and therefore, it may be that this leg-
> islation proceeds more from a desire to vex and annoy the "Heathen
> Chinee" in this respect, than to protect the people from the evil habit.
> But the motives of legislators cannot be the subject of judicial investiga-
> tion for the purpose of affecting the validity of their acts. It is the duty of
> the law-maker as far as his power extends, to enact laws for the conserva-
> tion of the morals of society, and to promote the growth of right thinking
> and acting in all matters affecting the physical or mental well-being of its
> members."[5]

The vehement and violent grassroots movement against Chinese immigrants put the federal government in an awkward position. The United
States was courting China as a trading partner—U.S. shippers saw a potentially huge market for their goods (Stelle 1981; Brummett et al. 1999). In
Washington, China was considered an important ally because of the size of
its markets. The situation became grave when Chinese merchants, outraged
at the treatment of their countrymen in the United States, began planning
a boycott of U.S. goods. Somehow the federal government had to improve
relations with China while not alienating the American public. The answer
lay in narcotics control. This was an issue of real interest to the Chinese
government. Opium addiction was widespread, thanks in part to Great
Britain's determination to maintain its profitable trade in that drug (Musto
1973, 28–53).

During the nineteenth century, the Chinese government had fought, and lost, two wars with Great Britain in an effort to close its harbors from further shipments. Britain had played the role of a big, aggressive drug cartel in forcing China to continue receiving opium from its Indian holdings in trade for silk and other goods. Chinese resistance had been met with British military might. When China lost the first war in 1842, Britain forced it to open up five new ports to the importation of opium. After China's second defeat in 1856, Britain expanded its market, and opium poured into China in unprecedented quantities. By the end of the nineteenth century, it was estimated that over one-fourth of the adult male Chinese population was addicted. In this situation, not surprisingly, the beleaguered Chinese government welcomed the strong U.S. stand against opium (Brook and Wakabayashi 2000; Hanes and Sanello 2002).

The growing presence of the United States in world affairs also drew it into the opium question. In 1903, the United States found itself confronted with a decision in the Philippines that illustrated the moral issues at stake. The Philippines had become a U.S. colony after the Spanish American War, but Spain continued to hold a monopoly on opium selling there. The U.S.-appointed governor of the Philippines, William Howard Taft, recommended allowing Spain to continue to supply the twelve thousand registered local addicts, most of whom were Chinese, not Filipino. The income from the opium sales could help fund community improvement projects, including education. Missionaries, however, argued that the United States must not maintain addicts, and President Theodore Roosevelt agreed, ending the arrangement without further ado. His decision was an early sign of the power that Prohibitionist arguments could pack in political debate (Musto 1992, 33).

International Agreement: Gateway to Criminal Controls

The realization was growing among anti-narcotics activists that their best option for achieving effective controls lay in international action. A treaty calling for curbs on the importation of dangerous drugs would force an indifferent Congress to create implementing legislation of national scope.[6] Such legislation would be much more efficient than pressuring Congress directly or, alternatively, working from the grass roots. The individual states had not been very successful in creating effective narcotics-control legislation (Cortwright 2001).

The activities of two individuals during this period stand out: Dr. Hamilton Wright and Bishop Henry Brent. The State Department appointed Wright, a specialist in tropical diseases, as its opium commissioner in 1908.

Brent, Episcopal bishop of the Philippines, was in charge of an investigative team whose mission was to offer narcotics policy alternatives to the federal government. Both men were dedicated drug prohibitionists with strong personalities. Wright, in particular, saw narcotics in absolutist, moralistic terms as an unalloyed evil. The two men lobbied for an international meeting to study the opium problem and make recommendations. They succeeded, and the Shanghai Commission was held in February 1909, with a mixture of European and other nations in attendance. Brent was elected president of the Commission, and Wright became its acting head. Wright then used the rather vague recommendations of the Commission to promote domestic legislation, while he and Brent pressed hard for more international meetings and stronger powers.

Wright used racism to his advantage in arguing for strong federal narcotics controls. In his 1910 report to Congress, he drew on the by-now familiar image of racial mixing between Chinese men and white women to make his point about the dangers of opium smoking in the United States: "One of the most unfortunate phases of the habit of opium smoking in this country is the large number of women who have become involved and were living as common-law wives of or cohabiting with Chinese in the Chinatowns of our various cities" (1910, 45). Wright reserved his strongest racial language for his discussion of cocaine, however. Including cocaine in his discussion was an attention-getting device. Cocaine was not a problem of international concern at that time, and it is not, pharmacologically speaking, a narcotic. Wright, as a medical expert, knew this. He also must have known that cocaine use had been in decline for several years (Helmer 1975, 51–52).

The Black Cocaine Threat: A Key to Southern Support

Wright focused on cocaine in his report to Congress, David Musto surmises, to help make narcotics control more appealing to southern members of that body, who were leery of federal drug legislation. The southerners feared that a strong federal tax law with regulatory purposes might be a precedent for federal civil rights legislation that could interfere with the system of racial apartheid that the South maintained under the rubric of states' rights. But many whites from the South were also fearful of cocaine use by local Blacks. Many agreed with the Memphis police chief who claimed that the effect of cocaine "is much more violent than that of whisky" (*New York Times* 1905, 14). It was widely believed that Blacks were using cocaine in epidemic proportions. State legislatures in Alabama, Georgia, and Tennessee had anti-cocaine bills under consideration in 1900, spurred on by fears that cocaine was giving younger Blacks a new sense of boldness (see, e.g., Spillane 2000, 94–104). A 1903 report sponsored by the American Pharmaceutical Association opined that "the negroes, the lower and immoral classes, are naturally most readily influenced, and therefore among them we have the greater number [of users], for they give little thought to the seriousness of the habit forming" (quoted in Morgan 1981, 92).

To gain southern support, Wright stressed the dangers of unregulated cocaine use in terms that sound almost contemporary: "It is the unanimous opinion of every state and municipal body . . . that the misuse of cocaine is a direct incentive to crime, that it is perhaps of all factors a singular one in augmenting the criminal ranks. . . . It is more appalling in its effects than any other habit-forming drug used in the United States" (1910, 48). Cocaine use among southern Blacks, especially those from among the "humbler ranks," posed particular dangers: "It has been stated on very high authority that the use of cocaine by the negroes of the South is one of the most elusive and troublesome questions which confront the enforcement of the law in most of the Southern States" (Wright 1910, 48–49). Wright blamed unscrupulous parties, presumably from outside the region, for the spread of cocaine in the South and for its use throughout the nation in large cities "to corrupt young girls" who shortly thereafter "fall to the ranks of prostitution" (Wright 1910, 49). Historian Martin Booth concludes that "for all his philanthropic intention, Wright was also a scaremonger playing upon xenophobic and racial unease, stressing the dangers drugs posed to white people" (1996, 198).

Wright's anti-drug campaign coincided with the high point of anti-alcohol fervor in the United States and abroad. The United States had grown more confident in playing a leadership role, and other nations were beginning to pay heed to its prohibitionist arguments (see, e.g., Morris 2002). Addictive and habit-forming drugs of all types were increasingly under attack. The Dutch, for example, were reconsidering their policy in colonial Indonesia, where they had long supported opium production as a way to raise revenue (Rush 1990, 255). And America was on the brink of war. The idea that the nation must gird for conflict and purify itself was in the air. There was a sense that the nation was surrounded by dangerous continents, with South America identified with cocaine, Europe with heroin and morphine, Africa with hashish, and Asia with opium. It was well known that the welter of state and local drug laws was chaotic and easily evaded. By 1914, H. Wayne Morgan argues, the national mood was such that national legislation seemed both logical and necessary (1981, 102, 106–7).

A public mindset increasingly open to regulation was not enough to overcome Wright's overbearing and uncompromising personality, however.

Although he drafted model legislation and circulated it in 1909, he proved to be an ineffective politician. His efforts faltered under pressure from the pharmaceutical industry and the medical lobby. The State Department eventually found an appropriate sponsor in Representative Francis Burton Harrison of New York, who served on the Foreign Relations Committee (Musto 1992, 34). When Congressman Harrison agreed to take charge of the legislative effort, Congress finally acted. The final legislation was considerably softer than Wright's first effort. Cannabis and chloral hydrate were dropped from the law, the proposed heavy tax on drug transfers became nominal, patent medicines received some exemptions, and record-keeping rules were eased (Cortwright 2001, 100). Like the Pure Food and Drug Act and most other Progressive-era legislation, the Harrison Act was born of strong beliefs, but full of compromises.[7]

The Rise of the Negro Cocaine Fiend

The media played a significant role in creating a sense of urgency about drugs in the period just before and just after the 1914 adoption of the Harrison Narcotics Act. Popular accounts of the drug problem, sometimes offering wildly inflated estimates of drug use, portrayed the United States as a drug-addicted nation. While the presence of medically induced addiction was acknowledged, the focus tended to be on the growing reach of unregulated recreational drug use in college dormitories, the workplace, and the ranks of the military, and especially among the very young. The *Literary Digest* warned that "school children, even at the ages of seven and eight are offered cocaine and heroin by peddlers about public-school buildings" (1914, 687). Popular accounts associated cocaine with the drug world and dissipation. Its easy availability in drug stores, bars, and even at soda fountains was condemned, and reformers were at work trying to ensure that all traces of it were removed from soft drinks.

The media often linked race, drugs, and crime, giving substance to white fears of the potential for Black drug-induced violence. The *New York Times* and other news media reported with concern, for example, that labor contractors in the South were distributing cocaine to their Black workers to increase productivity. In both the North and South, crimes committed by Blacks allegedly under the influence of cocaine were widely reported in graphic detail: "Most of the attacks upon white women of the South are the direct result of a cocaine-crazed Negro brain. Thousands of dingy hovels are scattered through the Negro sections of southern cities where 'snow' is retailed in dime boxes through back doors which are prevented by chains from opening more than three inches" (*Literary Digest* 1914, 687; and see generally Morgan 1981, 91–93).

Medical doctors played a significant role in the campaign against cocaine, often employing a racial subtext to bring home the dangers of cocaine in the hands of nonmedical personnel. In the example-filled style of scientific writing designed for popular audiences, doctors described horrific instances of murder and mayhem by cocaine-crazed individuals of the poorer classes of society and drew "scientific" conclusions about the "cocaine plague." In a 1908 article in the magazine section of the *New York Times*, for example, Dr. Leonard Corning described the cocaine habit as "the most terrible vice ever acquired by a civilized people" and the most rapidly widespread because of its accessibility to "the poorest and most depraved" in society: "There is little doubt but that every Jew peddler in the South carries the stuff, although many States have lately made its sale a felony." Corning recommended strong action against cocaine sellers because, once acquired, the cocaine habit is incurable.

Dr. Edward Huntington Williams wrote in the same vein, focusing on the South and the "Negro cocaine fiends" there: "There is no escaping the conviction that drug taking has become a race menace in certain regions South of the line" (1914b, 12). He claimed that cocaine frequently drove men insane, and the insane cocaine fiend could turn murderous. These drug users, he suggested, were virtually impervious to force and even to bullets: "Bullets fired into vital parts that would drop a sane man in his tracks fail to check the 'fiend'" (1914b, 12). Law enforcement personnel were reportedly acquiring guns with "greater shocking power" to deal with "cocaine-crazed Negroes." Like Corning, Williams was pessimistic about cures: "Once the negro has formed the habit, he is irreclaimable. The only method to keep him from taking the drug is by imprisoning him. And this is merely palliative treatment, for he returns inevitably to the drug habit when released." As he wrote in the *Medical Record* in the same year:

Once the Negro has reached the stage of being a "dope taker"—and a very few experimental sniffs of the drug make him a habitué—he is a constant menace to his community until he is eliminated. For his whole nature is changed for the worse from the habit. Sexual desires are increased and perverted, peaceful Negroes become quarrelsome, and timid Negroes develop a degree of "Dutch courage" that is sometimes almost incredible. A large proportion of the wholesale killings in the South during recent years have been the direct result of cocaine, and frequently the perpetrators of these crimes have been hitherto inoffensive, law-abiding

Negroes. Moreover, the Negro who has once formed the habit seems absolutely beyond redemption. Imprisonment "cures" him temporarily; but when released he returns to the drug almost inevitably. (1914, 247)

Such articles send a complex message. They draw their persuasive power from a potent combination of pseudoscientific gloss and bare-bones reporting, for example, "nine men killed in Mississippi on one occasion by crazed cocaine takers, five in North Carolina, three in Tennessee." Blacks on drugs are described in frightening terms, but with a hint of paternalistic concern. As ignorant, undisciplined people with weak moral standards, Blacks could be seen, in a patronizing way, as victims of cocaine. Williams, for example, blamed the politicians who had failed to control the availability of cocaine for forcing "a new and terrible form of slavery upon thousands of colored men—a hideous bondage from which they cannot escape by mere proclamation or Civil War."[8]

The image of the Negro cocaine fiend bears a striking resemblance to an earlier invention that played particularly well in the southern states: the alcohol-crazed Negro. Both of these stereotypes proceeded from the same idea: that drugs and Blacks are a dangerous, explosive mix. The underlying idea was that civilization had not quite taken hold in nonwhites. Drugs loosened what little self-control they had, threatening violence and, most serious of all, sexual predation of white women. The acceptability of such racist stereotyping in respectable publications is noteworthy. This was the era of Jim Crow legislation in the South, and of violence, occasional lynchings, and social separation throughout the nation. Mob violence against Blacks and Chinese was not uncommon. Racial attitudes, at best, were patronizing. Policy dialogue was a white-to-white form of communication in a white-dominated society. It is disconcerting to realize that some of these racialized images persist in contemporary drug-war rhetoric. White Americans have never abandoned the idea that drug taking in minority populations is particularly dangerous, despite the waxing and waning of fears about particular drugs.

Narcotics Control Becomes Police Work

The racial scare tactics that helped propel the Harrison Narcotics Act toward passage were less in evidence once the law went into effect in March 1915. Race and class nevertheless helped to determine how the law was enforced. Federal and state law-enforcement personnel concerned themselves with drug use by the urban poor and working classes (see, e.g., Bailey 1916, 314–16). Respectable members of society whose addictions were of long standing were quietly tolerated; most towns had resident addicts who refilled their prescriptions without interference. The public did not regard such people as real addicts because their cases did not fit the profiles of cases reported regularly by police agencies (Morgan 1981, 125, 127).

Attitudes toward drug takers were hardening in this period. With the help of the mass media and the tireless efforts of anti-drug activists, people were beginning to see drug addiction more as a vice than as a disease. It was often said that weak, immoral people tended to take up the habit, drugs destroying their already-damaged higher functions and rendering them unfit for society. Experts conceived the addict population as divisible into two parts: the medically addicted and mentally ill, who deserved sympathetic treatment, and the nonmedical addicts drawn to crime and violence—these "voluntary" addicts deserved prison.[9] Drug use was increasingly moralized as a matter of good and evil. The groundwork was being laid for strong federal controls.

Institutionalizing Federal Narcotics Law

The Harrison Act required doctors, pharmacists, and others who prescribe narcotics to register and pay a tax, and so enforcement responsibility was lodged in the Bureau of Internal Revenue of the Treasury Department.[10] It was not entirely clear, however, when narcotics prescriptions were permitted. The new legislation permitted physicians to prescribe narcotics "in good faith" and "in the course of his [sic] professional practice," but was silent on whether medical personnel could continue to give narcotics to addicted patients indefinitely, a crucial issue for doctors. This question received little attention in the hearings on the Act (Cortwright 2001, 104). The fact that enforcement authority was lodged in an agency accustomed to prosecuting smugglers, tax evaders, moonshiners, and other morals crimes, however, did not bode well for doctors.

Treasury agents, it turned out, were not inclined to see addicts as medical patients or drug use as a health problem (Nolan 2001, 28; Morgan 1981, 110). Early on, the Bureau decided that it would aggressively oppose programs that allowed addicts to maintain their addictions through controlled doses managed by physicians. Revenue agents began arresting physicians, but were soon rebuked by the Supreme Court in *United States v. Jin Fuey Moy*,[11] a 1916 decision ruling that the Harrison Act did not give government authority to prosecute addicts or the physicians who maintained them. That decision was the high-water mark of judicial resistance to the Harrison Act. No other case law developed that challenged Treasury's power to make arrests, however.

In response to the Court's decision, the Bureau did, for a brief time, relax its efforts to prosecute addicts and even supported clinics to dispense narcotics to registered addicts. Many of these clinics operated effectively, serving addict populations efficiently and with a high degree of medical supervision. They nevertheless lacked widespread support in the medical profession because they did not seem to lead to a cure (Morgan 1981, 112–13). In 1919, perhaps swayed by wartime jitters about the evils of "Seductive Chinese" and "Negro cocainomaniacs," the Supreme Court signaled that it no longer supported a physician's right to dispense narcotics simply to maintain an addict (Musto 1973, 134). Congress amended the Harrison Act that year to reflect this interpretation.[12] The Treasury Department used the new doctrine to move against the clinics it had previously supported, arresting doctors who resisted its interpretation of the law (Musto 1973, 247).

By 1925 the last clinic had closed, despite a Supreme Court decision holding that addicts had a right to medical care equivalent to other patients. Meanwhile, the Narcotics Division had banned all legal narcotics sales. This forced many addicts, for the first time, to buy from illegal street dealers. A robust black market in drugs developed as physicians abandoned their addicted patients (Musto 1992, 35–38; Inciardi 1992, 15–16). At this time, Nolan notes, "discussion of drug addiction, by both those inside and outside the medical community, leaned toward the moralistic rather than the therapeutic perspective" (2001, 30).

The number of narcotics addicts in prison was growing rapidly. By 1925 there were 2,569 narcotics convicts in federal prisons out of a total population of 7,710. Ten years earlier there had not been even one. Congress voted in 1928 to establish two farms for drug offenders, which were essentially prisons with some medical personnel on the premises. Throughout this period, the popular press continued to publish fearful stories, sometimes describing America as the most drug-addicted nation on earth, rivaled only by pathetic China. Narcotics were blamed for all manner of serious, violent crime. As a 1924 *Saturday Evening Post* article warned: "With the restraining forces of the higher nature gone, the addict feels no compunction whatever in committing any act that will contribute to a perverted supposition of his own comfort or welfare. And one of these acts, a characteristic one, is that the addict has an insane desire to make addicts out of others" (Lampman 1924, 41).

Doctors were mixed in their reactions to the hardening of federal narcotics policy. Critics argued that the Harrison Act was a tax act, nothing more, and that government had perverted the purpose of the Act in prosecuting doctors who prescribed narcotics to their patients. Representative John Coffee complained of "the persecution of perhaps a million victims of the diseased condition known as drug addiction" in a 1938 speech to the House of Representatives, attributing the criminalization of addicts to "bureaucratic action" (quoted in Williams 1938, xv–xvii). Dr. Henry Smith Williams wrote an impassioned defense of the doctors caught in the middle of the new prohibitionism. In *Drug Addicts Are Human Beings*, he describes addicts as unlucky victims of painful diseases, trapped by the new rules that prevented them from getting the medicines they needed to work and survive (Williams 1938).

Although doctors were divided on the culpability of drug addiction, they could hardly have resisted the new federal initiatives. The Narcotics Bureau commissioner, Harry Anslinger, was a smart, ambitious, determined bureaucrat who was a master at telling horrific stories of violence committed under the influence of drugs. Appointed in 1930 as commissioner in a newly created Federal Bureau of Narcotics, he dedicated himself to making his position as powerful as possible. Anslinger did not hesitate to bend facts and data to his cause. Thus in 1937, when the Treasury Department introduced a bill that would increase the penalties for repeat offenders, Commissioner Anslinger argued that when penalties are high, "your narcotic violations practically drop off to nothing." Without specifying what kinds of drug crimes were involved in these prosecutions or what segments of society were being prosecuted, Anslinger insinuated in his testimony that these were the most serious criminals in the nation:

Mr. Anslinger: I think that the greatest benefit of this bill would be to the general public to get the major criminals of the country out of the way.
Mr. Towey: Do I understand you correctly to say that you believe that the major criminals of today are drug addicts?
Mr. Anslinger: That is according to the reports of the Department of Justice, drug addicts and peddlers. (*Report* 1937, 8)

Throughout Anslinger's tenure, he did his utmost to convince the nation to increase drug penalties and reduce judicial sentencing discretion. He was a careful political operator, however, targeting only drugs that would advance the cause for tough federal controls. He did not at first foresee that, with enough negative publicity, even marijuana could qualify for the Harrison Act's list of substances requiring federal attention.

Marijuana Becomes a Dangerous Drug

The rapidity with which marijuana became a dangerous drug provides a useful object lesson in the power of a few skillful tacticians, aided by an uncritical mass media, to shape public policy. In less than a decade, marijuana rose from its lowly status as an ingredient in patent medicines to cure migraines, rheumatism, and insomnia to a source of insanity, suicide, and major crime. Racism played an important role in this transformation, as it had in earlier anti-drug efforts. Once again, the images of nonwhites high on drugs were cited over and over in accounts designed to arouse fears in white readers. As in earlier anti-drug campaigns, whites were invited to imagine that drug users, and the drug itself, were attacking their youth and their civilization (see, e.g., Fossier 1931, 249; Helmer 1975, 76).

Marijuana was vulnerable to attack by drug prohibitionists. Lobbyists for the pharmaceutical industry had defended it against Hamilton Wright's efforts to include it in the Harrison Act because they saw some value in marijuana for corn plasters, veterinary medicine, and nonintoxicating medicaments, but it had never garnered much support from organized medicine (Musto 1999, 216–17). The profession's lack of interest allowed prohibitionists to exploit the drug's long-standing association with Mexicans, who were increasingly regarded as an alien and unwanted presence. Mexican laborers had arrived in the western states during the 1920s in significant numbers, attracted by opportunities to do seasonal farm labor. For a time, they supplied essential labor in rural communities, particularly at harvest time. But the Depression slowed local economies, sparking widespread white resentment against local Mexican populations. Marijuana was thought to make them prone to fights and violence. Some expressed concern about marijuana use spreading to whites, especially to young people (Morgan 1981, 138; Bonnie and Whitebread 1974, 71).

The image of the marijuana user grew more dangerous in the mid-1920s when the Commissioner of Public Safety in New Orleans began a campaign for federal legislation. He and the news media used sensationalist imagery to portray marijuana use in graphic terms. Richard Bonnie and Charles Whitebread describe the change:

> In the border towns he was a Mexican laborer, indolent to some, volatile to others. Local authorities were, by and large, unable to generate any significant public or political interest, although there were no political objections to making the Mexican weed illegal. In the port cities, however, the marijuana user was a "dope fiend," the basest element of American society. He was a narcotics addict, a pimp, or a gambler; she was a prostitute. (1974, 43)

Elsewhere in the South, there began to be reports of heavy marijuana use among Black fieldhands. Police officers in Texas claimed that it incited violence and aroused a "lust for blood," while giving users "superhuman strength," a scare tactic that had earlier been attached to cocaine and would reappear in the 1980s in connection with PCPs. Mexicans were reportedly tempting innocent schoolchildren with the drug (Schlosser 2003, 19). Black communities in Harlem and other northern cities also were reported to be using it. Whatever reputation marijuana had as a medicine was lost in this period. By 1931, twenty-nine states had prohibited the use of marijuana for nonmedical purposes; four more states did so by 1933 (Bonnie and Whitebread 1974, 51).

The Federal Role in Criminalizing Marijuana

The Federal Bureau of Narcotics was uncertain about what approach to take in regulating marijuana. The idea of extending its reach to marijuana control was attractive. If the Bureau took on marijuana, it would increase its authority, riding a wave of anti-Mexican sentiment that was sweeping the nation. Indeed, the United States deported 400,000 Mexicans and Mexican Americans in the early 1930s (Ngai 2004, 135). On the other hand, a marijuana amendment to the Harrison Narcotics Act could provoke a judicial rejection of the entire statute. The courts might decide that because marijuana was a locally consumed drug, a familiar weed that had been used for generations for medicinal purposes, it was unsuited for federal legislation. Some within the Bureau also feared that marijuana was too widespread to eradicate or control through policing.

At first, Commissioner Anslinger's strategy was to press for state legislation. He promoted an optional clause in a comprehensive model law, suggesting that a seamless legal network at the state level could complement federal drug-fighting efforts. When he ran into public apathy and administrative obstacles, he knew he needed to change his approach. As Bonnie and Whitebread observe:

> The bureau needed to arouse public interest so that the professional objections would seem inconsequential beside a "felt need" of the legislatures. The "marihuana menace" was an ideal concept for such a campaign. Thus, beginning in late 1934, Commissioner Anslinger gradually shifted the focus of the Federal Bureau of Narcotic's publicity campaign away from the inability of federal law enforcement agencies to deal effectively with local drug problems toward the need to cope with a new drug menace—marijuana. (1974, 97)

Anslinger decided to back a separate marijuana statute at the federal level and began speaking out strongly about the marijuana threat across the nation (Helmer 1975, 54). The Woman's Christian Temperance Union and other women's organizations were interested in helping the cause and offered Anslinger platforms to spread the message. The media assisted in this effort, finding the marijuana menace to make good copy.[13] The *New York Times* played into the campaign to make marijuana seem more dangerous by eliding distinctions between marijuana and powerful narcotics (e.g., *New York Times* 1934b, 1934c, 1934d, 1934e, 1934h). Even when the *Times* did make a distinction between types of drugs, it portrayed marijuana "as appalling in its effects on the human mind and body as narcotics" and toxic enough to kill horses that eat it. For humans, the result of prolonged marijuana use was insanity, as the *Times* reported matter-of-factly in a 1934 news article:

> The raiders found the marijuana, or loco weed, which produces a pleasant, relaxed sensation when smoked, and eventually drives the habitual user insane, growing in abundance on a plot in the middle of the block bounded by Washington, Nassau, Adams and Concord Streets. (1934c)

That the *Times* got its inspiration from the Narcotics Bureau commissioner is obvious from its detailed coverage of the activities of the Bureau of Narcotics and the commissioner.[14] Anslinger kept a "gore file" of stories of suicide and violent crime to feed to the media. One theme was of white girls induced to have sex with Blacks under the influence of marijuana (Musto 1973, 23). Another was the association of marijuana with crime by minorities. As one Bureau release stated: "Fifty percent of the violent crimes committed in districts occupied by Mexicans, Spaniards, Latin-Americans, Greeks, or Negroes may be traced to this evil" (Bonnie and Whitebread 1974, 100).

Commissioner Anslinger, testifying before Congress in 1937, described marijuana as "dangerous to the mind and body, and particularly dangerous to the criminal type, because it releases all of the inhibitions" (1937a, 3). In his testimony before the Senate, he emphasized the power of marijuana to cause one person to attack another: "I believe in some cases one cigarette might develop a homicidal mania, probably to kill his brother. It depends on the physical characteristics of the individual . . . but all the experts agree that the continued use leads to insanity" (1937b, 16). As he said in a retrospective account, he "hammered at the facts," appearing on the radio and in public forums; writing articles for magazines; and giving hundreds of lectures, either himself or through his agents, always reporting "on the growing list of crimes, including murder and rape," associated with marijuana use (Anslinger and Oursler 1961, 38).

Congress passed the Marihuana Tax Act in 1937, when concern about the drug was at its peak. By that time, every state had enacted some form of anti-marijuana legislation. The new law, ostensibly another tax act, was really aimed at deterrence and facilitation of enforcement at the state level. Bonnie and Whitebread describe the Act as "hastily drawn, heard, debated and passed." It was "provoked almost entirely by the Federal Bureau of Narcotics and by a few hysterical state law enforcement agents hoping to get federal support for their activities; the law was tied neither to scientific study nor to enforcement need" (1974, 127). The pattern of emotional, reactive, quick-fire legislation would be seen again in the adoption of the federal anti-crack legislation.

Although the public still remained largely apathetic about marijuana, this was a significant victory for Anslinger. He continued to stress the danger of marijuana in later publications. In his 1953 book on the history of narcotics control, for example, he called marijuana "a scourge which undermines its victims and degrades them mentally, morally, and physically." He described the earliest stages of marijuana intoxication, in which "the will power is destroyed and inhibitions and restraints are released; the moral barricades are broken down and often debauchery and sexuality results. Where mental instability is inherent, the behavior is generally violent" (Anslinger and Tompkins 1953, 21–23). He offered stories to back up this conclusion:

> A gang of boys tears the clothes from two school girls and rape the screaming girls, one boy after the other. A sixteen-year-old kills his entire family of five in Florida, a man in Minnesota puts a bullet through the head of a stranger on the road; in Colorado a husband tries to shoot his wife, kills her grandmother instead and then kills himself. Every one of these crimes had been preceded by the smoking of one or more marijuana "reefers." (1961, 38)

During the remainder of his career as Narcotics Bureau commissioner, which spanned over thirty years, Anslinger was consistent in his approach. He dramatized drug addiction in stark terms as "murder on the installment plan" (Anslinger and Tompkins 1953, vii). He was a master of the horror stories of individuals ruined by drugs and the terrible crimes they committed, and he liked to describe drug moguls made rich by the trade. He blamed the Mafia, the Red Chinese, hoodlums, jazz music, and bleeding-heart judges for the continued use of drugs in the United States (Cortwright 2001, 155). The solution was always tougher enforcement of criminal penalties. He supported life sentences for the sale of narcotics to minors, for example. His leadership helped to establish the pattern of

heavy-handed law enforcement—single-minded, heavily reliant on infor-
mants, racially provocative, and wedded to long prison terms—that remains
in place today.

The medical profession, in the meantime, had effectively been outflanked.
Commisioner Anslinger was able to sway Congress with newspaper clip-
pings and anecdotes in arguing for a marijuana tax act, while medical
evidence, for example, was ignored. Mike Gray reports that members of
Congress excoriated the one medical expert they did permit to testify in
the 1937 hearings, Dr. William C. Woodward, who represented the American Medical Association (2000, 79). The efforts of the New York Academy
of Medicine to challenge Anslinger's claims about the dire medical effects
of marijuana with a blue-ribbon committee of experts were similarly stymied when the commissioner got wind of the project and began a smear
campaign against members of the committee as "dangerous" and "strange"
people long before the final report was released (Gray 2000, 83).

Racism and xenophobia figured into Anslinger's campaign to stir people
to action. He was circumspect about racially stigmatizing language in his
congressional testimony and in his books, but the implication was always
of upwardly mobile white youth ruined by criminal types, who, it was understood, were from the lower classes, often Blacks or unassimilated white
ethnics. The political cartoons of this period were similar in portraying only
white people as victims of the drug menace. In reading this literature, one
senses pervasive racism that excludes nonwhites from concern, except as
a danger to white lives and white sensibilities. Commissioner Anslinger,
whatever his personal beliefs about race, played to this audience.

Marijuana Is Displaced by Heroin

By the 1950s, politics had changed, but the sensitivity of white Americans
to the dangers posed by dark-skinned drug users had not. The new threat
was heroin. Its use appeared to be rising in some urban areas and in the
military. Commissioner Anslinger was convinced that the Communist Chinese were undermining American soldiers in Korea and Japan by giving
them heroin. He offered Congress details of Chinese "dope factories" and
plans for "chemical warfare" to fund their cause. He was equally adept in
playing to domestic fears of drug violence, describing most heroin addicts
as lower class people of low moral character: "We don't find addicts among
children from good homes." He believed that because they were usually
criminals or psychopaths, they should be "plucked out of the community
and quarantined" (Anslinger and Tompkins 1953, 170). At least ten years of

confinement was necessary, with automatic recommittal for any violation after release and life imprisonment for a second relapse (Anslinger and Tompkins 1953, 211–12). In a 1951 interview with members of Congress, Anslinger agreed that Blacks were more susceptible to narcotic drugs than whites (*U.S. News and World Report* 1951: 18–19).

The real fear, however, was that heroin could invade white, middle-class society, a fear that resonates with every drug scare. The press excitedly reported that heroin peddlers had left the slums and invaded middle-class neighborhoods (Morgan 1981, 146). Commissioner Anslinger's influence was behind much of the media hysteria. His face and words appeared often in *Reader's Digest, U.S. News and World Report, Time,* and other popular publications in the 1950s. *Time* described him as "a Pennsylvania Dutchman who knows more about the worldwide drug traffic than any other man on earth" (1955). Anslinger wrote his own copy, purporting to speak as an expert about everything related to drugs, from the hygienic habits of drug addicts (Anslinger and Tompkins 1953, 20–21) to the details of a Chinese Communist plot. He was, historian David Cortwright concludes, a man in the grip of a fixed idea (2001, 159).

The commissioner's effort to increase penalties for drug possession and sales paid off in 1951 and again in 1956 when he joined forces with Representatives Hale Boggs and Price Daniels, ambitious politicians who were looking for a safe, high-visibility issue for their upcoming campaigns. Anslinger's preoccupation was different: He was looking for something to blame for the failure of his agency to make significant inroads on the heroin problem. His dramatic congressional testimony and behind-the-scenes maneuvering helped shape the 1951 Boggs Act and the 1956 Narcotic Control Act and move them toward passage. The new laws lumped marijuana with other narcotic drugs and increased penalties across the board. This legislation, the harshest in the nation's history, reflected Anslinger's long-standing call for mandatory prison terms. Imprisonment was required for first-offense possession of heroin. Juries could recommend the death penalty for anyone convicted of selling to minors (Cortwright 2001, 156).

Conclusion

Harry Anslinger, Hamilton Wright, Henry Brent, and other anti-drug activists moved the United States firmly toward a punitive approach to drug use over the first half of the twentieth century. They succeeded because they knew who to lobby and what to say, and because they were then able to institutionalize their ideas as part of regular government operations. They

worked closely with a few members of Congress, a handful of top bureau-
crats, and, from time to time, the president of the United States. Sensationalist media coverage demonizing drugs and drug users helped them achieve
their goals. They did not get a lot of help from the public they courted.
A strong base of popular support for drug criminalization never material-
ized. The passage of the Harrison Act was a nonevent—it did not even get
newspaper coverage at the time (Musto 1973). The reception accorded the
Marijuana Tax Act and state narcotics laws was similar.

With or without strong public support, some form of meaningful regulation at the federal level was inevitable, given the growing scientific knowledge about the properties of narcotics and other drugs, and the obvious
problems associated with unrestricted use. The Harrison Narcotics Act,
with its tax-registration format, left open a range of enforcement strategies.
Anslinger masterfully moved into this opening, gaining the position, the
resources, and the rhetorical clout to shape the law to his own vision. Without Anslinger's determined leadership, the course that drug law took in the
United States would almost certainly have been much different.

Race was clearly a central element in the reconstruction of drug taking
from a medical problem to a crime. Advocates of criminal controls made a
strategic decision to paint drug use against a lurid, racialized backdrop of
sex and violence. This connection was important. Whatever ambivalence
Americans felt about pleasure-seeking through drugs, it became a frightening prospect when associated with people deemed dangerous and un-
trustworthy. The negative racial stereotypes that criminalization advocates
deployed clearly resonated with Congress and other key decision makers,
for if they had not, Anslinger, Brent, and Wright would not have relied on
them. That the media uncritically accepted and spread these images suggests a pervasive sense of white superiority at all levels in (white) society.

Stereotypes of cocaine-crazed Blacks and opium-purveying Chinese
were powerful because they aroused deep-seated emotions about race,
sex, and social control. The presumed capacity of habit-forming drugs to
change personality and to undermine the sense of social responsibility that
underlies productive work and self-control were especially threatening in
this context (Morgan 1981, 93–94). The fact that this did not, in fact, happen in most cases was ignored.[15] Anslinger and other activists were interested in conveying an emotional message, not facts about drug use. They
frequently evoked America's sense of national destiny as "a city on a hill,"
an image that has inspired generations since the Puritans with a sense of
holy duty. The criminalization of so-called hard drugs thus arose out of a
complex of related white fears that nonwhite "others" in American society,

assisted by drugs, could destroy this appealing vision of America's essential goodness.

The corruption of youth was another important element in the argument for criminalization. The frequency with which drug prohibitionists repeated the theme of youth ruined by drugs suggests the power of this image. This alarmist tale of youth led astray is invoked by today's advocates of harsh controls and remains a powerful influence. The story is always the same: A young person, full of promise, but naïve or insecure, allows him- or herself to be seduced by drugs and pays a fearful price. But there is another face to the image of youth ruined by drugs. Young people, scholars observe, are inherently threatening to the established order. They are one of civilization's "dangerous classes" because they can be tempted to challenge their subordinate status (Gordon 1994; and see Cohen 1972). The combination of drugs and youth makes the logic of criminal controls compelling.

Racial fears and stereotypes amplify and deepen white concerns about a declining social order. The experience of alcohol and drug prohibition is similar in this important respect: As the images of drug use became racialized, the case for criminal controls grew stronger. Advocates of criminal penalties understood the power of racial stereotypes and used them to achieve their ends. Alcohol and drug prohibition are thus sister movements, not just in their temporal proximity, but also in their political foundations.

Race is talked about differently now, but criminal controls on drug use continue to be harsh, and official attitudes toward drug users continue to be unremittingly hostile. Drugs remain, symbolically, a menace to white, middle-class values. But institutional priorities are also important in maintaining the status quo. Drug prohibition has not been only a "symbolic crusade." A colossal federal police apparatus has developed to sustain and extend punitive prohibitionism. Those professionally committed to this approach can be expected to do everything in their power to maintain it. Politicians and the media are also institutionally invested in constructing drug use as a crisis. It is these institutional priorities, rather than outraged public opinion or rising crime rates, that sustain punitive drug laws. As criminologists Katherine Beckett and Theodore Sasson note: "When it comes to concern about crime (and drugs), it appears that the public is following the leadership of politicians and the media, not the other way around" (2000, 126).

Those committed to maintaining criminal controls on drugs benefit from the acceptance of anecdotal advocacy in this policy realm. The argument for punitive prohibition was based from the beginning on stories and isolated examples. These appear to be much more politically compelling than

the scientific studies and medical knowledge relied on by supporters of regulatory and rehabilitative approaches. There has also been a long-standing
imbalance in the effort applied to each side of the policy debate. The professional groups that could have made a difference in the policy realm were
not as organized or as active as those in government and already committed
to criminal sanctions.

How significant is racism in maintaining the law-enforcement approach?
Robert Lieberman suggests that every political moment is made up of a
variety of patterns, each with its own logic and pace. These patterns "take
on lives of their own" and offer possibilities for change only when the gap
between ideals and institutions grows large enough to sustain an alternative
view (2002, 701–2). Such a gap occurred briefly in the 1970s when drug use
by college students and heightened sensitivities about racial injustice challenged the racialized demonization of drugs.[16] The rapid return to punitive
approaches to drug violations, however, suggests the tenacity of prohibitionism and a continuing willingness to punish and exclude those who fail
to conform to this nation's economic, social, and racial ideals.

| four | **Congress on Crack** |

*How Race-Neutral Language
Hides Racial Meaning*

The landscape of race relations has changed dramatically since the Anslinger era. The United States now makes a virtue of its racial mix, officially and often unofficially, embracing racial, ethnic, and other forms of diversity (Schuck 2003). "America," Timothy O'Neill observes, "is not only the most diverse nation in the world today, but for the first time in history, diversity has moved beyond being a fact to becoming a central social value.... What began in the mid-1960s as an effort to root out invidious discrimination against minorities has become part of America's central ideology" (2003). The depth of the changes in white attitudes and beliefs is, appropriately, a matter of sharp debate and thoughtful speculation. There is no question, though, that the standards for acceptable discourse about race have changed profoundly.

As openly racist language has disappeared from polite society, drug policies have grown even harsher and more disadvantageous to African Americans and other minorities. What is one to make of this disjuncture between the new enthusiasm for racial diversity and a drug policy that so disproportionately incarcerates impoverished nonwhites and Latinos? The United States appears to have sincerely accepted racial diversity as a desirable goal, but without coming to terms with its racist history and class prejudices. The ahistorical quality of the diversity commitment is particularly evident in drug policy. After all, punishment became the preferred approach to control drug abuse only with the help of overt racism. Yet the racist roots of criminal sanctions for drug abuse, and their ineffectiveness, seem to have been expunged from the collective consciousness. Presidents and members of Congress of both parties take extravagantly pro-punishment positions on this issue without a trace of irony.

This chapter focuses on the impact of the civil rights agenda on the nation's quixotic approach to drug abuse. The civil rights movement at first helped to loosen controls: Marijuana was reconstructed in the 1960s as a "white" drug, and even heroin, a "Black" drug, was recast in more humane terms. Racial disadvantage, for a brief time, became an argument against harsh criminal controls. The nation reverted to its previous approach with the conservative backlash of the Nixon and Reagan eras, however. As the nation began another war on crime, crack cocaine was "discovered" in America's urban ghettoes, making it an ideal choice for harsh government action.

Taking a "tough" stand on crack cocaine has been a bipartisan commitment in Washington since President Ronald Reagan spearheaded the war on drugs. Legislation criminalizing the possession and sale of crack cocaine quickly passed both houses of Congress in 1986 and 1988, with huge margins of both parties in support. The states were urged to follow the federal example and given inducements to do so. Most did. The well-known result is a very racially skewed pattern of arrests, convictions, and sentencing in drug cases, and subsequent disqualification of Black citizens from voting and other benefits of citizenship.

The aggressive legislative initiative against crack cocaine has been criticized as ill advised, expensive, and racist. This last charge is the most provocative, and the most important criticism of the policymaking process. Supporters of the legislation vehemently deny racial motives. The U.S. Supreme Court has taken the position that there was no invidious racial discrimination in either the passage or implementation of the legislation. The debate appears to be deadlocked, with both major political parties unapologetically remaining committed to strong criminal controls and denying any racial animus. Even as some states have begun to soften drug penalties with drug courts and other rehabilitation-oriented approaches, the rationale for policy change has been economic, not moral. The charge that the contemporary war on drugs, and specifically the war on crack, is racist nevertheless hangs in the air, suggesting the need for a national conversation about the role of race in criminal justice policy. This conversation should include scrutiny of the process that produced our crack laws, not just the implementation of these laws.

How does race shape the legislative process when overt racism has been banished from public debate? Specifically, how could Congress enact harsh penalties for a "Black" drug in a way that could later be defended as nonracist? The answer explored in this chapter is that members of Congress, presumably unintentionally, engaged negative racial stereotypes in considering the threat posed by crack cocaine and in determining what steps would be necessary to respond to it. Congress did not need to conger up a new set of racial images to justify uncompromising criminal penalties. The social location of crack in the urban ghettoes evoked a raced script written long ago by Henry Anslinger, commissioner of the now-defunct Federal Bureau of Narcotics, and other drug warriors of his era. The terms of debate were already well understood. The issue would have been complicated only if crack had been sold by college kids, housewives, or corporations.

The Politics of Drugs and Civil Rights

Criminologists mark the 1970s as a period when crime became a salient political issue and the federal government assumed a much larger role in fighting it. There was a rapid retreat from rehabilitative aspirations that had long informed sentencing practices in most areas of law (see, e.g., Garland 2001; Hagan 1995; Simon 1997). Developments in federal drug law were an important part of that process. The use of illegal drugs expanded greatly in the 1960s, though it was not at first perceived as a significant issue. Only 3 percent of those polled by the White House in May 1969 saw drugs as an important problem. Gallup polls on "national hopes and fears" did not even include drug issues until 1971 (Musto and Korsmeyer 2002, 39–40).

The federal government, under the leadership of Richard Nixon, seized on public apathy as an opportunity to reshape the public agenda. Nixon worked hard to arouse the public against illicit drug use, linking drugs to broader law-and-order themes. Both played well among middle-class voters. Drug abuse provided a rationale for federal controls that was missing in street crime, which had always been a local issue. Most important, drugs diverted attention from other problems. Musto and Korsmeyer speculate that the Nixon administration was well aware of the potent political symbolism a war on drugs would provide the fledgling administration:

> The campaign staff and White House advisors charged with securing Nixon's political future must have seen narcotic control policies as an irresistible opportunity to reduce crime, to codify disapproval of disruptive behavior by a substantial minority of the youthful population, and to deflect some of the attention from problems of the economy and of international conflict that consistently resisted any sort of politically satisfactory solution. (2002, 41)

Federal expenditures dedicated to the control of illicit drugs increased by more than 1000 percent during Nixon's first term. Significantly, however, two-thirds of the funds were for prevention and treatment (Manski,

Pepper, and Petrie 2001, 272). The nation was not in the frame of mind for a highly punitive, take-no-prisoners approach. The idea that heroin offenders could be rehabilitated had gained ground as a policy option in the 1960s, encouraged in part by the civil rights movement. Race had briefly become a reason for *not* punishing heroin addicts. And marijuana use had spread beyond the Mexican immigrant and Black populations to white middle-class youth, provoking serious arguments for decriminalization. White American youth, inspired by the civil rights movement, the Vietnam War, and their own experimentation with drugs, were questioning all the old assumptions. The situation called for alternatives to a strictly law-enforcement approach. For a brief time, the argument for rehabilitation gained some traction in Washington, more than it ever had before—or has had since.

Rehabilitating Heroin Addicts

The movement to rethink the nation's hard-line approach to illicit drugs was afoot even before Commissioner Anslinger retired in 1962. Britain had been maintaining opiate addicts as regular patients of physicians with no apparent ill effects. In the United States, the drive to establish a medical approach to drug policy was gaining some attention under the leadership of crusading professionals like Dr. Alfred Lindesmith and attorney Rufus King, both of whom advocated providing heroin to addicts. Even mainstream organizations like the American Medical Association and the American Bar Association were beginning to challenge the Department of the Treasury's Narcotics Bureau over the effectiveness of its hard-line approach. The Kennedy White House took note of these developments and pushed retirement on Commissioner Anslinger, who by then had completed over thirty years in his post as the nation's chief drug-enforcement officer. Within a month of his retirement, the White House sponsored a conference for scientists and leaders that took a more medically oriented view of appropriate drug policy. A year later, a presidential advisory group recommended research, elimination of some mandatory-minimum penalties, and transfer of enforcement responsibility away from the Treasury Department. Meanwhile, methadone was gaining support as a treatment for heroin addiction. By the mid-1960s, most cities had methadone clinics for heroin addicts.

During this period, heroin was thought of as a "Black" drug. Over 95 percent of the heroin addicts who visited the methadone clinic in the District of Columbia, for example, were African American. That characterization influenced public policy, but in a different direction than in the past: toward compassion, rather than punishment. As Wayne Morgan concludes:

The war against heroin ... became part of the struggle for civil rights. It became increasingly popular to believe that racism, poverty, and alienation among blacks caused drug use. These social forces ... were part of a larger social milieu that made susceptible people more likely to use drugs. That use in turn seemed both more inevitable and understandable than in affluent white society. Many of the decade's social programs were aimed at treating the addict and at eliminating the environment that allegedly caused drug use. (1981, 153)

By the end of the decade, observers were beginning to realize that whites were also heroin abusers. Addicted soldiers were returning from Vietnam. Heroin was "a soldier's drug" as opium had been in the Civil War. By 1971, half of the army's enlisted men in Vietnam had tried heroin (Cortwright 2001, 169). Heroin use had also spread to the white suburbs. The number of heroin users had grown from about 50,000 in 1960 to half a million in 1970 (Musto 1999, 248). The media devoted a lot of attention to the issue, encouraging President Nixon to declare a national state of emergency on drug abuse in 1972 and to make drugs "public enemy number one."

Nixon's instinctively punitive approach to drugs, however, was constrained by the circumstances of his era. Drug addiction had become associated with serving in the Vietnam War and with the civil rights movement. Punitive prohibitionism was not politically feasible. So Nixon emphasized prevention and treatment, including methadone for heroin addicts and mandatory treatment for Vietnam veterans, and he implored television executives to reinforce his message (Johnson et al. 1996, 185). He set up a White House office for drug abuse prevention and poured resources into treatment. The budget for law enforcement did grow significantly, from $43 million in 1970 to $292 million in 1974, but the prevention and treatment budget grew even faster, from $59 to $462 million during the same period (Johnson et al. 1996, 182). The number of methadone patients grew from 9,100 to 73,000 between 1971 and 1973, a period that has been dubbed the "Camelot period" of drug policy. As Dr. Jerome Jaffe, a respected expert on drugs and the first White House advisor on drugs, ruefully observed: "For one brief period in the history of drug policy, investment in demand reduction was given priority over supply control and law enforcement" (quoted in Jaffe 2002, 53; and generally Musto 2002).

Opposition to methadone soon developed from those accustomed to a more punitive approach and, ironically, from some quarters of the civil rights movement. Militant voices within the Black and Puerto Rican communities decried enslavement to methadone and the government's failure to combat poverty and social marginalization in minority communities. While methadone allowed addicts to function better, it did not reach the problems that brought about addiction, and it created dependency in some users. Support for methadone eroded before a coherent national policy could emerge.

By the late 1970s, the nation's attention had shifted toward marijuana and cocaine abuse. Treatment was becoming more controversial, and the traditional law-enforcement approach was regaining momentum. A general toughening of attitudes toward law breaking had replaced the tolerance of the 1960s and early 1970s. The contrast was clear in a 1988 White House conference on drugs, where methadone was excoriated as part of the drug problem, despite clear evidence that it had reduced the spread of HIV/AIDS. As Cortwright observes, "Utility was out, symbolism was in" (2001, 175). By 1986, 80 percent of the federal drug-fighting budget went for interdiction and law enforcement, rather than treatment. The federal drug budget was never again to see such a high proportion of its resources devoted to treatment as in the early Nixon years (Kleber 2002).

The "Whitening" of Marijuana

Federal policy to deal with marijuana also underwent an important transformation in this period. The growing popularity of marijuana among college students in the 1960s raised a new set of racially charged issues for drug prohibitionists. This "whitening" of the marijuana-smoking population helped to explode old myths about its dangerousness. Marijuana did not appear to be addictive, despite its federal classification as a narcotic, and despite Anslinger's assertions that it was "the assassin of youth" and "as hellish as heroin" and (Anslinger and Cooper 1937; Gerber 2004, 8). No longer could the drug be associated solely with Blacks, Mexicans, Latin Americans, and others who had been denigrated as foreign, unassimilated elements in American society. Commissioner Anslinger's earlier racial allusions to "ginger colored niggers" using pot and to its tendency to produce insanity were rejected, often derisively. *Reefer Madness*, a 1936 film built on this theme, became a cult classic and a shorthand way of expressing skepticism about the government's honesty in portraying the dangers of drugs. Meanwhile, scientific support for marijuana prohibition, never strong, had begun to erode as the demographic profile of the drug user changed.

This period marked the breakdown of the old consensus that marijuana use inevitably led to dangerous abuse and criminal behavior. Yet the old criminal controls, including mandatory minimum sentences of five years for sellers and two years for users, remained in place. Juvenile arrests rose by 800 percent between 1960 and 1967. The Nixon administration was challenged to deal with a new type of drug dealer and drug user. In a June 1970 speech on "Preserving the American Way of Life," Vice President Spiro Agnew articulated the dilemma as the Nixon administration saw it. For Agnew and those he represented, the problem was that drug use had moved out of the ghetto and into the suburbs, where harsh penalties were ruining promising young lives and creating disrespect for the law (Kerr 1973, 234–35).

The new demographics of marijuana smoking meant that there was, for the first time, a political base that could challenge the old racially stereotyped view of marijuana as a dangerous, addictive drug associated with crime and dissipation (Bonnie and Whitebread 1974, 222–26). The issue was explosive because marijuana smokers were not just numerous, but also privileged, educated, and articulate. User groups such as BLOSSOM (Basic Liberation of Smokers and Sympathizers of Marijuana) and NORML (National Organization for the Reform of Marijuana Laws) had formed to actively argue for decriminalization. The American Civil Liberties Union weighed in for decriminalization. Students were holding large demonstrations at state houses around the nation. Respected members of the community—including war veterans, well-known academics, and even a few members of Congress—were willing to testify against criminal penalties.

The buildup of respectable opinion in favor of marijuana bore some resemblance to the gathering middle- and upper-class storm against anti-alcohol laws that helped bring an end to Prohibition. Once again, Congress scheduled hearings, though this time the chorus of complaint had fewer wealthy aristocrats and more youthful voices than in the earlier successful effort to end Prohibition (see, e.g., Kerr 1973; Schlosser 2003).

But marijuana's new respectability had its limits. It symbolized youth in rebellion against established norms, including the war in Vietnam and limits on free speech, including pornography. It stood for sexual experimentation and privacy, women's liberation, environmentalism, and cultural relativism. Marijuana, in short, came to express youth's generalized dissatisfaction with adult values. As Representative Shirley Chisholm told her fellow members of the House of Representatives in a 1969 hearing:

> I think that the war on "pot" is being intensified because it is now readily apparent that it is seemingly having a greater effect on middle-and upper-class white American youth. The generations that are the heirs-apparent who will some day rule the Republic now seem to want to abdicate their positions unless there are significant changes made and we the legislators

and leaders seem bound and determined to force them to acquiesce to
our designs and plans for them. (quoted in Kerr 1973, 265)

The Nixon White House was in a delicate position. Knee-jerk prohibitionism would not work politically, but neither would decriminalization, even of
marijuana. As Gerber notes, "By 1970, crime generally and drugs in particular were becoming code words in some conservative groups for racial hos-
tility, cultural stereotypes, and suburban isolationism. Right-wing religious
voters also expressed alarm at cultural turmoil, social disarray, and ethical
relativism" (2004, 20). Here was an opportunity for law-and-order politics.
Nixon saw his base as people angry at hippies, women's liberation activists,
pot smokers, Black nationalists, and other rebellious elements (Baum 1996,
10). He wanted to reach this "silent majority," but he could not afford to put
thousands of college students in prison for drug felonies. The long-standing
policy of criminal penalties must stand, but it had to be softened to avoid
egregious sentences.

In 1970, at Nixon's urging, Congress passed the Comprehensive Drug
Abuse Prevention and Control Act,[1] which eliminated mandatory-minimum
sentences for drug offenders, reduced the penalty for first-time possession
of marijuana to a misdemeanor, and allowed for the expunging of criminal
records for minor offenses. At the same time, the administration resisted recommendations that marijuana be distinguished from the dangerous narcotic
drugs with which it had been classified in the Anslinger era.

In an effort to bolster support for its approach, the administration em-
panelled a carefully selected National Commission on Marijuana and Drug
Abuse. To Nixon's surprise, the conservative members of his commission
recommended decriminalization, a recommendation he quickly rejected.
Nixon was personally, as well as politically, antagonistic to both hard and soft
drugs, seeing them as the key to the troubling transformation of America's
youth into unruly, anti-authoritarian peaceniks. Other conservatives also
weighed in against the Commission's decriminalization recommendation,
but eleven states and a number of cities did change their laws to reduce
penalties for marijuana possession. Others, partly in recognition of the difficulty of enforcing marijuana strictures, rewrote sentencing rules to allow
for greater judicial discretion (Jensen and Gerber 1998, 12–13; Bonnie and
Whitebread 1974, 240).

Support for a new approach to marijuana, though stronger than it had
ever been, was still politically risky for those in public office. Public officials
who expressed the opinion that marijuana should be decriminalized could
be dismissed or subjected to critical scrutiny from legislative committees, as

was the director of the Food and Drug Administration, James Goddard. Researchers were prevented from testing the effects of marijuana on humans because of concerns about congressional and public reaction. The Federal Bureau of Investigation, under J. Edgar Hoover's leadership, showed no reluctance to arrest drug offenders. Hoover saw drug arrests as a means of clamping down on anti-war protesters and "leftists." Marijuana arrests rose from 18,000 in 1965 to 188,000 by 1970 (Gerber 2004, 19).

The Federal Bureau of Narcotics was another agency that refused to accept any softening in its opposition to marijuana, although it did adjust its anti-marijuana propaganda to fit the new user profile. Officials now focused on public health as the central problem. The marijuana user would no longer to be portrayed as a criminal, but rather as troubled and emotionally unstable, suffering from lack of motivation and alienation. Federal officials began to emphasize what they did *not* know about marijuana as an argument against decriminalization. They stressed the potential for marijuana to serve as a gateway to more serious drug use. At the same time, they made enforcement selective, avoiding middle-class users. As one wag observed, "In California, it is illegal to smoke marihuana unless you have your hair cut at least once a month" (Morgan 1981, 161). There was no support, however, for removing criminal controls. As Bonnie and Whitebread conclude: "Officialdom had very little faith in the nation's young. In their view the entire generation was unstable" (1974, 229).

The continuing spread of marijuana through college campuses and beyond, to soldiers, young professionals, blue-collar youth, and high school students, led to increased pressure to clamp down. By 1979, over two-thirds of the nation's eighteen- to twenty-five-year-olds had tried marijuana at least once (Cortwright 2001, 175). The Carter administration, which had initially proposed removing criminal sanctions for possession of small amounts of marijuana, was forced to retreat by newly formed white, middle-class parents' groups like the Parents' Resource Institute for Drug Education, or PRIDE, and the National Federation of Parents for Drug-Free Youth. These groups, which had their largest base of support in the white suburbs of the southern states, were immediately influential with the White House and Congress. The parents were alarmed by the glamorization of drug use in the media and by their own children's attraction to drugs. Their goal was more attention to the dangers of drugs, strict enforcement, more interdiction, and zero tolerance of drug use. They were indifferent to the problems of inner-city drug use and addiction (Musto and Korsmeyer 2002, 230–35; Cortwright 2001, 175).

With Ronald Reagan's ascension to the White House in 1980, these conservative voices gained a receptive hearing. They also gained an able advocate in First Lady Nancy Reagan with her "Just Say No" campaign. The momentum toward a law-enforcement approach to marijuana grew significantly in the Reagan years and has sustained itself since then. Marijuana arrests now constitute nearly half of the nation's annual total of 1.5 million drug arrests. A recent study by Ryan King and Marc Mauer found that between 1990 and 2002:

> 82% of the increase in drug arrests nationally (450,000) was for marijuana offenses, and virtually all of that increase was in possession offenses. Of the nearly 700,000 arrests in 2002, 88% were for possession. Only 1 in 18 of these arrests results in a felony conviction, with the rest either being dismissed or adjudicated as a misdemeanor, meaning that a substantial amount of resources, roughly $4 billion per year for marijuana alone, is being dedicated to minor offenses. (2006, 6)

The current policy of arrest and prosecution in some parts of the nation, and mandatory treatment or de facto decriminalization in others, preserves the veneer of punitive prohibitionism that conservative drug politics demands, while providing police with enormous discretion for harassment and arrest without too much interference with established social hierarchies (Jacobs 1999, 38–39; and see Musto 2002).

Racial Symbolism

The paradoxes of drug regulation described here contain a racial thread that is relevant to what came after. While this quick review of the methadone-maintenance effort and of the struggle over decriminalizing marijuana can hardly do justice to the complexity of the regulatory issues at stake in the 1960s and 1970s, it does show how racial images played themselves out. It is no accident that changes in legislation concerning heroin and marijuana occurred at the high point in the modern civil rights movement. The movement, along with growing opposition to the war in Vietnam, fostered experimentation with all traditional social mores. It also helped to complicate traditional images of Black depravity and white innocence. White youth were using drugs without risking their class and race privileges. The media was glamorizing drug use, something that had occurred in the past, but not as openly. Youth, rather than social marginality, was becoming the scapegoat of the era.

This reconfiguration of hard-line attitudes toward drugs is also instructive at a structural level. Tens of millions of Americans, including much of the political leadership of the day, had used marijuana without ill effect.

Scientific evidence about the harms of the drug remained scant. And yet marijuana use remained a crime. This account of frustrated reform should make it clear that the battle between those who would maintain criminal controls and those who would abolish them will always be unequal, even when politically empowered constituencies argue for decriminalization. Repeal of a criminal law is a rare occurrence because of what it symbolizes. Legislators fear that any action they take to reduce or eliminate penalties will be taken as an endorsement of unacceptable behavior.

The repeal of Prohibition was an exception in part because the assault was led by some of the nation's wealthiest and most influential citizens, but even more significantly because alcohol use had a more mainstream American past than marijuana use. Alcohol, unlike marijuana, is a quintessentially American drug. Had marijuana had a different genealogy, Bonnie and Whitebread suggest, the issue of criminalization might never have arisen. We will never know if they are right, of course. The decades of marijuana's classification as a narcotic; the implication that it causes addiction, crime, and insanity; and its association with the Black and Latino underclass, instilled too much unease for the decriminalization argument to be taken very seriously, even when advocates for repeal emerged (Bonnie and Whitebread 1974, 295).

The marijuana saga also presages the more subtle racialized framework currently used to assess the dangers of drugs and of street crime more generally. Crude racial labels have been replaced by a race- and class-specific geography that pinpoints the source of dangerous drugs in the (minority/poor) ghetto and speaks of contagion spreading to (white/middle-class) suburban areas. When Vice President Agnew spoke of "preserving the American way of life," for example, he made no apology for locating the greatest danger in the spread of drugs beyond the ghetto. He was articulating an approach that takes for granted that poor urban areas are hopeless places whose potential for corrupting the entire society must be contained.

The Nixon administration also helped to paint drug use and street crime generally as a form of defiance against legitimate authority, signalling that its sympathies were with the white, adult, voting public that was uneasy with the freedom-oriented movements of the youth-oriented 1960s, including the movement for Black civil rights. Nixon's emotionally charged, moralistic rhetoric soon came to dominate and impoverish public discourse about crime and drugs. By constructing crime and illicit drug use as willful rejection of mainstream values, he was able to focus concern on street crime and lifestyle violations, rather than corporate or white-collar crime. Nixon's moralism and Nancy Reagan's "Just Say No" campaign also limited solutions because they suggested that the root of the problem was youthful defiance of authority. The logical response was punishment.

From the Administration's perspective, the fact that Black and other minority populations were disproportionately affected by drug laws was regrettable, but not really surprising. The United States has always relied on criminal sanctions to control African Americans, as Jonathan Simon points out, so when Blacks go to prison at much higher rates than whites, it does not seem unusual:

> The problem of race has been intertwined in the practices of crime and punishment almost since the beginning of the European settlement of the North American Atlantic coast. Today the real and imaginary links of violence (and street crime generally) with young African American men are helping to drive the imperative of governing through crime. Whether or not voters acknowledge such motives to pollsters, it is hard to ignore the continuities between the present situation and a traditional preference for governing predominantly African American populations in distinct and distinctly less respectable ways. (1997, 180–81)

The continued emphasis on criminal controls for drug violations complements the logic of individual choice and responsibility that increasingly dominates contemporary American political thought and justifies government's retreat from a welfare state. As long as they involve society's social marginals, drugs and street crime provide easy and compelling grist for the news media and for politicians seeking consensus-building issues. Presidential campaigns have repeatedly played on fear of crime, even as rates of violent offending have fallen. Simon dubs the current strategy of regulating through criminal controls "governing through crime" and suggests that, while the retreat from more nuanced modes of governing is a global phenomenon, the logic of rules and sanctions is particularly attractive in the United States (1997, 2007). Our incarceration rate is evidence of this. We imprison five to eight times as many people on a per capita basis as most European nations.

Negative attitudes toward African Americans remain a potent, though generally unstated, motivator for tough criminal penalties. Empirical research has established that support for highly punitive policies correlates with the tendency to think that Blacks have inherently criminal tendencies (see, e.g., Chiricos, Welch, and Gertz 2004). The pattern is consistent at the state level: The size of a state's Black population is a stronger prediction of the prison population and its propensity to adopt the death penalty than its rate of violent crime (Greenberg and West 2001; Jacobs and Carmichael

2002). Racial beliefs not only make people more afraid of crime, but also tend to narrow the options people consider appropriate for dealing with it (see Mauer 2004, 80). By establishing the criminal as undesirable and probably irredeemable, racial stereotypes deflect support for regulatory or prevention-oriented alternatives.

The Rise of Crack and a New—Blacker—War on Drugs

The trend toward more punitive attitudes toward crime and punishment that began in the 1970s grew stronger in the 1980s. Republicans took over the Senate and pushed a variety of crime bills, including the Sentencing Reform Act,[2] which later was to play a significant role in enhancing criminal penalties for crack. Public opinion about drugs and crime was hardening, and the tenor of debate was moving from deterrence to retribution. In the words of a British observer: "An ideology, encouraged by the administration, took hold that the public would be safer and better protected from the risk of victimization by incarcerating those who had offended against them for as long a time as possible" (Windlesham 1998, 24–25). And indeed, between 1975 and 1989, the average prison term per violent crime tripled. To be tough on crime became a political necessity (Belenko 1993, 9).

At the urging of the Justice Department, President Reagan officially announced his administration's war on drugs in October 1982, a period of sharp spending cuts throughout most of the federal government. Officials in the Justice Department and in other federal agencies associated with law enforcement soon realized benefits from President Reagan's commitment, however. The Department of Defense budget for drugs more than doubled. The Customs allocation grew by over 300 percent and continued to rise into the early 1990s. The FBI overcame its initial resistance to new drug-fighting assignments when it became clear that the alternative was budget cuts. Between 1980 and 1984, FBI anti-drug monies increased from $8 million to $95 million. Money available for drug treatment, on the other hand, was reduced (Beckett and Sasson 1997, 42–43).

The Reagan administration's anti-drug policy followed the well-worn pro-criminalization script pioneered by Harry Anslinger, but honed to the racial standard of modern times by Richard Nixon. Explicit racial stereotyping and slurs could no longer be deployed to stir up emotion, but somehow the public had to be encouraged to focus on those it feared. The Reagan administration did not fully realize this at first. When it took office in 1980, at the urging of parent groups, it focused on youthful marijuana smoking (Musto 1999, 266). But its association with white, middle-class youth was problematic. Marijuana was no longer frightening enough to justify dramatic federal intervention. Cocaine, on the other hand, was once again becoming fashionable, largely because prices were falling precipitously. By 1984, it was cheap enough to be affordable to even the poor and homeless, and its purity had increased enough to make it smokable. At about this time, the media began reporting on a new solid form of cocaine available in poor Black urban neighbourhoods (Cortwright 2001, 176). The Reagan administration had stumbled on the ideal drug to facilitate its policy goals.

Crack as a "Poster Drug" for Pursuing the Republican Agenda

President Reagan was determined to put street crime, welfare fraud, and drug dealing on the public agenda, not because these were popularly perceived as serious threats at the time, but because of the political message they communicated. Focusing on types of misbehavior associated with poverty and racial minorities offered significant political dividends for Republicans. The political goal was to support and expand the Republican Party's post-Watergate base, which included fiscal conservatives as well as moral conservatives. The fiscally conservative wanted "to replace social welfare with social control as the principle of state policy" (Beckett 1997, 5; and see Belenko 1993, 9). Religious conservatives found recreational drug use sinful. Newly powerful in Republican politics, they were anxious to strike a blow for moral responsibility and against the loosened moral standards of the 1960s (Cortwright 2001, 178–79).

This political strategy took advantage of racial tensions without ever openly revealing a racial agenda. The policies chosen for special attention targeted Blacks and minorities without reference to race, but in a way that would nevertheless tend to polarize the electorate along racial lines (Edsall and Edsall 1991, 138–39; Elwood 1994). The message stressed individual responsibility for the moral choice of drug taking and the scourge of drug selling, while downplaying the structural factors associated with the drug trade (see Reeves and Campbell 1994, 2–3). Those who would be subject to the new initiatives would be in no position to mobilize against the rhetoric of punitive prohibitionism.

Crack was perfectly suited for Reagan's anti-drug campaign because of its potency, transportability, and low cost, but most importantly because media attention ensured that no one would miss its connection with the terrifying inner city and its restless Black youth. As had occurred in every past drug scare, the media hyped the addictive potential of crack and its association with violence. Crack was, in Reinarman and Levine's words, "a godsend to the Right":

> They used it and the drug issue as an ideological fig leaf to place over the unsightly urban ills that had increased markedly under Reagan administration social and economic policies. . . . For the Reagan administration and others on the right, America's drug problems functioned as opportunities for the imposition of an old moral agenda and the appearance of a new social concern. Moreover, the remedies that followed from this view were in perfect harmony with "traditional family values"—individual moral discipline and abstinence, combined with police and prisons for those who indulged. Such remedies avoided all questions about the economic and political sources and solutions to America's social problems. (1997, 38)

President Reagan invested heavily in the anti-drug strategy. On October 28, 1986, he signed the $1.7 billion Drug-Free America Act.[3] The president's new drug czar, William Bennett, announced that prison capacities would be doubled and that users, as well as dealers, would be incarcerated (Jensen and Gerber 1998, 19; Reinarman and Levine 1989, 536; Gordon 1994). A second, even more expensive spending bill was adopted just before the 1988 election. Democrats, on the defensive, competed with Republicans to be tough on drug crime. It was, after all, election time.

The Media and the Message about Crack

Crack cocaine proved the key to rekindling public interest in tough punishments for illicit drugs. Public concern about illicit drugs had stayed at a low ebb in the early years of the Reagan administration, despite the president and Nancy Reagan's efforts to focus public attention on the issue (Jensen, Gerber, and Babcock 1991, 655–56). In 1985 and through most of 1986, Gallup public opinion surveys rated drugs a distant fourth among all problems facing the nation (Gallup Institute 1986). Crack, though on the streets in some large cities, was largely unknown to the American public. This changed dramatically in the spring of 1986 after the cocaine-related deaths of two celebrity athletes: Len Bias, a University of Maryland basketball star who had just signed a contract with the Boston Celtics, and Don Rogers, a member of the Cleveland Browns who died the day before he was to be married. Crack was initially blamed for their powder-induced fatalities.

Orcutt and Turner (1993) describe an unprecedented "media epidemic" of coverage in 1986 that began with the deaths of Bias and Rogers. In July, the three networks offered seventy-four evening news segments on drugs, half about crack. In the three months before the 1986 election, there were one thousand stories discussing crack. Fifteen million viewers watched a CBS documentary on crack in the fall of 1986, the highest on record for a news documentary. The competition for audience spawned other primetime and news programs. NBC, for example, produced four hundred separate stories devoted to crack. *Newsweek* called it the biggest story since Vietnam and Watergate, describing crack as "the most addictive drug known to man," while *Time* made crack its issue of the year in 1986 (Szalavitz 1999; see generally Reeves and Campbell 1994, 162–83). Several media outlets ran stories suggesting a pandemic of crack use. Public concern about drugs rose in tandem with media coverage (Shoemaker, Wanta, and Leggett 1989, 77–79). Buried in all the attention devoted to crack were a few dissenting voices who suggested that the extent of the recent wave of drug abuse had been seriously exaggerated (Reinarman and Levine 1988, 252). For the most part, however, and in keeping with previous drug wars, there was a lack of critical attention to the actual incidence of crack abuse and to the reliability of the government sources on which the media depended for its stories.

The crack issue returned to the airwaves in 1988, another election year. In April 1988, ABC described crack as "a plague that was eating away at the fabric of America" (Reinarman and Levine 1995, 153). The *Washington Post* ran 1,565 stories on the drug crisis between October 1988 and October 1989. News coverage, as in the past, typically framed the issue of drug abuse in terms that promoted a criminal justice response (Beckett and Sasson 1998, 30; Reeves and Campbell 1994). The tone grew increasingly moralistic and dramatic over time. News stories included many misleading and inaccurate claims about an "epidemic" of drug use, about crack as a violence-inducing drug, and about pathetic "crack babies" destined to struggle with addiction. The principal theme—that immoral, mostly nonwhite users and dealers were laying siege to middle-class white America—resonated with earlier anti-drug rhetoric and supported the government's expansionist, law-enforcement approach (Beckett and Sasson 1998, 30–33).

Reeves and Campbell looked at 270 news reports broadcasted on the major networks between 1981 and 1988. They found a "cocaine narrative" that spoke menacingly of the drug's dangers. Cocaine was presented as a pollutant, threatening the purity of vulnerable groups, particularly children, teenagers, and mothers. Important segments of the economy were deemed at risk in these portrayals, especially professional sports and college campuses. Hollywood was infected and might spread its infatuation with drugs more broadly (1994, 15, 19). These news reports, Reeves and Campbell showed, were also clearly raced: "Perhaps the central finding of this study is the disparity in news treatment of 'white offenders' and 'black delinquents.' ... Whites were generally depicted as 'repentant deviants' while blacks were often branded as 'enemy' or 'contesting deviants'" (1994, 42).

The Federal Role in Fomenting Fear of Crack Cocaine

Federal officials actively encouraged the media to focus on crack, but they also benefited from its own fascination with this new threat. The National Institute for Drug Abuse carried out an active campaign in 1986 to "increase public awareness" of the drug problem, offering public service announcements, numerous news releases, and "ride alongs" on federal drug busts. The New York representative of the federal Drug Enforcement Administration (DEA), Robert Stutman, gave hundreds of interviews to encourage media interest. He recalls: "I began a lobbying effort and I used the media. The media were only too willing to cooperate, because as far as the New York media was concerned, crack was the hottest combat reporting story to come along since the end of the Vietnam War" (quoted in Beckett 1997, 56). All of the major networks followed the reports of these agencies closely in their news programs (Reeves and Campbell 1994, 165).

Katherine Beckett demonstrated the extent of government influence on media coverage of drug issues in the Reagan period by analyzing "interpretative packages" in television stories between 1982 and 1991. Each of these packages has a set of "signature issues" that identify it, and a core frame that makes the package coherent, such as "zero tolerance," or "need more resources," or "get the traffickers." She found that most drug stories had their basis in government information, such as footage provided by law-enforcement organizations. These stories tended to be more favorable to escalating the effort than those produced through private sources:

> The ascendance of the discourse of law and order in the news ... was largely a consequence of officials' capacity to call attention to and frame discussions of the crime and drug issues. Conservative politicians and law enforcement personnel were particularly successful in defining themselves as the relevant "authorities" on the crime and drug issues. (1997, 65–76, 77)

Government officials, including the president, went as far as staging events to promote the idea that crack posed an imminent threat to the nation. To gain support for his $7.8 billion National Drug Control Strategy, newly elected President George H. W. Bush, in his first national television address in September 1989, dramatically held up a bag of crack that he claimed had been bought in Lafayette Park, directly across from the White House. The clear implication was that crack could be bought anywhere: "It's turning our cities into battle zones, and it's murdering our children" (George Bush Presidential Library and Museum). The truth was that federal agents had been unsuccessful in finding anyone in the Lafayette Park selling crack. They resorted to luring eighteen-year-old Keith Timothy Jackson there to make the sale with a promise of $2,400 and with a DEA agent driving him there. The staged sale required two attempts because of initial difficulties with the filming (Lusane 1991, 66–67; and see Elwood 1994, 41; Reinarman and Levine 1997, 23). The strategy was nevertheless successful. Shortly after President Bush's speech, 64 percent of those responding to a *New York Times/CBS News* poll labeled drugs the nation's most important problem. In January 1985, only 1 percent had held that opinion (Reinarman and Levine 1995, 156; Jensen and Gerber 1998, 20).

The period in which Congress adopted its most important anti-crack legislation was thus one of anti-drug extremism, promoted through the determined efforts of Presidents Reagan and Bush and their supporters and through amplification of the pro-punishment message by an uncritical mass media. As in past periods of drug hysteria, the issue was framed as a moral imperative to protect traditional American values. Suspicion of racial minorities and fearful assumptions about instant addiction and dangerous highs were essential parts of the message (Reinarman and Levine 1995, 147–48). Accurate information about the actual incidence of drug use and its effects were somewhat beside the point, as they have always been.

The quotidian facts were that crack "was the drug of choice in the inner city and nearly nowhere else" (Jacobs 1999, 128; and see Bourgois 1995). And even there, the consensus was that it was a harsh and unsatisfactory drug; many people tried it once and rejected it (Reinarman and Levine 1997, 4). Regular use rates were less than 1 percent throughout this period, and monthly use rates were less than 2 percent and declining through the late 1980s. The people who did use crack regularly tended to be those who were also attracted to heroin and other harmful drugs (Goode 1990, 1091; see also Jacobs 1999; and Elwood 1994, 12). The range of the drug was limited because most sellers lacked the social capital to move into suburban areas.

Reading the Legislative Mind

At this time Congress was competing with the White House to put its own stamp on the problem of drug abuse. Crack was the obvious target to express its concern. To create incentives for the Department of Justice to go after major traffickers, the House Subcommittee on Crime created two levels of mandatory sentences based on the quantity of the drug mixture found at the time of arrest (Sterling 1995, 409). This law passed easily, despite the fact that it departed sharply from Congress's earlier commitment to flexible sentencing guidelines designed by a commission that it had created just two years earlier. The 1986 Anti-Drug Abuse Act[4] provides that 5 grams of a mixture containing measurable amounts of crack cocaine receive a five-year minimum term in federal prison; 50 grams require a ten-year term.

As the politician- and media-inspired furor over crack continued, Congress decided that it needed to go after users, not just dealers. The 1988 Anti-Drug Abuse Act[5] created more mandatory minimum penalties. Possession of a mixture of 5 grams containing crack cocaine would be punished by a minimum of five years in prison. The cutoff was 3 grams for a second possession conviction, and 1 gram for a third. No other drug is penalized with mandatory-minimum sentences like this. Possession of any amount of heroin, for example, can draw no more than one year in prison under the 1988 Anti-Drug Abuse Act.

Were members of Congress aware that they were attacking a racially specific target in setting particularly harsh criminal penalties for crack cocaine offenses? The 1986 and 1988 Anti-Drug Abuse Acts are famous for their draconian mandatory-minimum sentences, and virtually everyone has heard that it requires one hundred times more powder than crack cocaine for the same punishment. But the racial dimension of the enactment process is not well understood. Members of Congress deny any racist leanings in voting for these penalties. The public record reveals no crude racial stereotypes or slurs. The effort was bipartisan, and the legislation passed by wide margins. Yet suspicions linger because the brunt of these harsh penalties has fallen almost entirely on African Americans, and even when that became evident, Congress made no move to change the law.

Any inquiry into the emotional state of a legislative body is bound to be risky and filled with imprecision. Congress is a complex institutional actor, leaving behind only indeterminate signs of its motivation and decision-making processes. This is particularly true in the case of the mandatory-minimum legislation that put crack in a category all by itself. The legislative record is sparse, almost bereft of discussion. House Speaker Thomas P. "Tip" O'Neill, obviously shaken by the June 1986 death of Len Bias, set a five-week deadline for the completion of all committee work on an omnibus anti-drug bill. The usual procedure, which involved introducing a bill, holding hearings, inviting comment, going through markups and amendments, and reintroducing a clean bill, were mostly bypassed in this case (Sterling 1995, 408; and see Everett 1998, 95). News articles, rather than debate, fill most of the relevant pages of the *Congressional Record*. The speeches that were published are full of enthusiasm about the bipartisan spirit of the effort. The record was hardly more robust for the 1988 penalties for simple possession of 5 grams or more of crack. There are, nevertheless, many clues about congressional intent in this record.

The available evidence suggests that Congress knew it was going after a poor, largely Black, often addicted population in criminalizing small-scale sales and possession of crack cocaine. Members of Congress were certainly aware that crack cocaine was part of a thriving drug business in the poor, nonwhite areas of big cities. While wealthier, largely white users bought various drugs, supporting the market with their purchases, they were seldom targeted for enforcement. Given the vitality of the drug market, Congress must also have known that those arrested for selling drugs would be replaced by other unemployed, undereducated youth who had few prospects for decent employment. Less than twenty years earlier, Congress had acted on this belief, dropping mandatory minimums for virtually all drug crimes after hearing testimony from the Katzenbach Commission, which demonstrated that mandatory minimums for these crimes have a disproportionate impact on impoverished racial minorities (1967, 6).

That the poor suffer more from criminal penalties simply because they are poor was also well known. Edwin Sutherland, a leading criminologist, had declared in 1939 that "if two persons on different economic levels are equally guilty of the same offense, the one on the lower level is more likely to be arrested, convicted, and committed to an institution" (179). His claim, published in standard textbooks with many citations, had been backed up consistently by research since that time (see, e.g., Reiman 1995, 138, note 6). There was also the question of the effectiveness of harsh criminal penalties for drug use. Congress could hardly have thought that this drug war, after so many other failed attempts, was destined to wipe out crack abuse.

How did members of Congress think about impact when they adopted the mandatory-minimum legislation? The fact that this large body of decision makers moved quickly and in virtual unanimity to create especially harsh penalties for crack reveals a common mindset. There are also indications of this shared frame of mind in speeches members delivered to colleagues and in the published material that supporters of the legislation inserted into the record. The articles and speeches almost uniformly focused on the dangers of crack in the strongest terms. Looking at the colloquy, it is clear that the alarmists received positive feedback from other members, while those few with critical reservations were ignored.

The 1986 Anti-Drug Abuse Act

On September 8, 1986, Representative James Claude Wright of Texas introduced HR 5484 to the House of Representatives. The 250-page bill acquired 301 cosponsors, attracted 260 proposed amendments, and touched on 207 subjects. Members of Congress were enthusiastic in their endorsement, hailing it as a significant bipartisan effort to deal realistically with the perceived crisis in illicit drug use through interdiction, education, rehabilitation, and increased spending on law enforcement. New criminal penalties for trafficking crack cocaine were a very small part of this bill. They were noncontroversial. The little debate that occurred focused on a proposed death-penalty provision for drug dealers and creation of a overarching "drug czar" to manage the federal government's efforts in this area. Congress approved HR 5484 on October 17, 1986, with no significant resistance from either the House or the Senate. Ten days later—less than two months after this bill was introduced—President Reagan signed into law the 1986 Anti-Drug Abuse Act.

Most of the short time this bill was under consideration was spent within House committees, though there were some brief exchanges in both chambers. Many of the remarks were self-congratulatory. Arizona Senator Dennis DeConcini, for example, praised the legislation and bipartisanism more generally. He waxed eloquent about the virtues of the U.S. Congress, the House, the Senate, his colleagues, members of the Democratic Party, the Speaker of the House, the Republican leadership, and several additional Democrats.

There were, however, a few criticisms en route to enactment. Senator Patrick Moynihan debunked the argument that crack causes crime, calling it a scapegoat: "If we blame crime on crack, our politicians are off the hook. Forgotten are the failed schools, the malign welfare programs, the desolate neighborhoods, the wasted years. Only crack is to blame. One is tempted to think that if crack did not exist, someone somewhere would have received a Federal grant to develop it."[6] This pungent observation was ignored in subsequent discussion, though Senator Evans criticized the rush to legislate and suggested that the crisis had been overdrawn. Concerned about the cost of the new drug bill, he offered an amendment to finance the bill through user fees for alcohol and tobacco.[7] Representative Barney Frank of Massachusetts was the most critical: "I am afraid that this bill is becoming the legislative equivalent to crack. It is going to give people a short-term high, but it is going to be dangerous in the long run to the system and expensive to boot."[8] These concerns were brushed aside in an atmosphere of overwhelming accolades. New York Representative James Scheuer, for example, described it as "a great bill" and praised the "great consensus" on which it was built.

Congress had clearly made up its mind about crack before the bill came up for discussion in September. There was only one hearing, in July, consisting mostly of a lengthy testimonial from a young woman recovering from addiction to a combination of crack and Valium. The words *crack* or *cocaine* did not appear at all in the *Congressional Record* until March 21, 1986. At that point, members of Congress began to offer brief, alarmist speeches and news articles for the consideration of their colleagues. These articles, which came from a wide variety of media sources, all described crack cocaine in dramatic terms as a plague, a major cancer, a wildfire, and a "true epidemic" spreading uncontrollably through American society. It was, several members announced, "The most serious problem facing our country" with every segment of society "under attack."[9]

The problem was so vast ("Men have given up their paychecks. Women have prostituted themselves. Children have stolen from their parents"[10]) that the only solution was to impose very tough criminal penalties. Florida senator Paula Hawkins picked up on the complaint of some police officers that the courts were too lenient in dealing with these cases: "All too many of our judges still avail themselves of the wide sentencing discretion allowed them under these watered down laws to let major drug dealers off with a tap on the wrist even after conviction."[11] Senator Hawkins was also critical of the "voices of permissiveness" that allegedly thwarted legislation to stop drug abuse: "We hear them singing their same old tired tune about civil liberties, about the hopelessness of really stopping the drug traffic. . . ."[12]

The matter of penalties was mentioned only a few times in either the House or Senate discussion. The difference among penalties was alluded to only once, in a September 26 speech by one of the prime movers in the enactment process, Florida Senator Lawton Chiles:

> Those who possess 5 or more grams of cocaine freebase will be treated as serious offenders. Those apprehended with 50 or more grams of cocaine freebase will be treated as major offenders. Such treatment is absolutely

essential because of the especially lethal characteristics of this form of cocaine. Five grams can produce 100 hits of crack. Those who possess such an amount should have the book thrown at them.[13]

No one took issue with Chiles's sentiments about penalties or his pharmacological assertions. The small African American representation in the House, judging from its voting pattern, was mixed in its assessment, but no one addressed the sentencing issue directly for the *Congressional Record*. Black Congressional Caucus leader Charles Rangel, representing New York, was an active supporter of the legislation as a whole; others were silent. Yet only eleven of the House's twenty-one African American members voted in favor of HR 5484.

Compassion was definitely *not* the order of the day. The fact that many dealers were themselves addicted to crack failed to move advocates of harsher penalties. In a June 17 speech, for example, Senator Chiles indicated his awareness of the problem of addition. He cited expert opinion that the addict will "sell, deal, or steal" to get rock cocaine, noting that "once addicted, scruples and morals disappear and addicts with no criminal records become thieves and killers." This did not prevent him from going on to argue that "those dealing in rock and crack cocaine should face the stiffest penalties that law allows."[14]

That the Senate's two most ardent crusaders for the legislation were working from a raced understanding of the problem is clear from the news articles they introduced into the *Congressional Record* for the edification of their colleagues.[15] Analysis of this material[16] suggests three racial themes:

Theme #1—Crack is moving from the Black ghetto to the white suburbs of America:

- "Even though sellers usually set up shop in predominately black neighborhoods, their customers tend to be white. The ability to sell cocaine in rock form has lowered the price to where it is affordable to the middle class" (Blythe 1986).
- "Street sales of cocaine rocks have occurred in the same neighborhoods where other drugs were sold in the past: run-down black neighborhoods ... but the drug market is also creeping into other neighborhoods. ... Less than a block from where unsuspecting white retirees play tennis, bands of young black men push their rocks on passing motorists, interested or not. 'Rock houses' where the drug is sold but not smoked also are appearing in all kinds of neighborhoods" (Blythe 1986).

- "Crack has captured the ghetto and is inching its way into the suburbs.... The police are losing the war against crack, and the war is turning the ghettos of major cities into something like a domestic Vietnam" (McKillop 1986).
- "There are ominous signs that crack and rock dealers are expanding well beyond the inner city" (McKillop 1986).

Theme #2—Crack dealers are Black men:
- "Most of the dealers, as with past drug trends, are black or Hispanic, police said. Haitians also comprise a large number of those selling cocaine rocks, authorities said.... Whites rarely sell the cocaine rocks" (Blythe 1986).
- "'I got some ear ring. You know, make yo' ears ring. It so good.... We goin' to smoke 'em good. Get you high.... Hey, you want girls, I'll get you girls, black girls ... I swear. I ain't jivin' you.' For the growing numbers of the white middle class who have become hooked on cocaine rock, buying the drug can be like stepping into a foreign culture" (Blythe 1986).
- "Although police said most dealers are Black, cocaine rocks are sold in all types of neighborhoods by all types of people" (Blythe 1986).
- "Dealers—'ounce men' as they are known in LA—organize small cells of pushers, couriers and lookouts from the ghetto's legion of unemployed teenagers" (McKillop 1986).
- "West 107th Street in Manhattan is a fringe neighborhood populated by low-income blacks and Hispanics—and one of New York's open-air drug markets." ... West 107th Street sees a steady stream of limos, taxis, and out-of-state cars. 'Sometimes you get the impression we're in New Jersey," says Deputy Inspector Frank Bihler.... He jokes about blowing up the bridges and tunnels to keep the suburbanites out" (McKillop 1986).
- "Selling crack is where the ghetto's inverted social pecking order begins.... These people are very, very into the 'in' thing.... The rock business is now the largest employer in the Los Angeles ghetto" (McKillop 1986).

Theme #3—Promising (white) young people are at risk:
- "So the pretty young girl with dirty-blonde hair, deep blue eyes and a model's figure says she started stealing. She needed money to buy the rock" (Blythe 1986).
- "Art F was a 40ish San Francisco lawyer when cocaine took over his life.... He smoked $1000 worth of rock a day. Somewhere along the way he lost his wife, his two children and his Marin County home" (McKillop 1986).

That this racially explicit framing of the problem drew no reaction at all from Congress is striking, especially in light of the penalties they adopted. As table 4.1 shows, these thresholds were much lower than for most of the other drugs listed in the penalty section of the new legislation. This table sets forth the penalties for manufacturing, distributing, dispensing, or possessing with intent to commit those acts. Penalties apply to mixtures containing "a detectable amount" of each of the following drugs:

Table 4.1 Five- and ten-year federal prison terms for varying amounts of illegal drugs

Substance	At least 5 years of imprisonment[a]	At least 10 years of imprisonment[a]
Marijuana	100,000	1,000,000
Cocaine or derivatives	500	5000
Heroin	100	1000
PCP	10	100
N-phenyl-N	40	400
Cocaine base	5	50
Methamphetamine	5	50
LSD	1	10

[a] Mixture amounts in grams.

Although the new mandatory minimums attempt to differentiate between low-level dealers and drug kingpins, they do not calibrate penalties according to the relative harmfulness of the various drugs included in the legislation. The House Subcommittee on Crime had consulted with law-enforcement personnel in the Department of Justice about the quantities needed to focus law-enforcement efforts on high-level dealers, but had not gone beyond this. Nor did it contact anyone besides federal drug enforcement agents, such as the Judicial Conference, the Bureau of Prisons, or the Parole Commission (Sterling 1995, 409–10).[17]

Congress's own Sentencing Commission was generally left out of this process. Members of Congress did not seek its input when debating what penalties to impose (Sterling 1995, 409–10). Once the mandatory minimums had been adopted, Congress offered little guidance on how to accommodate them to the Commission's comprehensive plans for rational sentencing. The ultimate result, which was to become evident within a few years, was that the Commission understood its mission in a way that further ratcheted up sentences in cases involving crack cocaine, even beyond what Congress may have intended.

More of the Same: The 1988 Anti-Drug Abuse Act Criminalizes Possession of Crack

Congress revisited drug policy in 1988, a period of continuing urban violence, much of it associated with gang conflicts over drug profits. Fanned by constant media attention, concerns about the dangers of crack and other drugs was growing. The State Department reported that production of coca, opium, and marijuana had increased over the past two years and that the price of cocaine was dropping as its purity increased. Hospital emergencies and cocaine deaths had increased. Most members of Congress were convinced that they needed to do more. In the words of Representative Julian Dixon, a member of the Black Caucus, "The simple truth is that almost two years later, we are losing the war."[18] The most powerful argument for a new, tougher federal law, in short, was that the 1986 law had failed to deter drug abuse.

The 1988 legislation was, again, an omnibus affair covering many separate issues related to the use of illicit drugs. Several sections were concerned, for example, with cutting off federal benefits, such as student loans, to people convicted of drug dealing. The 1988 bill also made the death penalty available for the most serious drug-law offenses. This was too much for several African American members of Congress, who were familiar with studies showing racial disproportion in the imposition of the death penalty and aware that, just a year before, the Supreme Court had turned down a constitutional challenge on this grounds. In response to this decision, and out of concern with this latest death-penalty provision, Representative John Conyers attempted to convince his colleagues to adopt the Racial Justice Act, a bill designed to reestablish evidence of racial disproportion as a constitutional issue in death-penalty cases. His effort failed, suggesting the frustrating situation of minority members sensitive to the likelihood of racial oppression in the new law, but stymied by the prevailing punitive mindset.

Proponents of the new mandatory minimums argued that higher fixed penalties for crimes involving crack were necessary in light of the growing supply of the drug and its links to violent crime. The new penalty most relevant for ordinary offenders, however, was at the lowest end of the offense scale and had no link to violent crime: The 1988 bill would impose five years of imprisonment for simple possession of cocaine base, with no evidence of intent to sell. This sentence would apply to first-time offenders. Such a severe penalty, a few critics pointed out, was entirely out of keeping with penalties in the federal system. One year of imprisonment had been the maximum for possession of *any* amount of any other drug. The new penalties were also criticized as inconsistent with the philosophy of the guidelines approach that Congress had adopted when it created the federal Sentencing Commission (Sterling 1995, 316–17).

Those advocating the new mandatory minimums, however, easily dominated this discussion. The section on the new penalties, according to the bill's legislative history, was adopted by voice vote. The final vote on the whole legislation was 346 to 11. Six of those negative votes came from the Black Congressional Caucus.[19] The Caucus was mixed in its assessment. Some members, concerned about drug sales in minority communities, were strong proponents of tougher penalties. Others may well have been concerned about racial impact. Congress had not left itself much time to discuss such matters. Public Law 100-690 had taken only one hundred days to become law.

Conclusion

The "crack attack" that stirred Congress to enact harsh mandatory-minimum sentences for possession and sale of small amounts of crack cocaine has been dubbed a moral panic (Beckett 1997; Reinarman and Levine 1995, 1997; Steiner 2001). Sociologist Stanley Cohen popularized this term in describing the reactions of the media, law enforcement, and the public to youth disturbances in Britain during the 1960s. For Cohen, a moral panic occurs when

> a person or group of persons emerges to become defined as a threat to societal values and interests; its nature is presented in a stylized and stereotypical fashion by the mass media; the moral barricades are manned by editors, bishops, politicians and other right thinking people; socially accredited experts pronounce their diagnoses and solutions. . . . (1980, 9)

Moral panics create "folk devils," elements in society who are stripped of all favorable characteristics and blamed for the condition. These harm-causing characters are selfish and evil; they must be stopped (Goode and Ben-Yehuda 1994b, 29). In the 1986 epidemic of concern over crack, the folk devil was the drug dealer and, to some extent, the drug itself. As in other moral panics, media hype was an essential element in the mobilization of public opinion about crack. The press, as Reinarman and Duskin observe, has developed "a cultivated incapacity for understanding drug problems" that "prepares the public to believe false stereotypes about drug dealing and to support endless drug wars" (2002, 41).

Political officials also played a predictable role, describing crack in dramatic terms and exaggerating its impact. Constant reliance on the term *war* to describe the government's strategy ratcheted up the rhetoric considerably. Political scientist Murray Edelman labels *war* a potent "condensation symbol," evoking the need for implacable action against a serious, potentially lethal enemy (1988, 73). Officials reinforced the message with references to "our children," "our cities," and "our values," comforting symbols of group solidarity against a common enemy. The despised rhetorical target was painted in terms of utter disgustingness, as child predators would be in a latter criminalization episode (Lynch 2002, 561). Media scholar James Hawdon found many examples of extremist drug rhetoric in his study of 167 drug-related speeches and public statements by Presidents Reagan and Bush between 1981 and 1992: "President Reagan masterfully incited the public and helped create a moral panic." Hawdon found that President Bush was less gifted in stirring these passions, which may explain why, by 1992, the panic was winding down (2001, 438; see also Goode 1990; Tonry 2004).

As previous chapters have shown, harsh penalties are always justified with demonization rhetoric. A racialized subtext usually amplifies the message of infection of youth by exposure to the dissipation of the underclass. The vulnerability of the underclass itself is never a matter of concern. Consider, for example, Representative Bertram Podell's February 3, 1970, speech in support of toughening legislation to control heroin: "Like an epidemic whose symptoms remained unrecognized until hundreds and thousands were infected, drug abuse and the problems that go with such abuse have infected almost every community in the United States."[20] The House was at the time considering a "beast of prey" bill to punish drug dealers, whom another member of Congress described as the "most depraved of the criminal elements . . . ready to wreck the lives of children in order to obtain enormous income."[21]

Drug scares pay handsome political benefits by encouraging quick, emotionally satisfying fixes in times of rapid social change. There is little tolerance or even interest in critical inquiry and careful deliberation in these manufactured states of crisis (see, e.g., Lynch 2002, 557). Poverty can be blamed on drugs, and the fact that they tend to be most visible in the poorest neighborhoods of our nation only reinforces the point. Every president, Franklin Zimring and Gordon Hawkins note, acts confident that the problem can be eradicated with enough law-enforcement effort—it is "an amnesia that seems to affect political leaders in regard to drug control" (1992, 48).

Race framed the legislative reaction to crack, as it always frames penal prohibitionism. The nation's racial hierarchy helps to determine which drugs will be considered dangerous and which will be accepted as a normal part of society, regardless of their cost in death and disability (Lauderdale and Inverarity 1984). It is an essential ingredient in the rhetoric of danger and disrespect for middle-class norms that underlies concern about illicit drugs. The inconvenient reality, of course, is that middle-class white Americans have always been major consumers of illicit drugs. That is why the drug-war message has always been two-pronged: The main theme is corruption by drugs and drug dealers, but with a counterpoint of redemption for those who admit their seduction by drugs. The public can thereby be reassured that the drug problem can be stopped without bringing things too close to home.

By focusing public wrath on those who sell drugs rather than those who buy them, the spotlight stays on the most marginal elements in society. Our failure to deal with the lack of opportunity in poor minority areas, criminologist John Hagan suggests, ensures that this business will always attract sellers:

> Until we confront the social and economic roles played by deviance service centers and vice industries in America's racial and ethnic ghettos, we will not be able to reduce the scale of their associated activities and stubborn persistence in these distressed minority settings. This is especially true in the context of the economic slowdown and transition that has characterized the last quarter of this century." (1995, 39)

What is distinctive about the anti-crack campaign is not its focus on impoverished African Americans in economically depressed urban areas, however, but its harshness. The buildup of Black citizens imprisoned for drug offenses represents an unprecedented assault on a ghetto vice industry, a high-water mark in the nation's episodic wars on drugs. The punitiveness is equivalent only, perhaps, to the cruel treatment accorded African Americans in the post-Reconstruction South, a shameful era of penal servitude, chain gangs, and racist law enforcement.

The amounts spent are also unprecedented. Between 1987 and 1998, the federal budget for fighting drug abuse rose from $6 billion to $20 billion (Gest 2001, 115). Two-thirds of this money went to law enforcement and prisons, and only one-third to prevention and treatment. Congress gave law-enforcement agencies powerful inducements to arrest by authorizing forfeiture of drug-related assets, while judges lost discretion to reduce sentences in light of extenuating circumstances. Those convicted of drug offenses, in addition to long sentences, have been stripped, often for life, of important rights. The collateral damage to African American communities has been enormous.

five

The Racial Impact of
the War on Drugs

How Government Coped

The 1986 Anti-Drug Abuse Act[1] and its 1988 counterpart[2] had immediate and noticeable impacts on the pattern of drug arrests and prosecutions throughout the nation. Congress intended, and law-enforcement agencies received, a powerful message: Focus as many resources as possible on crack arrests, including arrest and prosecution of small-time users and sellers (U.S. Sentencing Commission 1995a, 118–21). Fourteen states rewrote their drug laws to target crack, although only Iowa adopted the federal level's 100:1 differentiation.

Strong economic incentives encouraged states to focus on crack, including increasingly generous forfeiture provisions throughout the 1980s and the 1986 introduction of the Byrne Program, a federal grant program that created multi-jurisdictional drug task forces. State and local agencies and the multi-jurisdictional task forces grew rapidly with these new resources. By 1991, there were 904 task forces covering 83 percent of the population. Some of these units became dependent on monies from drug seizures, which they pursued aggressively.[3] The task forces seized over $1 billion in assets between 1988 and 1992 and have remained a powerful force in drug-law enforcement (Blumenson and Nilsen 1998).

Crack cases soon dominated other types of drug offenses in both state and federal court systems. Almost all of these defendants were African American. A 1992 Sentencing Commission survey found that in sixteen states, including populous states like New Jersey and Illinois, not a single white had been charged (U.S. Sentencing Commission 1995b, xi; Wexler 1995). In over half of the federal district courts that had tried drug cases, according to another study, all of the defendants were minorities (Weich and Angulo 2000, 193). State courts were also seeing vastly increased numbers of drug cases involving minorities, some of which had been referred by federal agents.

Young African American men were going to prison for drug crimes in record numbers. Judges complained that these cases were swamping their dockets, and expressed concern that the prosecutions were overwhelmingly against young African American men. Like Judge Cahill in the *Clary* case,[4] they found the situation morally troubling and deeply discouraging. A few federal district judges retired in protest. Some judges on senior status refused to include drug cases in their dockets.

As the racial dimensions of the aggressive assault on crack began to draw public attention, Congress became involved. Prisoners' rights groups argued for repeal of the mandatory minimums, and many federal judges spoke out on the issue. These critics found a surprising ally in the U.S. Sentencing Commission, which proposed that the penalties for crack offenses be lowered to be at parity with those for powder cocaine. The Commission's parity recommendation had the support of members of the Congressional Black Caucus, which spoke eloquently in its favor. Yet the parity proposal failed when it was put to a vote, and by a large margin. Subsequent compromise proposals to reduce federal penalties for crack cocaine have met the same fate.

Why have critics of the mandatory minimums gotten no traction in Congress, even when they have had the backing of the experts on the Sentencing Commission and members of the Black Congressional Caucus? How could the racial significance of the crack cocaine penalties be denied? The answers to these questions may lie in the ideology of color blindness that dominates U.S. discourse about race. Color blindness is both a prescription for behavior, and an approach to the analysis of racial difference. The color-blind perspective is intentionally simple-minded about racial beliefs and attitudes, based on the belief that good people can, and will, ignore race in making decisions. When outcomes differ by race, the color-blind approach assumes that they are either the result of intended discrimination or an indication of "real" racial differences. Racism, in other words, is a purely personal matter unanchored in institutions or habits of mind. This perspective leads to inaction and indifference about sentencing disparities and other indications of persistent racial inequalities. As one group of observers explains:

> Today, many white Americans are concerned only with whether they are, individually, guilty of something called racism. Having examined their souls and concluded that they are not personally guilty of any direct act of discrimination, many whites convince themselves that they are not racists and then wash their hands of the problem posed by persistent racial inequality. (Brown et al. 2003, 4)

Color blindness prescribes only a very limited role for government when racial differences are found to exist. If those differences are the result of overt, conscious, or deliberate racial discrimination, government must intervene. But government has no responsibility to go further in seeking to understand why racial differences occur. Color-blind ideology does not envision unconscious racism born of stereotypical thinking or irrational racial fears. Nor does this present-oriented, intention-bound approach allow much room for structural constraints or institutional practices that can bias outcomes. The idea that society constructs race and that much of this is not consciously intended is foreign to color blindness.

This chapter argues that color-blind ideology has guided Congress in refusing to change its crack cocaine penalties. Every public policy, Howard Winant argues, has an implicit theory of race and racism (1998). Color blindness can explain why Congress refused all pleas to change the mandatory minimums in crack cases, even the repeated requests of its own Sentencing Commission. Winant's observation suggests that we should also look at the Sentencing Commission's theory of race and racism to see how it differs from that of Congress. This chapter accordingly begins with a close look at the Sentencing Commission and the evolution of its proposal for parity in sentencing crack and powder cocaine offenders instead of the law's 100:1 differential between the two drugs.

The U.S. Sentencing Commission and the War on Drugs

The decision to create a sentencing commission was a major departure for Congress and an institutional innovation at the federal level. Historically, judges have been at the helm of the sentencing process, exercising broad discretion over punishment within a very wide range of possible outcomes set by the legislature (U.S. Sentencing Commission 1991a). Inserting a commission's expert judgment into the process could be expected to create more uniformity across the system as a whole, but at a significant cost to judicial power. The commission's sentencing experts would determine appropriate punishment ranges, based on specified criteria related to the crime and the criminal. Judges would be required to sentence within a greatly narrowed range.

The idea of a sentencing commission had been talked about seriously since 1973, when a former federal judge, Marvin Frankel, broached the idea in a crusading book, *Criminal Sentences: Law without Order* (1973). At that point, a few members of Congress had begun to scrutinize disparities in sentences handed down by federal judges, and several states were experimenting with commissions, most of which allowed judges to retain considerable sentencing discretion. Congress, however, was not so positively inclined toward the federal judiciary; it wanted to "send a message" to "out of control" judges.

Congress created its Commission with the 1984 Sentencing Reform Act,[5] which was part of the Comprehensive Crime Control Act. The effort brought together unlikely political bedfellows. Senator Edward Kennedy, who had been among the first to push for reform, became a leader on the liberal side (Stith and Koh 1993). His idea was to rely on the courts' own governing body, the Judicial Conference, to create a body of experts that would develop voluntary sentencing guidelines for the federal bench. Liberals were concerned about racial and class discrimination in sentencing, geographical differences in sentences, and overincarceration. They wanted to constrain, but not eliminate, judicial power to set sentences. The agenda of the conservatives involved in the sentencing policy debate was much different. They saw the commission idea as a chance to demonstrate their opposition to "intolerable levels of crime" and to eliminate a judge-controlled system "incompatible with effective crime control" because of overlenient sentencing.[6]

The result was a victory for the conservative vision. The new law abolished parole and required offenders to serve at least 85 percent of their sentences. The commissioners were to be presidential appointees approved by the Senate. Only three of the seven would be judges. The commission would produce mandatory, not discretionary, sentencing rules. Sentencing judges could make some adjustments, but only on grounds not addressed in the Sentencing Guidelines. Departures from prescribed sentences, limited to 25 percent of the authorized sentence, had to be justified and were appealable. Conservatives added a provision requiring "a term of imprisonment at or near the maximum term authorized" for repeat violent offenders and for drug offenders. There was no requirement, however, to take prison capacity into account (see Stith and Koh 1993, 266–68).

The mission of the Commission was to develop a rational system that could provide sentences of comparable severity for comparably serious crimes across the federal system, while taking appropriate account of the criminal history of the defendant. There was no specific guidance from Congress on how to balance conflicts between the retributive and rehabilitative goals of sentencing, though Congress had signaled a strong concern for public safety, particularly with respect to gun violations, child sexual abuse, and drugs. The task that Congress set for the Commission was essentially legislative. U.S. Supreme Court Justice Antonin Scalia referred to them as "a junior varsity Congress."[7]

The Commission dealt with the contradictory messages it received by developing a sentencing grid system that allowed judges to locate the proper sentence range by factoring in offense and offender characteristics (Breyer 1988). The prosecutor would play a major role in this process as the source of the relevant information about the case (Denzlinger and Miller 1991, 51). "The Guidelines make the US attorney the most powerful person in the courthouse," explained Alan Johnson, a former U.S. attorney in western Pennsylvania, expressing a widely shared opinion (quoted in Flaherty and Biskupic 1996a; and see Cabranes 1992). Judges did retain authority to deviate from the Guidelines, but within rules that prevent consideration of factors like a background of poverty or a lack of education. The emphasis, in short, was on creating more uniform sentencing outcomes by reducing judicial, but not prosecutorial, discretion.

Guidelines versus Mandatory Minimums in Crack Cases

The Commission began to work on its Guidelines sentences for crack cocaine before Congress adopted legislation mandating five- and ten-year mandatory-minimum penalties for designated offenses. The Commission solicited ideas from stakeholders in a variety of areas, including the Drug Enforcement Administration (DEA), which wanted all drug offenders, except those who cooperated with the prosecution, to get some prison time. But the DEA envisioned that federal authority would be exercised only in the most serious cases, with sentences of three years or more reserved for those who distributed very large quantities of drugs or who were ringleaders or financial backers. Had Congress not acted, the Commission probably would have taken this approach.

Congress's 1986 mandatory-minimum legislation, however, changed everything. Remarkably, some members of Congress appear to have believed that they were aiming at big-time drug dealers with their five-year penalty for offenses involving 5 grams (0.176 ounce) of material containing crack cocaine and ten-year penalties for 10 grams (0.353 ounce). Senator Mack Mattingly, for example, equated a gram of crack with fifteen potential sales. Senator Robert Byrd suggested that the ten-year minimums would get the "kingpins—the masterminds who are really running these operations," while the five-year terms would be for the "middle-level dealers."[8] (See generally Sterling 2005.)

Politics, however, finally determined how the mandatory minimums would work. One representative, fearful that his rural district might be ignored in favor of those with bigger drug sales, asked that the amounts required for prosecution be lowered (Sterling 2005). Congress compounded the problem by specifying that sentencing would be based on the total weight of the mixture containing the drug, rather than the amount of the drug itself, a sharp departure from previous practice that promised enormous consequences for small-time dealers (see Meierhoefer 1999, 34–36).

In creating mandatory-minimum sentences for crack offenses, Congress followed a well-worn script. Mandatory minimums have been used on occasion since the founding era. Throughout the nineteenth century, Congress established them for a variety of crimes on an occasional basis (U.S. Sentencing Commission 1991a). Drug offenses became a target for mandatory minimums in 1951, at the height of the McCarthy era, and again in 1956, in the Narcotics Control Act,[9] when Congress imposed them for most drug importation and distribution violations. By the late 1960s, however, a consensus had emerged in both parties that the mandatory-minimums approach to drug control was a failure (Schlosser 2003, 43). The 1970 Comprehensive Drug Abuse Prevention and Control Act[10] repealed virtually all of them. The moral panic over crack cocaine brought back mandatory sentences, but this time they would be required to coexist somehow with Guidelines sentencing and the U.S. Sentencing Commission.

The surprising outcome of the confluence of mandatory minimums and Guidelines sentencing was even more severe punishments than Congress may have intended. In attempting to maintain proportionality across all drug amounts, the Commission raised penalties for drugs not covered by the mandatory minimums. The result was higher penalties than Congress had prescribed for some amounts of the drug. The Commission also adopted a "relevant conduct" standard that made low-level offenders responsible for all the drugs found in the operation, as if they were involved in a coordinated conspiracy (Meierhoefer 1999, 35).

The impact of the mandatory-minimum legislation on the Guidelines is most evident when sentences for crack and powder cocaine are compared. The penalties for powder cocaine violations reflect the relatively nonpunitive judicial sentences set in earlier years. As it had in other areas, the Commission used these older sentences to establish its baseline for powder offenses. For crack, a new drug, there was no sentencing history, but there *was* a clear congressional mandate. The significance of the disparity in the treatment of the two pharmacologically identical drugs was apparently unnoticed in the rush to approve the new Guidelines. Approval occurred after a one-day hearing in the Senate and a six-day hearing in the House.

The crack/powder disparity did not at first draw much attention from the federal bench, which seemed to have been caught off guard by the advent of the Sentencing Guidelines. The judges focused at first on the defects they saw in an administratively guided sentencing system. In its 1991 conference, the Ninth Circuit, the largest on the federal bench, voted 172 to 28 to recommend that the Guidelines be nonbinding. Stith and Cabranes estimated that three-fourths of federal trial judges and two-thirds of the appellate bench opposed the Guidelines when they were enacted (1998, 5). Most saw the prosecutor emerging as the most influential participant in sentencing (Federal Judicial Center 1996). A spate of lawsuits tested the system on constitutional and other grounds, but the Supreme Court upheld the system in its entirety in 1989 in *Mistretta v. United States*.[11] A few judges resigned, some took senior status, and many continued to criticize the system from the bench.[12]

Despite these protests, the Guidelines became part of the fabric of the criminal justice system, growing more complicated with time. Congress continued to tinker with the system to reduce the number of downward departures by judges, though the Supreme Court, as it turned out, would have the last word on the matter.[13] Meanwhile, the penalties that Congress and the Commission had set for crack offenses began to have their effect.

Imprisonment quickly became the new standard in drug cases, in spite of the fact that nearly two-thirds of the federal prosecutions were for relatively small amounts of crack cocaine, less than 23 grams. The elimination of parole meant that every offender served at least 85 percent of his or her sentence; the earlier average had been 47 percent. Average sentence length increased from 47 months to 77 months. This meant that actual time served increased to an average of 65 months and that overall sentence length in drug cases increased by an average of three years, or 248 percent, from 1984 to 1990 (U.S. Sentencing Commission 1991b, 378). The rate of incarceration was growing dramatically at both the state and federal levels. By 2003, it had reached 482 per 100,000 population, higher than any nation in the world.

In monitoring these changes, both the Sentencing Commission and the Federal Judicial Center noted a change in the racial makeup of the drug offender population. Research also revealed that the new legislation was not being evenly applied. A 1992 study conducted by the Federal Judicial Center found that about 40 percent of the defendants subject to mandatory minimums were actually receiving lesser sentences (Schwarzer 1992; Meierhoefer 1992a). Prosecutors were apparently negotiating away the crime originally charged to encourage guilty pleas and information sharing. As the Center's director, Judge William Schwarzer, concluded: "It is not that the sentencing scheme is not tough or rigid enough, but rather that the tougher and more rigid it is, the more determined the effort (and the greater the need) to circumvent it" (1992, 407).

From the outset, the Justice Department contributed to the steep rise in drug arrests and convictions by allowing its local offices to focus on minor cases, which could, and arguably should, have been handled by the states. But the federal law's low threshold for arrest and its wide-open standards for prosecution created incentives for low-level arrests, which are easier to obtain. The result was that less than 7 percent of all federal cocaine convictions in 2000 were high-level dealers, while more than 70 percent were at the bottom end of the drug distribution network—street dealers, lookouts, couriers, and so on. Street-level crack dealers were serving longer sentences on average (104 months) than powder cocaine importers and high-level suppliers (101 months) (U.S. Sentencing Commission 2002).

The Racial Impact of the Anti-crack Initiative

As the number of drug arrests grew, so did the proportion of African Americans in the state and federal systems, rising from 24 percent in 1980 to 39 percent in 1993 (Tonry and Hatlestad 1997, 246). In state prisons, their proportion grew from 7 percent in 1986 to 25 percent in 1991 (Tonry and Hatlestad 1997, 232). Changes at the federal level have been even more dramatic, largely because of crack prosecutions, almost all of which involve African American defendants. Between 1980 and 1999, their incarceration rate in federal prisons more than tripled, from 1,156 per 100,000 to 3,620 per 100,000 population.

Blacks have historically received higher penalties than whites for all types of crimes, but the gap widened between 1986 and 1990, largely because of the new crack law. In the federal system, the racial difference in average sentence length grew from 11 percent in 1986 to 49 percent in 1990, while the racial difference in sentence length for "other drug offenders" grew from 6 percent in 1984 to 93 percent in 1990. Figure 5.1 shows the rising numbers of African Americans in state and federal prisons between 1980 and 2003.

These patterns were not the result of white disinterest in crack cocaine. The majority of users have always been white. The 1991 National Survey on Drug Abuse, for example, found that 65 percent of those reporting crack use in their lifetimes were white, while 26 percent were African American and 9 percent were Hispanic (U.S. Sentencing Commission 1995b, chap. 3; and see Substance Abuse and Mental Health Services Administration 1999, 37–39). Whites not only were successfully avoiding prosecution, but they also were benefiting from sentence reductions, despite the mandatory-minimum legislation. As Federal Judicial Center researcher Barbara Meierhoefer notes:

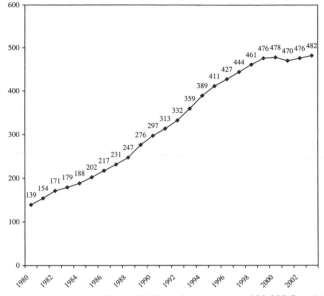

Figure 5.1 Rising Incarceration Rates of African Americans per 100,000 Population in State and Federal Prisons

In 1990 lower-scale drug offenders who were black were more than twice as likely as others to receive a sentence of five or more years. Among those with mandatory minimum behaviors, black offenders were twenty-one percent and Latino offenders were twenty-eight percent more likely than whites to receive a sentence of at least the minimum term. The sharp divergence begins in 1987, suggesting an effect of the mandatory minimum statutes. (1992b, 391)

It was becoming evident that race remained relevant in sentencing, even after adjusting for the type of drug, drug amount, weapon use, prior record, age, drug use, and gender, a pattern that has continued (see, e.g., Kautt 2001–2). The racial impact of sentencing in drug cases, Kautt's work and other research suggests, extends beyond the crack/powder disparity to a broader racial bias in sentencing. White defendants more often avoid going to prison, and when they do go, they serve shorter terms than their African American counterparts. It also seems clear that some of the factors considered legitimate in sentencing, such as prior criminal history, create a vicious circle of sentencing disadvantages for African American offenders (Harcourt 2003).

By 1993, a number of civil rights, religious, criminal justice, and grassroots organizations had become interested in the crack/powder issue. Twenty-five of these groups formed themselves into an alliance: the National Coalition against the Discriminatory Crack Law. The group held briefings for members of Congress and supported legislation introduced by Congressmen Charles Rangel and William Hughes to equalize crack and powder cocaine sentences. Each of these representatives, for differing reasons, could afford to press his convictions. Rangel had a safe seat, and Hughes had announced plans to retire. The bill they jointly sponsored, however, did not make it out of the Democratically controlled Judiciary Committee, despite the efforts of Subcommittee Chairman Hughes. Opponents of the amendment—including some Democrats—argued that the way to achieve equity was to *raise* the penalties for powder cocaine (Taifa 1998, 201). Sensing the possibility of a cure that would be worse than the disease, Hughes acquiesced in an amendment mandating that the Sentencing Commission study the matter and that it submit its recommendations to Congress by the end of the year. The vote was unanimous. It was an election year, and the Commission had already embarked on a review of cocaine penalties anyway.

The Experts Consider the Crack/Powder Disparity

From the Sentencing Commission's perspective, the racial pattern in drug sentencing was not just unfortunate. It was also embarrassing in a professional sense. The Commission was established to bring greater fairness in sentencing and to prevent factors like racial disadvantage from making a difference in the sentencing process. As its first chairperson, Judge William Wilkins, explained:

> The United States Sentencing Commission was created by Congress to promulgate and refine sentencing guidelines, to serve as the expert research agency in the area of Federal sentencing, and to provide technical assistance and information to Congress, the criminal justice community, and the public. (1991, 30)

The emergence of egregious racial differences in sentences suggested that the Commission had failed in its basic mission of bringing fairness to the process. The validity of its expertise was at stake.

But the Commission was at first unsure what was happening. Crack cocaine was known to be a "Black" drug associated with the inner city, so racially disproportionate enforcement patterns were to be expected. But the possibility of discriminatory treatment could not be dismissed out of hand.

And so the Commission staff read widely to learn more about the pharmacology of crack cocaine, distribution networks, "crack babies" and "boarder babies," as well as the relevant sentencing literature. Staff members collected and studied news reports of racism in federal drug cases to document possible cases of prejudicial treatment. It ultimately dismissed studies suggesting that bias might be at work in arrest, prosecution, or sentencing. The Commissioners focused instead on one study that argued that if the crack/powder disparity were eliminated, racial differences in drug sentencing would disappear (Meierhoefer 1992a, 162).

The Commissioners appear to have realized that they were entering politically volatile territory. As one of them remarked, "the racial thing" had attracted the public's interest: "The racial flag gets you great support in some areas, but strong opposition in others."[14] The problem was that the racial disparities were too obvious to dismiss or explain away as a function of enforcement problems. Almost 90 percent of the federal crack offenders were African American. Defendants convicted of simple possession of powder cocaine, on the other hand, were over half white.

The difference between penalties for low-level offenses involving crack and powder cocaine, some of the Commissioners concluded, was the heart of the matter. How could the Commission justify an arbitrary one-hundred-fold difference in penalties for drugs that were pharmacologically identical, particularly in light of popular understanding that crack was a "Black" drug and that cocaine powder was a "white" drug? Crack might be more dangerous in how it was used, but how much worse could it be? How could social impact be measured scientifically and rationally factored into a penalty system?

The solution the Commission finally agreed on, after much discussion and a 4 to 3 vote, was to suggest parity in punishments for the two drugs, with the powder cocaine penalty structure in the Guidelines being the point of reference for both drugs. The minority wanted to keep some distinction, but no one favored more than a 5:1 ratio in penalties. Parity had the advantage of being defensible on the grounds that the drugs were identical in their chemical makeups. This "scientific" approach to the problem provided a quick, but honorable, retreat from the disturbing fact that Blacks were being arrested in record numbers and sentenced to prison terms of unprecedented length.[15]

The Commissioners realized, however, that racial impact would not be a persuasive argument to use with Congress to change the penalty structure. Opponents of the change would claim that racial differences in offending explained the racial impact. So, in anticipation that the color-blind ideology prevailing in Congress would doom any positive resolution of the crack controversy, the Commission decided to downplay racial impact as a reason for changing the law. As one staff member observed: "It leads nowhere we want to go."[16]

The Commission's 1995 report to Congress reflects this determination. The book-length report devoted only a single page to the racial disparities between crack and powder cases. The Commission also revealed its understanding of the risks it was taking in the way it introduced the parity proposal. Because color-blind ideology attributes racial differences in outcomes either to intentional discrimination or to racial differences in behavior, it was important to offer reassurance that the parity proposal was not meant to be critical of Congress's motives in enacting the mandatory minimums. The Commission offered this preamble to its recommendation: "There is no evidence that Congress or the Sentencing Commission acted with any discriminatory intent in setting different statutory guidelines penalties for different forms of cocaine" (1995b, xii).

The problem, the Commission suggested, was the perception that others might have that the 100:1 ratio was racially discriminatory. Commission chair, Judge Richard Conaboy, stressed the theme of appearances and unintended effects:

> Fifth and finally, because there is such a clear impact of those high penalties on minority defendants, the policy, the 100-to-1 ratio, leads to very strong perceptions of unfairness. Crack is cheap, and it is thus distributed and attractive to the poor, many of whom are minorities. With a 100-to-1 ratio we have, we think, unintentionally developed the anomaly of punishing the poor and minorities more severely under the guise of trying to protect them.[17]

The Commission had consulted with other federal officials in making its parity proposal, and it had the backing of some influential people who had reputations for being tough on crime. Even the Department of Justice, which did not want parity, supported a significantly reduced ratio (Bergman 1998, 199). A former director of the president's Office of National Drug Control Policy, Lee P. Brown, was in favor of parity. He and his counterpart in office at the time, General Barry McCaffrey, another hardnosed anti-crime advocate, attempted—but failed—to get the Clinton White House on board with the parity proposal. It was ironic that these two drug warriors supported parity, but were unable to get a racially sensitive Democratic president to agree with them. But it also indicated the political delicacy of the situation.

Congress Considers Race in the War on Drugs

The Commission's parity recommendation and the publicity it engendered forced Congress, finally, to address the issue of race in its war on drugs. The recommendation would become law on November 1, 1995, unless Congress took the unprecedented step of rejecting it. Congress had already considered over five hundred previous Commission recommendations and allowed all of them to take effect. To reject this particular proposal would make Congress look less sensitive to racial issues than its Sentencing Commission. Some members of Congress were furious that they had been put in this position. Senator Hatch's office, for example, threatened to cut the agency's funding.[18]

Supporters and opponents of the proposal formed quickly, and along racial lines. The Black Congressional Caucus endorsed the parity recommendation. Their principal opponents were white Republican members of Congress from the deep South. These opponents rested their arguments on the dangerousness of crack, its cheapness, and its availability. In Representative Bill McCollum's words: "Any retreat at this time in our battle against the evil of illegal drugs, and in particular crack cocaine, would be a mistake this Congress would long regret. Congress must not lose its resolve."[19] Representative Don E. Bush countered by charging that the bill to kill the Commission's parity proposal was racist: "Is there a conspiracy among the Republican majority to incarcerate as many African-American males as possible? . . . It is dishonesty, if not intellectual heresy, to introduce a bill such as this."[20]

There was much jockeying for advantage in this discussion. Anti-parity spokespeople claimed to speak for the true interests of Black Americans. Thus Representative Burton Barr, a white Republican from Georgia, noted that he had spoken with impoverished residents of housing projects, who told him to "get those people off the streets and put them away for a long period of time."[21] Representative Clay Shaw, also white and a Florida Republican, argued similarly that we should "put them in jail and throw the key away. That is the voice of America. That is the voice of the minorities in the areas that are responsible who want to get their areas up out of poverty, get out of the gutter, get the problems out of their neighborhoods. . . ."[22] These testimonials prompted sarcastic replies from some African American members, including Representative Maxine Waters, a California Democrat: "I am surprised at much of the rhetoric and all of these so-called conversations that my friends on the other side of the aisle have been having in minority communities."[23]

Some conservative members of the House used the debate to argue for stiffer penalties for powder cocaine. Representative Jeff Flake of Arizona, for example, advocated equally severe sentences for both drugs on the grounds that penalties for powder cocaine were too light.[24] Those who supported the Commission's proposal rejected this logic, emphasizing the damage done in poor and African American communities by the harsh sentencing rules.[25] Some of this rhetoric was sharply critical of Congress. A Democratic Representative from Pennsylvania, Chaka Fattah, was blunt: "The American people can see the sheet being pulled away from what is a racist implementation of the criminal justice system in this country, and we shall reap what we sow."[26] Representative Melvin Watts, a Democrat from North Carolina, drew his inspiration from the recent Million Man March and the president's address to its participants that accompanied it:

> We cannot say to black people in the country, you deserve to go to jail for something that white people do not go to jail for. It is unfair. It is outrageous. It is despicable that we would sit here on this floor of Congress, two days after the President has talked about fairness, two days after a million people have come here and begged for fairness, and we say, let us go do business as usual, let us keep this in effect while we study it some more.[27]

When others tried to drain the racial dynamic from the issue, Massachusetts Representative Barney Frank countered by labeling both the law and its implementation racist. For Frank, the racial impact could not be dismissed as irrelevant in evaluating the legislation, especially when Black colleagues were calling for reform:

> The sentencing disparity is overwhelmingly objectively a racist one. Now maybe my colleagues think it is justified, but no one has denied that the effect of the policy is to treat young black men much more harshly.... I can think of no policy which we have which in fact ends up so racially distorted. I have to say this to the overwhelmingly white majority of which I am a part in this House. When our African-American colleagues come here in large numbers and plead with us to allow a non-partisan body of experts to change this racially disparate policy ... do not tell them "Oh, this is in the interest of your community, this is what the people who you represent really want."[28]

Frank's idea that a law could be judged by its effects stirred up his colleagues, revealing a strong sentiment in favor of color-blind justice. Representative Stephen E. Buyer, for example, asked members to imagine what would happen if the prosecution of white-collar crime had to be racially balanced or domestic abuse had to be gender balanced.[29] Other members were equally dismissive, suggesting that Frank's argument was "weightless," and arguing against "prosecution by quota," with some pressing for an increase in penalties for powder cocaine to eliminate the problem.[30]

Representative McCollum took strong issue with Frank's insinuation that Congress had acted insensitively toward African Americans in creating the special mandatory minimums. The race of those incarcerated, he argued, can never constitute evidence of racism. McCollum used color-blind logic in rejecting Frank's position. One must prove racist intent, McCollum argued, in order to blame Congress for the impact of its actions: "It is not, in my judgment, at all racist. If you think about those words, the idea of racism implies prejudice. It implies that we in Congress, or those in law enforcement, are out there intentionally attempting to put somebody in jail because of the color of their skin or to make them serve a longer sentence. That is not so."[31]

The debate never moved beyond this point. The members of the House who fought to maintain the mandatory minimums addressed the issue with color-blind logic, treating racial prejudice as an evil based solely in individual bad intentions. The supporters of parity, most of whom were anxious to avoid calling their colleagues racist, were unable to take control of the debate. As the *Congressional Quarterly* reported: "Republicans said that the tougher sentences for crack have nothing to do with race. . . ." The problem is "people are not enforcing them properly."[32]

Those on the pro-parity side never fully articulated the fundamental point that law can insidiously promote unfairness by constructing a framework that leads inexorably to racially oppressive results (Frymer 2005, 373). Nor did the pro-parity side speak clearly to the possibility that Congress might have been motivated by unconscious racial prejudices, fears, and stereotyping when it singled out crack cocaine for special penalties. Their vagueness around these key points led to a debate that produced more heat than light. Howard Winant suggests that such ambiguity about race and racism is emblematic of our era: "The understanding we have of racism, an understanding which was forged in the 1960s, is now seriously deficient. . . . In fact, since the ambiguous triumph of the civil-rights movement in the mid-1960s, clarity about what racism means has been slipping away" (1998, 757).

For most members of Congress there was no irony in voting against parity and, at the same time, supporting a resolution that nineteen members of the House offered to express the resolve of Congress to take an active role in eliminating racism. The resolution was acceptable, even desirable, because it was framed in the reassuring language of color-blind justice:

When we are divided by racism, we are weakened as a Nation; in the beginning our government played a role in perpetuating racism, but for almost 140 years it has worked at great length to address the problems of racial inequality. . . . It is not enough merely to acknowledge that all races possess equal rights. . . . Action must be taken to guarantee that equal opportunity and respect are afforded to all people through the enforcement of laws that prohibit discrimination on the basis of race."[33]

The House of Representatives rejected the parity proposal by an overwhelming 332 to 83 vote, sending the matter back to the Commission for further study. This time Congress asked the Commission for nonbinding recommendations. It left the Commissioners with a directive: "The sentence imposed for trafficking in a quantity of crack cocaine should generally exceed the sentence imposed for trafficking in a like quantity of powder cocaine." This outcome was a compromise crafted by Senator Edward Kennedy "to keep alive the hope that this Congress will someday soon address the festering issue of racial disparity in our Nation's cocaine sentencing laws." He described the problem, much as the Commission had, as one of "maintaining the confidence of the country that it is free from racial bias," and warned that "we may have inadvertently created an injustice—the much harsher sentences imposed for crack cocaine than for powdered cocaine."[34]

Reactions to the Rejection of the Parity Proposal

Judge Conaboy was surprised at the failure of his Commission's recommendation for parity. He recalled legislators who had told him that they agreed with the proposal. But they had then voted against it. "I was naive. There was a remarkable feeling in Congress that time takes care of everything. It was tragic."[35]

At this point the coalition of groups that had organized around the parity proposal weighed in, lobbying President Clinton to veto the congressional rejection of the parity proposal. Had he done so, the Commission's position would have become law. Representatives of the group met with Justice Department officials, members of Congress, the attorney general, and the president, but President Clinton stood with Congress on the issue. On October 30, 1995, he signed into law a bill that maintained the original mandatory minimum penalties for those found possessing crack cocaine (Dewoy 1995).

President Clinton's endorsement of the mandatory minimums created outrage and violence in federal prisons around the nation. Within a few days of the congressional vote, hundreds of prisoners in at least five federal facilities set fires and broke windows to display their unhappiness with the result. Federal prison officials locked down more than 100,000 inmates across the United States (Isikoff 1995; see also K. Johnson 1995). Kathleen Hawk, director of the Bureau of Prisons, blamed the outbreaks on a pervasive sense of unfairness in federal sentencing:

> After extremely intensive reviews of what happened, we believe the initial disruptions were triggered by news reports that Congress would not lower crack penalties to equal penalties for powder cocaine. The disturbances spread because of widespread inmate perceptions that sentencing laws are unfair and because inmates were already agitated over such issues as mandatory minimum sentences, loss of funding for prison programs, and media reports of racial biases in sentencing. (1996, 11)

Meanwhile, the Commission returned to work, stung by the clear-cut rejection of its proposal. In April 1997, it proposed a compromise calling for a 5:1 ratio. This would mean increasing the number of grams of crack required to trigger the five-year mandatory minimum from 5 to between 25 and 75, and reducing the required number of grams of powder from 500 to between 125 and 375. The Commissioners also proposed that the five-year mandatory minimum for simple possession be drastically reduced.

As in its earlier report, the Commission carefully avoided suggesting that racism might have played a role in the rush to create mandatory minimums for crack offenses. The problem, the Commission asserted once again, was that people might *perceive* racism to be operating:

> While there is no evidence of racial bias behind the promulgation of this federal sentencing law, nearly 90 percent of the offenders convicted in federal court for crack cocaine distribution are African-American, while the majority of crack cocaine users is white. Thus sentences appear to be harsher and more severe for racial minorities than others as a result of this law. The current penalty structure results in a perception of unfairness and inconsistency. (1997, 8)

Vice Chairperson Michael Gelacak joined his colleagues in the 5:1 recommendation, but filed a dissent complaining about the willingness of the Commission to bend to the will of Congress on the penalty issue. He charged his colleagues with caving in and dodging their responsibility to speak directly to the race issue: "I believe that the country would be better served by our dealing more directly with these issues. Political compromise is a function better left to the Legislature" (1997, 1). Gelacak acknowledged the delicacy of the race issue, but argued that it had to be confronted:

It is a little like punishing vehicular homicide while under the influence of alcohol more severely if the defendant had become intoxicated by ingesting cheap wine rather than Scotch whisky. Although a discussion of the nation's drug abuse problem and the impact of penalties on African Americans and other people of color is often uncomfortable and elevates the profile of the issue as well as the political consequences, we cannot choose to ignore it or act as if it is of no concern. (U.S. Sentencing Commission 1997, 2–3)

Commissioner Gelacak was more pointed in his assessment of the issue a few months later. It was racist, he argued, *not* to discuss impact. Intent was irrelevant. But for Congress, he noted ruefully, 100:1 is "a dead issue."[36]

Gelacak was right—the issue was dead. President Clinton was steadfast in his refusal to revise the mandatory minimums, despite a strong letter from Attorney General Janet Reno and the former White House drug czar, General Barry McCaffrey, recommending a 10:1 ratio:

A sentencing scheme that treats crack 100 times more harshly than powder undoubtedly has become an important symbol of racial injustice in our criminal justice system. We cannot turn a blind eye to the corrosive effect this has had on respect for the law in certain communities and on the effective administration of justice. When communities lose faith in the fairness of the legal process, our ability to enforce the law suffers.[37]

The mood in Washington at this time was harshly punitive, according to Eric Sterling, a member of the House Judiciary Committee's senior staff. Congress was considering various tough-on-crime proposals, including three-strikes legislation that mandated life imprisonment for certain crimes. It responded to a series of California forest fires by doubling the sentence for arsonists convicted under federal law. There was enthusiasm for boot camps for delinquent minors and criminal sentences for their parents. Representative Jay Dickey of Arkansas proposed to allow public flogging and supported the trial of thirteen-year-olds as adults. Legislation to give life imprisonment to drug felons and violent criminals convicted a third time was passed with virtually no discussion and no recorded vote. No one seemed worried about the growing cost of imprisonment (Sterling 1995, 412–13; Miller 1996, 218).

With Congress and the White House fixated on punishment, some pro-parity activists turned once again to the Sentencing Commission. A group of federal defense attorneys, the Practitioners Advisory Group, suggested that the Commission change the Guidelines without congressional approval.[38] They argued that this would focus federal resources on major and mid-level dealers, Congress's original target. The Commission could hardly take such advice. It was at this point fighting for its life. Congress had become an indifferent sponsor, ignoring the need to appoint new members. Those remaining were forced to operate without a chairperson.

In 2002, after a lengthy series of hearings, the Commission issued yet another report critical of the mandatory minimums. It focused on the failure of the law to achieve its ostensible purposes—tough prosecution focused on high-level dealers: "Contrary to the intent of Congress, the five and ten year minimum penalties most often apply to low level crack cocaine traffickers, rather than to serious or major traffickers."[39] The median amount of crack involved for those receiving ten-year sentences, for example, was 52 grams (0.834 ounce), hardly the stuff of big-time trafficking. The Commission was also critical of the mandatory minimums as a response to drug-related violence. A study of thousands of federal cocaine cases had found that weapons were involved in only 2.3 percent of crack cases and 1.2 percent of powder cases. The Commission argued for eliminating the mandatory minimums and using its Guidelines instead. The Guidelines could ensure that there was some differentiation between crack and powder cocaine, but within a penalty structure more responsive to specific crimes than the crude mandatory minimums.

In 2004, the Commission reiterated its criticisms, arguing that "reduction of unsupportable adverse impacts" on minority racial groups had become even more important with time. It attempted to compromise with Congress, recommending a 20:1 disparity (2004a, 113, 131–32).

This debate took an important turn in January 2005, when the U.S. Supreme Court held in *United States v. Booker*[40] that the compulsory features of the federal Sentencing Guidelines violate constitutional guarantees. Henceforth, the Sentencing Guidelines would be advisory only. The case dealt the Sentencing Commission a serious blow, but did not deter it from continuing its efforts to do something to reduce the crack/powder sentencing disparity. In April 2005, Commission members sent a long letter to members of the Senate Subcommittee on Crime, Terrorism, and Homeland Security urging them to protect the core principles of the Sentencing Reform Act and cautioning, once more, against a quantity-based penalty structure for crack cocaine offenses.[41]

Conclusion

The crack/powder saga shows how color-blind ideology constrains debate about racial justice. The framework invites angry denials of racist intentions, but does nothing to encourage people to take responsibility for social injustice. The racial dimensions of the crack penalties have been strikingly evident to tens of millions of Americans—but color-blind ideology made the issue too hot to handle in the halls of Congress when Congress was finally forced to confront it. Discussion swung uncomfortably between avoidance of race and angry allegations of racial insensitivity. In the estimation of one observer, neither recognition of racial difference nor denial of its relevance works very well in congressional debate:

> When this issue is framed primarily as one of race, only 80 members of Congress will vote accordingly. While such a vote may provide a welcome opportunity for public debate, it can also be polarizing. When true parity in sentencing is framed as the only *just* position, any argument that does not acknowledge race is at risk. (Bergman 1998, 199)

The conundrum was that race gave the argument for changing the mandatory minimums much of its moral force, but only with some members. The vast majority, however, embraced color blindness, which eviscerated any discussion of racial impact and perceptions of racism. Color blindness encouraged them to see racial impact as a slippery slope leading to racial entitlements and demands for reparations. An indication of the prevalence of this mode of thinking is the absence of significant political repercussions from the government's repeated refusal to abandon the mandatory minimums. Members of Congress made no effort to hide their decision, nor did the White House. Holding steady with this obviously flawed policy was obviously good politics.

Had Congress seriously considered the Commission's parity approach, it might have led to a worthwhile discussion about the broader failure of the sentencing system to deliver racial justice. The Sentencing Commission was established because the old rehabilitative arguments were no longer persuasive and the old rehabilitative tools—judicial sentencing discretion and parole—looked arbitrary and open to abuse. But it was becoming obvious that neither bureaucratic sentencing nor legislative intervention were doing any better. In the words of Michael Tonry and Kathleen Hatlestad:

> The cruelest irony of the modern American sentencing reform movement is that the diminution of racial discrimination in sentencing was a primary aim, and exacerbation of racial disparities is a major result. The aim was to make it less likely that officials would exercise broad unreviewable discretion in ways harmful to minority defendants and offenders. The result has been the establishment of rigid rules and laws that narrow officials' discretion, but that also punish minority offenders disproportionately harshly. Racial disparities in the justice system that are unprecedented in American history, and steadily getting worse, are the result. (1997, 217)

six

Racial Justice

The Courts Consider
Sentencing Disparities

Courts were destined not just to process crack cases, but also to play a role in legitimizing racially disparate impact. Soon after the mandatory-minimum penalties were enacted, lawyers for the accused, enjoying few other options, began to challenge the constitutionality of the differential sentences for crack and powder cocaine. They found a receptive audience in a few federal judges at the trial level. These judges were seeing the racial pattern in drug sentencing firsthand, and like many others in the federal system, they were already angry about the new Sentencing Guidelines and the mandatory minimums that further reduced judicial discretion.

The constitutional challenges centered on the amount of punishment prescribed for crack cocaine, definitional weaknesses in the description of the drug, and, most significantly, the racial implications of the huge differential in punishments for crack and powder offenses. For a brief time, some advocates and some judges convinced themselves that the constitutional limits had been breached. But in the end, these turned out to be easy questions for the federal appellate courts. Courts of appeal across the country considered the issues and found that they were all in agreement that the Constitution does not bar the mandatory minimums, despite their racially disproportionate effect. The only appellate court that agreed with the argument that laws that punish crack more severely than powder cocaine are racially discriminatory was a state supreme court, and it decided on state-law grounds.[1] The U.S. Supreme Court did not find it necessary to weigh in on such a settled matter of law. The litigation campaign thus clarified one important point: The fact that a sentencing law disproportionately affects a traditionally disadvantaged group is, by itself, irrelevant under the now-prevailing interpretation of the federal Constitution.

Courts at all levels nevertheless had an impact on the debate over racial justice in sentencing. The crack/powder lawsuits were salient to all the relevant elites involved. Civil rights activists publicized the early court victories and noted their losses on appeal. Experts in the federal and state sentencing commissions studied the federal cases in detail and discussed them in their publications. State and federal legislators maintained their own communications with judges and interested law-enforcement organizations.

The litigation campaign also subtly focused controversy over the massive changes in sentencing policy that were occurring to narrower questions about the racial implications of the 100:1 disparity. The more generalized critique of mandatory minimums as inefficient, ineffective, and mean-spirited moved to the background in the late 1980s and 1990s. There was a similar channeling of attention away from the Sentencing Guidelines, helped along by *Mistretta v. United States*, the 1989 Supreme Court decision that found no fault with the Guidelines as an exercise of congressional authority.[2] Thus by 1995, when Congress and its Sentencing Commission came into conflict over the Commission's parity recommendation, courts had done their part to make that conflict the rallying point for protest and debate.

The clear-cut failure of this challenge in the courts, as in Congress, suggests the inadequacy of our current approach to racial discrimination. Defense counsel had asked the courts to reconsider the traditional discrimination paradigm, to think more broadly than in the past about subtle discrimination that is not directed toward particular individuals and that may not be fully thought through, or even conscious. The force of these arguments lay in the overwhelming numbers of African Americans put in legal jeopardy by the new regime. The problem was that this was a precedent-shattering approach. Defendants were, in effect, asking judges to abandon precedents that made racist intent the center of inquiry in favor of a more psychologically up-to-date line of attack.

These cases also put the courts in direct conflict with clearly expressed congressional will, a situation courts always strive to avoid. The problem is not only judicial commitment to the separation of powers and respect for precedent. The structure of the system also encourages adherence to familiar formulae. Judges normally reason, after all, from decisions in past cases, and appellate judges, who are completely removed from the day-to-day experience of justice, have the final say in every case. Whatever insights might inhere in seeing witnesses, litigants, and evidence firsthand are lost in the legal process. The hierarchical system of courts thus filters out messy lived experience, while it reinforces the myth that law provides clear answers to profoundly complicated questions.

This institutional conservatism has an impact on American politics. The nation's fascination with legal decisions tends to narrow public discourse on topics like racial discrimination to parallel what the courts say about it. As Timothy O'Neill observes: "Law language narrows the debate and helps to simplify complexities, but it may also impoverish public understanding of serious controversies" (1981, 634). The judicial handling of crack appeals is a good example of this phenomenon. The courts have reinforced the color-blind perspective that denies the complexity of racial disadvantage, not just in law, but in politics and public debate.

More specifically, the current legal approach gives those who charge racism the near-impossible burden of proving intentional discrimination, while courts avoid coming to grips with the operation of the system as a whole. Statutes are presumed neutral, no matter how damning their impact, unless there is some evidence of intentional wrongdoing in a particular case. The courts, in short, fall into the same pattern of color-blind racism found in Congress. Consider, for example, how Senator Charles Grassley, chair of the Senate Judiciary Committee, dismissed concerns about racial discrimination during the crack/powder debate: "If [disparities based on race] exist, they are wrong, but that doesn't, it seems to me, come from the system. That could come from the predilections of the people involved" (Flaherty and Biskupic 1996b).

This chapter takes a careful look at how courts at all levels in the federal system have handled constitutional challenges to the crack/powder disparity. The goal is both to critique current doctrine and to return to the moral dilemma Judge Clyde Cahill faced in sentencing Edward James Clary. There is sometimes no easy way to bridge the divide between law and justice. The chasm has made many judges deeply uncomfortable about their obligations in crack cases. The situation they face bears some significant similarities to another time when courts were caught in a racial dilemma: the pre–Civil War period in cases arising under the Fugitive Slave Law. That parallel is explored in this chapter.

The crack controversy highlights a central problem in contemporary equal protection doctrine. The legal framework that currently prevails, developed in the 1940 to 1960 period of civil rights activism, has become dangerously out of date. The current problem is not so much overt individual racism, but the institutional incentives that produce racially oppressive outcomes (Frymer 2005; Wang 2006). Scientific understanding of how racial prejudice works in modern society has also advanced and now provides a potentially valuable opportunity for rethinking discrimination doctrine. In light of these changes, the old intentionalist framework should be abandoned, as "separate but equal" was abandoned in *Brown v. Board of Education*.[3] Judicial unwillingness to be more realistic about racism has absolved decision makers from responsibility to design policies that promote racial fairness, and has done nothing to promote the democratic debate the nation requires to confront some of the most deeply entrenched problems facing American society (Guinier and Torres 2002, 37, 58).

Defending the Accused

Litigation to promote some kinds of social change can follow a somewhat leisurely agenda that allows a progression of cases to burnish an issue for the consideration of higher courts. Cases on the criminal side of the docket have no such luxury. The obligations of representing the accused force them to move quickly. The challenge to the mandatory minimums, however, had a cooperative aspect.

The key player in bringing defense counsel together and coordinating their attack was the National Association of Criminal Defense Lawyers (NACDL). The Association's headquarters maintained comprehensive files of motions filed, lawyers to contact, and favorable precedents that it shared with defense counsel around the nation. It offered support in promising cases and filed *amicus* briefs in some, helping defense lawyers to connect arrest statistics to law-enforcement decisions that targeted African American neighborhoods, and citing prior cases that took racial impact into account.[4] NACDL also reached out to civil rights organizations concerned with sentencing issues. Its magazine, the *Champion,* carried regular updates on cases, developments in Congress, the Department of Justice, and the U.S. Sentencing Commission. The director issued press releases to influence public debate.

Behind this effort was a profound conviction among many in the defense bar that the approach Congress and the administration had taken to control crack abuse was racist and unworkable. This perspective was strikingly evident in a September 1989 hearing before Representative Charles Rangel's Select Committee on Narcotics Abuse and Control. Rangel had invited testimony from William Bennett, director of the Office of National Drug Control Policy, colloquially known as the "drug czar," and from Randolph Stone, a public defender in Cook County, Illinois. The topic was "The Federal Drug Strategy: What Does It Mean for Black America?" Race figured into both accounts, but with vastly different implications for public policy in each of them.

Bennett, representing the government's approach, emphasized the negative impact of drugs on Black communities in dramatic terms: "There is no doubt ... that 'crack' has destroyed more families than poverty did, that 'crack' has done perhaps what the Ku Klux Klan tried to do but couldn't do."[5] The law-abiding majority that does not use drugs are "fighting for their lives"; they are the "invisible men" who struggle and do "prevail against this plague" in their neighborhoods. Drug-law enforcement was an essential first step in rescuing these communities: "When the fire is burning, get the hoses in and put out the fire. That's the situation with 'crack' in many of our communities. ... The problem is: What do we do tomorrow?" Bennett answered his own question: "Call in the police, and if more police are needed, call in more police. If more jails are needed, more prisons are needed, build them. ... It costs a lot of money to keep a drug dealer out of jail. If that person isn't in jail, they're going to continue to inflict damage cost on the community."[6] He defended the diversion of $50 million that had been earmarked for renovating federal housing to drug-law enforcement by arguing that "the first priority is to rid public housing of the 'rats,' of drug dealers ... because there's not much sense in making these kinds of improvements for drug dealers."[7]

Randolph Stone, on the other hand, spoke from the perspective of someone who dealt with drug cases on a daily basis. Drug arrests had increased exponentially in the Chicago metropolitan area where Stone served as a public defender, creating an enormous backlog of cases: Forty-two percent of all cases in the criminal courts in the city were drug cases in 1989, and three out of four of those arrested were juveniles. Every day, about 120 people were charged with possession or delivery of drugs.

For Stone, the increasing number of arrests was part of the problem, not an indication that the solution was at hand: "I am here to say that ever-increasing arrests and building more courtrooms and jails will not resolve the problem."[8] He envisioned more than a million people locked up, about half of whom would be young African Americans: "Our criminal justice system every day is looking more and more like South Africa's criminal justice system. ... It is a fundamental mistake to believe that the drug wars can be resolved by the criminal justice system" because "poverty and suffering will produce an endless demand for drugs." Committee Chair Rangel responded in exasperation: "Could you not agree that there are some bums that should be in jail?" Stone's answer returned to his main theme: "The criminal justice system is the wrong place to fight the war on drugs. That's my only point. Of course I understand that there are some people who deserve to be in jail, no question about it. It's a question of emphasis and a question of focus."[9]

Defense lawyers who see matters as Randolph Stone described them sometimes have an opportunity to press their point of view in a criminal case. The pre-plea process in the federal system leaves room for participants to manipulate penalties, though the prosecutor holds most of the power in this situation. Trial judges are also in a position to facilitate sentence reduction on fairness grounds. They sometimes do this by stepping out of normal routines, for example, by demanding that a drug bust be reweighed before sentencing or by telling jurors before their deliberations what the mandatory sentence would be for the crime charged. There are reported instances of judges defying the Guidelines by giving a reduced sentence, with the prosecution waiving its right to appeal, an implicit acknowledgment of the injustice of the prescribed sentence (Bromwich 1999). As two *Washington Post* journalists concluded in 1996: "Judges from Washington state to Washington, D.C. have refused to hand down heavy sentences required under the law because of concerns about racial disparity" (Flaherty and Biskupic 1996a). Law professor Daniel Freed labels this "informal noncompliance" a form of institutionalized protest against the sentencing laws (1992, 1754).

Often, however, the only potentially effective move available to the defense is to attack the sentencing law outright. Lawsuits challenging the crack penalties began in 1987, shortly after the Sentencing Commission announced how the Guideline system would work. The number of suits grew quickly until the mid-1990s, when their numbers began to level off in the wake of adverse appellate decisions (see fig. 6.1).

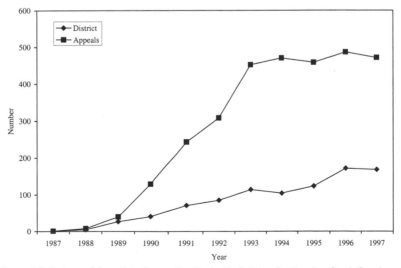

Figure 6.1 Pattern of Growth in Cases Decided with Opinion Challenging Crack Cocaine Penalties

Constitutional Issues and Their Fate in the Appellate Courts

Judge Cahill's 1994 decision in the *Clary* case[10] was one of perhaps a dozen that found constitutional fault with the crack legislation. Most federal district courts turned down these claims. The constitutional issues raised by those who wrote opinions justifying their decisions boil down to three:

1. The harsh mandatory minimums for crack offenses offend the Eighth Amendment's prohibition on cruel and unusual punishments.
2. The sentencing standards are unconstitutionally vague, in violation of due process standards.
3. The 100:1 disparity offends the Fourteenth Amendment requirement of "equal protection of the law" without regard to race.

None of these arguments were persuasive in any of the federal courts of appeals. The Eighth Amendment argument foundered on the weight of precedent from prior drug cases. In 1982, for example, the U.S. Supreme Court had upheld forty years of imprisonment for possession and an attempt to sell 9 ounces of marijuana in *Hutto v. Davis*.[11] Nine years later, in *Harmelin v. Michigan*,[12] the Court cited that precedent in upholding a sentence of life imprisonment for a defendant with no prior convictions who attempted to sell 672 grams of crack cocaine. The vagueness argument was similarly unsuccessful. When the defense claimed that the term "cocaine base" in the statute was inadequate as a description of crack, appellate courts uniformly rejected the argument. As the Third Circuit Court of Appeals said in *United States v. Frazier*: "This court joins the unanimous judgment of at least nine other circuits in holding that the distinction made in the federal statutes and Sentencing Guidelines between 'cocaine base' and 'cocaine' is sufficiently precise not to be constitutionally void for vagueness."[13]

Appellate courts rejected the equal protection arguments on the strength of *McCleskey v. Kemp*,[14] a 1987 Supreme Court precedent in which a defendant had relied on statistical evidence to demonstrate that the death penalty in Georgia disproportionately disadvantages African American defendants charged with killing whites. Defendant McCleskey, however, had provided no evidence of discriminatory behavior by officials involved in the case. The Court accepted the statistical evidence of racial differences in sentencing outcomes, but held that disproportionate racial impact is not enough to invalidate legislation on equal protection grounds. The Court ruled that the defendant loses, even if the legislature was aware that a racial impact is likely. To prevail, the Court held, the claimant must show that the legislature consciously intended to disadvantage racial minorities:

"Discriminatory purpose" implies more than intent as volition or intent as awareness of consequences. It implies that the decisionmaker, in this case a state legislature, selected or reaffirmed a particular course of action at least in part "because of" not merely "in spite of" its adverse effects upon an identifiable group. For this claim to prevail, McCleskey would have to prove that the Georgia Legislature enacted or maintained the death penalty statute because of an *anticipated* racially discriminatory effect.[15]

The *McCleskey* decision had a powerful impact on equal protection claims in many areas of law. It gave courts a tough standard that instructed them to deny relief without evidence of intentional wrongdoing. This was an impossible standard for defendants who had no evidence of racist acts in the prosecution of their cases. The severity of the racial effect, *McCleskey* holds, is by itself irrelevant, and so is a legislature's obliviousness, or lack of interest in, the racial consequences of a law. As the Eighth Circuit Court of Appeals stated in *United States v. Clary*, the case that reversed Judge Cahill: "[E]ven if a neutral law has a disproportionate adverse impact on a racial minority, it is unconstitutional only if that effect can be traced to a discriminatory purpose." Discriminatory purpose "implies that the decision-maker, in this case Congress, selected or reaffirmed a particular course of action at least in part 'because of' not merely 'in spite of,' its adverse effects upon an identifiable group."[16]

The Supreme Court implicitly reaffirmed its position when it denied *certiorari* in *Edwards v. United States*,[17] a case in which the defendant claimed that the differential between crack and powder cocaine sentences unconstitutionally targets African Americans, especially males from the inner cities. The defendant, a decorated Persian Gulf veteran with no criminal record, faced a ten-year mandatory-minimum sentence for trafficking in crack cocaine. The constitutional arguments were that the crack/powder disparity violated due process and that the severity of the law constituted cruel and unusual punishment.

The *Edwards* appeal attracted two high-profile lawyers, Johnnie Cochran, famous for his role in successfully defending O. J. Simpson, and Harvard Law professor Charles Ogletree. Their passionate argument for constitutional relief fell on deaf ears. The Department of Justice, which could have filed a brief in opposition, did not even bother to respond. The Supreme Court was also unimpressed. It issued a one-sentence order declining to hear the case.

The Court took *McCleskey* a step further in *United States v. Armstrong*.[18] This case makes it nearly impossible to gather evidence of prosecutorial wrongdoing in crack cases. Defense lawyers had convinced the trial judge, Consuelo Marshall, that the prosecution should be obliged to explain why all twenty-four of the crack cocaine cases they closed in 1991 involved African American defendants. The Ninth Circuit Court of Appeals considered the matter important enough to decide, *en banc*, with the whole court participating. In a 7 to 4 decision, it agreed with Judge Marshall that the discovery order was within the trial judge's purview.[19]

The Supreme Court, however, took up the case and reversed, agreeing with the dissenters in the *en banc* decision that Judge Marshall's discovery order "effectively collapses intent into effect."[20] In an 8 to 1 decision, the Court ruled that a trial judge must have more convincing evidence than statistical disparities to open the door to an investigation of possible prosecutorial misconduct. To invoke the court's help in uncovering racism, the Court held that "a defendant must produce credible evidence that similarly situated defendants of other races could have been prosecuted, but were not."[21] Justice Rehnquist was concerned that prosecutors might otherwise be exposed to unwarranted litigation. He chided the trial judge for presuming "that people of all races commit all types of crimes," implying that the all-Black pattern of crack prosecutions should not be considered out of the ordinary.[22]

Trial Judges Confront the Ethics of Disproportionate Sentencing

The pattern of consistent reversals on appeal was becoming clear by the fall of 1995. Eric Sterling, coordinator for the National Drug Strategy Network, a loose association of organizations fighting the crack penalties, sent a memo to the group on October 11:

> *Bottom line on the constitutional arguments:* At this point in time, no federal court has held the crack statute affixing penalties at 100 times that of powder cocaine unconstitutional. The D.C. Circuit has rejected the notion that the Guidelines' different treatment of cocaine powder and crack violates the equal protection clause. . . . This is the position taken by every circuit that has addressed the question. The Supreme Court of Minnesota invalidated their state statute. . . . No other state court has followed suit.[23]

The situation in Congress was equally discouraging for the reformers. The Senate had rejected the Sentencing Commission's parity recommendation. The House of Representatives was poised to do the same in a few days. It planned to uphold the mandatory minimums and at the same time adopt a Sentencing Commission recommendation to "enhance" sentences of those who used weapons in drug cases.

As the effort to reform crack sentencing faltered, the mood in many trial courts became bleak. Federal authorities estimated that in 1993 about 50 of the 680 senior federal judges were refusing to take drug cases. Among the regular-duty judges, however, withdrawal was not an option. A few found other ways to register their disapproval. The *Wall Street Journal* described a "low-key rebellion" in which judges "are devising ways to get around the rules in their own cases" (Moses 1993, B12). A few judges resigned. Judge Harold Greene, an early opponent of congressionally prescribed sentences, noted "a profound and severe sense of wrong" in being required to impose sentences that did not seem to fit the crime (Treaster 1993).[24] Judge John Curtin expressed the view of many in describing the war on drugs as unwinnable: "In spite of the expenditure of billions of dollars, we have failed to reduce consumption, to reduce violent crime, to cut importation, and to lessen huge profits gained by organized criminals. We have repeated the mistakes of Prohibition with far more serious consequences. Criminal sanction has made for increased drug use rather than the opposite" (1997, 3).

Judge Jack Weinstein, who had become famous for presiding over the Agent Orange trial, provoked an angry response from several members of Congress when he publicized his own small rebellion against the crack penalties. He let it be known that he had refused to sentence one drug defendant because she might lose custody of her child. A few months later he quite publicly refused to take any more drug cases, describing "a sense of depression about much of the cruelty I have been a party to in connection with the 'war on drugs'" and calling himself "a tired old judge who has temporarily filed his quota of remorselessness" (Treaster 1993). At this point, the Republican leadership of the House of Representatives sent him a letter of rebuke, warning him that his action "repudiates the legislative process at the heart of representative democracy." The letter, bearing the signatures of Newt Gingrich, Dick Armey, Tom DeLay, and others, suggested that if Weinstein disagreed with the policy, he must resign his position or face impeachment.[25]

With the help of Weinstein and other judges who "went public" with their views, the dilemma of the judge forced to impose a long sentence on a minor drug dealer was becoming a news story. Most attractive to journalists was the anguish of Republican judges with well-established reputations for sternness. Thus Judge Stanley Marshall, a Reagan appointee, attracted media attention when he imposed a five-year sentence on a mother in Washington, D.C., after police found crack in a locked box that her son had hidden in her attic. He was quoted as saying: "I've always been considered a fairly harsh sentencer, but it's killing me that I'm sending so many low-level offenders away for all this time" (Carmody 1993, 10). Several journalists reported on a similar California case:

> U.S. District Judge William W. Schwarzer, a Republican appointee, is not known as a light sentencer. Thus it was that everyone in his San Francisco courtroom watched in stunned silence as Schwarzer, known for his stoic demeanor, choked with tears as he anguished over sentencing Richard Anderson, a first offender Oakland longshoreman, to ten years in prison without parole for what appeared to be a minor mistake in judgment in having given a ride to a drug dealer for a meeting with an undercover federal agent. (Taylor 1990, 65–66)

As these stories suggest, judges faced difficult choices. They could impose sentences they found unjust, or they could retire or resign from their posts. The only other alternative was to develop creative alternatives to Guidelines-prescribed sentences that could survive on appeal. The conflict was not unlike what judges faced over a century ago in adjudicating cases brought under the federal Fugitive Slave Act. That law required criminal justice officials in northern states to return escaped slaves to their southern masters. In both instances, it is easy to find judicial opinions expressing anguish over the conflict between law and morality. Effective action to resist the legal imperative, however, was also rare in both instances.

Resolving Conflicts between Law and Racial Justice

When legal scholar Robert Cover studied fugitive slave cases, he found that judges generally implemented the law in every respect, turning the defendants back to their owners, albeit reluctantly: "Time and again, the judiciary paraded its helplessness before the law; lamented harsh results; intimated that in a more perfect world, or at the end of days, a better law would emerge, but almost uniformly, marched to the music, steeled themselves, and hung Billy Budd" (1975, 5–6).[26] Situations like this are relatively rare in law, at least on the grand scale of national policy that pushes large numbers of judges toward a particular decision they do not want to make. The crack cocaine sentencing dilemma may be the first clear-cut instance since the Fugitive Slave Law.

The parallel proved helpful in my own research. Professor Cover developed a typology of judicial responses in his reading of fugitive slave cases. He found three related "responsibility-mitigation mechanisms":

- Elevation of the formal stakes (sometimes combined with minimization of the moral stakes involved);
- Retreat to a mechanistic formalism;
- Ascription of responsibility elsewhere. (1975, 199)

My methodology, like Cover's, was to look for cases in which the defense requested reconsideration of the sentencing formula and the request got a written response. These are relatively rare: Most cases simply summarily reject these arguments, leaving no trace of the thinking involved. To find appropriate cases, I pursued three strategies. I began by examining all of the cases the Sentencing Commission cited in its report on legal challenges to the penalties (U.S. Sentencing Commission 1995b, app. C). I also searched the sentencing-policy literature and NACDL case files for citations. I looked for any signs of sympathy for defendants or criticisms of the sentencing laws, even if the results were unfavorable to the defendants. I used these cases to find more recent cases on point.

I found the same pattern of complaint and acquiescence that Cover described in fugitive slave litigation:

- **Elevation of the formal stakes.** Judges sometimes justify inaction by noting the severity of the drug problem, or the dangers inherent in departing from the rules. In *United States v. Angulo-Lopez*,[27] for example, the court justified life imprisonment without parole in terms of the dangers of drugs: "The evidence before the trial court at sentencing establishes the rapid addiction of crack users. The gravity of the offenses of manufacturing and distributing crack is quite severe. No doubt thousands of lives have been ruined and even lost as a result of crack use and dependence."[28] In *United States v. Thompson*,[29] the court suggested a parade of horribles: "If the disparate racial impact of the guideline ranges for 'crack' offenses warranted a departure in *any* case, it would warrant a departure in *every* case. One could hardly justify granting departures only for African-American defendants and not for defendants of other races, since the same offense would then lead to different punishments based solely on the defendant's race."[30]
- **Retreat to a mechanistic formulation.** Judges who take this route in drug cases usually cite binding precedent as their primary reason for denying relief. In *United States v. Dumas*,[31] for example, Judge Robert Boochever expressed "shock" that 92 percent of federal prosecutions for crack involved African American defendants, but was "compelled to concur" with the court's refusal to grant relief: "If it were an open question in this circuit, one might find that the imposition of the 100 to 1 ratio with its

invidious racial effects is so arbitrary and capricious as to lack a rational basis. We have resolved that issue, however. . . ."[32]

Some judges simply expressed regret in denying relief. In *United States v. Haynes*,[33] for example, Judge Richard J. Cardamone described the defendants as two young black friends with promising futures—Haynes had been a star high school athlete with a scholarship to college. But friends of the defendants had persuaded them to become involved in drug dealing. They were eligible for sentences of twenty-seven years and thirty years to life. The judge refused a defense motion to depart from the Guidelines, despite his belief that they were "draconian." He expressed regret about the length of the sentences, and so did the appellate court in upholding the sentences.[34]

- **Ascription of responsibility elsewhere.** *United States v. Singleterry*[35] illustrates how some judges use their opinions to critique the rules, while nevertheless applying them: "[T]he absence of a constitutional command is not an invitation to government complacency. Although Singleterry has not established a constitutional violation, he has raised important questions about the efficacy and fairness of our current sentencing policies for offenses involving cocaine substances. We leave the resolution of these matters to the considered judgment of those with the proper authority and institutional capacity."[36]

In considering judicial capacities to bend law to moral judgment, it is important to recall that courts sometimes use informal, even extra-legal, means to avoid judgments that offend the moral sensibilities of participants. Some of these techniques are noted in this chapter. In the fugitive slave cases too, there is at least anecdotal evidence that courts sometimes avoided making adverse decisions. In Syracuse, for example, it is reputed that the local prosecutor checked himself into a mental hospital for a time to avoid prosecuting fugitive slave cases.

There seems to be somewhat more legal innovation in the crack cases than in the fugitive slave cases that Cover analyzed, at least at the trial level. In *United States v. Lattimore*,[37] district court judge James Rosenbaum decided that defendant was entitled to the sentence Congress had provided in the mandatory-minimum statute, rather than the longer Guidelines sentence. In *United States v. Davis*,[38] district court judge J. Owen Forrester held that Congress had not sufficiently differentiated crack from powder cocaine, which forced him to apply the rule of "lenity," a pre-Guidelines rule of thumb that prescribes the lesser penalty when two statutes are not clearly distinguishable.[39] In a handful of other cases, judges found constitutional violations in the way the crack rules are applied.

Other cases find fault with the mandatory minimums at their conception. Judge Louis F. Oberdorfer held in *United States v. Walls*[40] that the crack minimums amounted to cruel and unusual punishment. He was perturbed that drug-control officers had set defendants up for harsher penalties by demanding that they turn the powder cocaine they were selling into crack. He drew support from the history of racism in drug legislation and from *Robinson v. California*,[41] a case from the Warren Court era that declared punishment for being a drug addict unconstitutional. Judge Cahill, as noted in chapter 1, also used the history of racial injustice in drug laws to challenge congressional judgment on equal protection grounds in *United States v. Clary*.

Judge Harold Greene in *United States v. Shepherd*[42] held that the due process clause of the Constitution had been offended by the way the government was pursuing crack cases. The defendant in *Shepherd*, as in *Walls*, had been required by the arresting officer to turn cocaine into crack. Judge Greene saw in this police action and the system that supported it an unconstitutional draining away of judicial authority: "This case demonstrates that, because of the mandatory minimum sentences and the rigid Sentencing Guidelines, effective control of sentencing—from time immemorial in common law countries a judicial function—has effectively slipped, at least in some cases, not only to the realm of the prosecution but even further to that of the police. This development denies due process and is intolerable in our Constitutional scheme."[43] Judge Greene also found a due process violation in *United States v. Spencer*,[44] where the mandated sentence was thirty years for possession of less than 8 ounces of crack cocaine.

Each of these decisions, except Judge Forrester's in *Davis*, was reversed on appeal, and *Davis* has been sharply criticized at all levels.[45] Rejection in the courts of appeals was invariably respectful, but also unwavering. Nearly every opinion was unanimous.[46]

By the mid-1990s, the constitutional challenges had more or less ended. The upper tier of the judiciary had successfully resisted pressure for change from the bottom. The roadblock to change was clearly doctrinal, not evidentiary. The empirical evidence that the defense bar had produced was strong, with much of it coming from the government's own studies. The most affected constituency, uneducated inner-city African American youth, was clearly vulnerable to abuse by lawmakers. Nor was there any hiding the fact that the legislation had been passed in haste, with palpable fear of the consequences of this "Black" drug.

The Supreme Court's Roadblock to Constitutional Relief

"No State shall . . . deny to any person within its jurisdiction the equal protection of the laws." This brief phrase, somewhat obscure in its precise meaning, concludes the first section of the Fourteenth Amendment, which lays out
several other important rights of citizenship. Congress adopted the Fourteenth Amendment in 1868 to guarantee the civil rights of the nation's newly
freed slaves. The necessity for a federal guarantee was obvious. The southern
states had subordinated the former slaves economically, socially, and politically through the notorious Black Codes. President Andrew Johnson had
vetoed the first congressional effort to turn back this tide of incapacitating
state law, the 1866 Civil Rights Act (Perry 1999, 51). The Fourteenth Amendment provided the necessary legal foundation for the reconstruction effort
that was then taking shape, but its major significance came much later, after
a long period of Jim Crow legislation segregated facilities of all sorts in the
South—from water fountains to cemeteries and orphanages.

The Supreme Court arrived late to the problem of racial disadvantage,
and its engagement since that time has been fitful. Not until 1938 did the
Court acknowledge that it has special responsibilities toward "discrete and
insular minorities" like African Americans.[47] It failed to fully embrace this
standard, however, until the 1960s, bypassing an obvious opportunity in its
1954 school desegregation decision, *Brown v. Board of Education*.[48] The
Court finally became actively engaged with equal protection doctrine at
about the same time that Congress was developing the 1964 Civil Rights
Act.[49] As the justices began to demand a higher standard for government
action, they also expanded the coverage of the guarantee to other disadvantaged groups, including white women.

The early emphasis on alleviating oppression of powerless groups, Evan
Gerstmann and others have argued, was turned on its head in the 1980s, as
the Supreme Court developed a generalized suspicion of classifications based
on group membership.[50] The concern, in other words, shifted from protecting powerless minorities by requiring a high level of scrutiny of any rule that
affected them, to a presumption against *any* racial classification, including
those designed to benefit long-oppressed minorities. The Constitution's equal
protection guarantee, in effect, has become a broad mandate for government
not to arbitrarily single out any individual or group (Perry 1999, 83).

How can courts determine whether government is acting against a minority out of spite or without any legitimate purpose? Legislatures never
announce invidious intentions. Courts must draw their own conclusions on
the basis of the legislature's handiwork. In the early civil rights era, this task

was made easier by the presumption that white southerners would always attempt to preserve their race privileges. Officials might deny discriminating, but the evidence of racial exclusion spoke louder than their words. The absence of Black voters in a district, for example, undermined the credibility of local officials who claimed that their rules were neutral.

The problem of intent arises not just in Fourteenth Amendment equal protection claims, but also in the enforcement of the 1964 Civil Rights Act's equality guarantee. The Supreme Court came closest to letting evidence of impact alone justify intervention in a 1971 race discrimination case arising under the Civil Rights Act. In *Griggs v. Duke Power Company*,[51] the Court declared that the company's newly imposed test requirement violated the Civil Rights Act because it excluded almost all local Blacks in the area from decent jobs. There was no dissent from this result or reasoning.

By 1976, however, the Supreme Court had retreated. In *Washington v. Davis*,[52] it reversed a court of appeals decision that had relied on *Griggs* in finding disparate racial impact sufficient to establish a constitutional violation. The issue was whether a verbal aptitude test that the District of Columbia was using in hiring police officers violated the Constitution's equal protection guarantee. The test disproportionately excluded African American applicants from consideration, but the Court decided that racial disproportion alone was not enough to violate the Constitution's equal protection clause: "A law, neutral on its face and serving ends otherwise within the power of government to pursue, is [not] invalid under the Equal Protection Clause simply because it may affect a greater proportion of one race than another."[53] While litigants might still use impact-based arguments to show violations of statutory guarantees, these arguments would not be sufficient to invalidate rules or procedures on constitutional grounds.[54]

The Court attempted to clarify its position by reviewing prior litigation involving racial distinctions in setting up and administering schools, legislative apportionment, jury service, and the distribution of public benefits. Justice Byron White, writing for the Court, claimed that the rulings had been consistent in requiring a persuasive demonstration of discriminatory intent along with evidence of pernicious effects:

> Necessarily, an invidious discriminatory purpose may often be inferred from the totality of the relevant facts, including the fact, if it is true, that the law bears more heavily on one race than another. . . . Nevertheless, we have not held that a law, neutral on its face and serving ends otherwise within the power of government to pursue, is invalid under the Equal Protection Clause simply because it may affect a greater proportion of

one race than another. Disproportionate impact is not irrelevant, but it is not the sole touchstone of an invidious racial discrimination forbidden by the Constitution.[55]

Admitting that the line of demarcation had not always been clear, the Court summarized its reading of previous cases in guarded, negative terms: "Our cases have not embraced the proposition that a law or other official act, without regard to whether it reflects a racially discriminatory purpose, is unconstitutional solely because it has a racially disproportionate impact."[56]

The Supreme Court has been reasonably consistent since *Washington v. Davis* in ruling that there must be evidence of intent to discriminate before the government's action will be deemed to violate the equal protection clause. The Court's 1987 decision in *McCleskey v. Kemp* reaffirmed this line of cases and has become the major point of reference in subsequent cases. One study found that in the decade following *McCleskey*, not a single claimant had prevailed in a claim alleging racial discrimination by government—*McCleskey* is usually cited in denying relief (Blume, Eisenberg, and Johnson 1998, 1808).

Cognitive Psychology on Racism in Law

How does the reasoning in *McCleskey* stand up to what is currently known about the psychology of racial discrimination? Should discrimination be conceptualized as typically intentional, as *McCleskey* and its companion cases presume? Law is biased toward willed behavior because it is less morally problematic to assume that what we do is under our conscious control. But as a theory of discrimination, does this approach leave out most of what it should contain? If the life of the law has been experience, as Justice Oliver Wendell Holmes famously proclaimed, shouldn't the experience of life inform the law?

The past thirty years of social psychological research, Linda Krieger and Susan Fiske (2006) assert, offers several major insights relevant to antidiscrimination law. One of them is that unconscious expectations, including stereotypes, influence perception. Perception, this research suggests, is not passive. It is highly selective in making sense of reality, relying on cues that derive from preexisting frameworks, or schemas. The irony is that we are completely unaware of all this. "We experience the world," Susan Fiske and Shelley Taylor assert, "as if our schemas have added nothing to it" (1991, 99).

Controlled experiments suggest that people use visually prominent physical features, such as race, gender, age, and apparent occupation or region of origin, to cue schemas, which in turn evoke certain expectations that have measurable effects on thinking. Schemas associated with race, age, and so on are, in effect, stereotypes. They may be simple or complex, for example, "white southern Baptist" might function as a schema for some people. One indication that schemas are operating is that people are dramatically slowed down in their mental processing if there is a mismatch between their stereotypical expectations and the reality they encounter in a test (Banaji and Greenwald 1995). Words alone (for example, *female* or *old*) influence reaction times in directions suggestive of stereotypes and prejudice (Dovidio, Evans, and Tyler 1986; Perdue and Gurtman 1990; see generally Wegner and Wenzlaff 1996).

This research proceeds from the starting point that modern racism is less hostile than its antecedents, but probably no less widespread. Some researchers propose the term *aversive racism* to describe attitudes commonly held by white Americans who are genuinely committed to tolerance, but who, at the same time, hold negative stereotypes about African Americans and other racial and ethnic groups: "These factors converge to produce attitudinal ambivalence, uncertainty and fear in interracial encounters, and . . . racist behavior that is manifested in indirect and subtle ways" (Eagly and Chaiken 1998, 285; and see Dovidio and Gaertner 2000). The invocation of racial and other stereotypes affects thinking in at least four ways, according to Eliot Smith's review of mental representation and memory in the *Handbook of Social Psychology*:

- Ambiguous behaviors may be interpreted as confirming the stereotype.
- Stereotype-consistent behavior will tend to reconfirm the stereotype while inconsistent behavior will be thought exceptional or attributable to chance.
- The stereotype, rather than the individual's behavior, may be used for the basis of judgment.
- Recall will be affected, and stereotype-inconsistent characteristics will tend to be forgotten. (1998, 405)

Racial stereotypes tend to persist not just because of selective information processing, but also because of the way people differentiate themselves from others, what cognitive psychologists call the outgroup homogeneity effect. Individuals tend to accentuate differences from groups they perceive as different from themselves, at the same time minimizing the differences among individuals in the out group. The effect is robust, occurring across various kinds of ingroup/outgroup combinations, including students in neighboring colleges, members of related professions, and racial groups.

Another processing error relevant to racism is "the fundamental attribution error," a tendency to attribute another person's behavior to character, rather than situation. We make this error in judging others, but tend to forgive our own lapses: "Instead of realizing that there are situational forces, such as social norms or roles, that produce particular behavior, people generally see another's behavior as freely chosen and as representing that other person's stable qualities" (Fiske and Taylor 1991, 67).

All of these processing errors are made worse by a human tendency to assume that everyone else sees things as we do, what cognitive psychologists call the false consensus effect: "People not only overestimate how typical their own behavior is, they also overestimate the typicality of their feelings, beliefs, and opinions. The false consensus effect may be a chief vehicle by which people maintain that their own beliefs or opinions are right" (Fiske and Taylor 1991, 78–79). It also helps people justify imposing their own beliefs on others.

These findings suggest the difficulty of eliminating prejudice, rooted as it is in basic modes of thought. The question of how to uproot it has engaged researchers for at least two decades. A basic finding is that negative stereotypes must be actively resisted to be avoided. Patricia Devine likens the process to breaking a bad habit: "The individual must (a) initially decide to stop the old behavior, (b) remember the resolution, and (c) try repeatedly and decide repeatedly to eliminate the habit" (1989, 15). The old stereotype remains, but it is no longer used. Resisting old stereotypes requires effort and is not always successful: "The non-prejudiced responses take time, attention, and effort. To the extent that any (or all) of these are limited, the outcome is likely to be stereotype-congruent or prejudice-like responses" (1989, 16; and see Devine et al. 2002).

This brief survey suggests a fundamental conflict with the legal approach to discrimination. The racism that law treats as exceptional, psychology considers mundane. Law looks for motives to discriminate, while psychology postulates that the architecture of our thinking predisposes us to racism and other forms of stereotyping by group. Were judges to acknowledge in their decisions what psychologists have established in their experiments, what would discrimination law look like?

Reconceptualizing Racism and Disparate Impact in Law

If the U.S. Supreme Court were to accept the idea that racial stereotypes and prejudice are endemic in society, courts would look differently at disparate-impact claims. Judges would be more ready to attribute racial disadvantage to individual "wiring" problems and to institutionalized practices built on stereotypical thinking, rather than intentional prejudice. They would not accept assertions of nonprejudice at face value, even from Congress. They would be interested in helping to ferret out discrimination. *Armstrong v. United States*, with its dismissive approach to racially lopsided prosecution statistics, would be rejected as an example of wrong-headed racism characteristic of an unenlightened era, as the Supreme Court's 1896 decision upholding segregation, *Plessy v. Ferguson*,[57] is now.

Were the judicial branch to accept the reality of unconscious racism, the whole tenor of public debate about racial discrimination would change. Policymakers would have to be concerned about disparate racial impact and embedded racism. They would need to monitor their own decisions to avoid racial stereotyping. There would be a premium on designing institutions that operate stereotype-free. If decision makers took these responsibilities seriously, public debate about race would be more engaged with policy design than name calling, and government would be pressing institutions to measure the impact of their procedures to avoid institutionalizing disadvantage.

In its early years under the Johnson administration, the Equal Economic Opportunity Commission took this approach, pressuring companies to address patterns of exclusion, rather than focusing on specific acts of discrimination. This policy was carried forward under President Nixon (see Katznelson 2005, 146–47). Although impact is still relevant in the government's enforcement actions, courts have become less willing to press for change in the past two decades. Linda Krieger, a law professor and employment rights litigator, writes of the difficulty of winning Title VII employment discrimination cases with only disparate impact data. Courts, she has found, are looking for evidence of prejudice because they assume that discrimination is intentional. She noted the difficulty of making this kind of showing in a case she litigated: "To be blunt, to establish that my client had been wronged, I would have to prove that the plant manager was a racist and a liar" (1995, 1163).

The courts have applied a standard more in keeping with current psychological knowledge about discrimination in cases arising under the Age Discrimination in Employment Act (ADEA).[58] The language in the two anti-discrimination statutes is similar, but judges interpret them differently because they believe that Congress meant to distinguish age and race discrimination:

> The legislative history of the ADEA suggests that the Congressional framers thought that non-willful discrimination directed towards an individual

was quite possible. Unlike race discrimination, age discrimination may simply arise from an unconscious application of stereotyped notions of ability rather than from a deliberate desire to remove older employees from the workforce: [now quoting Rep. Burke] "Age discrimination is not the same as the insidious discrimination based on race or creed, prejudices and bigotry. Those discriminations result in non-employment because of feelings about a person entirely unrelated to his ability to do a job. This is hardly a problem for the older jobseeker. Discrimination arises for him because of assumptions that are made about the effects of age on performance. As a general rule, ability is ageless."[59]

Conclusion

A comforting myth about the American system of government is that, over time, judicial decisions help us move progressively closer to our nation's foundational values. The way the Supreme Court has handled the problem of racial discrimination, however, belies that myth. Instead of broadening and deepening American understanding of discrimination in line with our core commitment to racial equality, the Court has narrowed and rigidified its approach in the past two decades. Current constitutional doctrine makes only the most blatant type of discriminatory treatment actionable, which means that the judiciary has little to contribute to the resolution of contemporary racial inequities.

The conflict between law and justice is certainly felt within the lower reaches of the judicial branch, among the judges and magistrates who see drug defendants face to face as they impose punishment. "Justice," as one acute observer noted, "is personal. It always begins and ends with specific, concrete persons" (J. Johnson 1995, 201). We talk about justice as part of translating it into actual practice: "The talking represents our own internal dialogue with the world and our place in it" (J. Johnson 1995, 202). Judge Cahill shared that dialogue with the world when he wrote his opinion in the *Clary* case.

Racial profiling, one law-enforcement practice that has received critical attention from government and the media, is only the tip of a constitutional iceberg. The whole architecture of the anti-drug effort is vulnerable to criticism for racial bias. If courts and policymakers were to go in this direction, they would also be obliged to consider the long tradition of particularly harsh punishment for other crimes committed by Black citizens.

Taking impact seriously would also extend courts into forms of discrimination outside the criminal justice system. Racial impact is a source of useful information wherever there is evidence of disadvantage—for example, public education, land use, and employment. The absence of courts from the struggle for racial justice allows many old wounds to fester.

epilogue

Individuals are both actors on the stage of political life, and products of impersonal institutional processes that shape their ideas. No individual or group can truly be held responsible for the racism and punitiveness that inhere in our drug laws. Critical policy analysis should look in a different direction, toward honest acknowledgment of the consequences of political decisions, and toward corrective action guided by democratic principles. The problem is much broader than the current war on drugs. Too many policies today target unfortunate populations with harsh treatment, creating outcomes that are harmful to democracy.

The United States appears addicted to incarceration. By the end of 2005, the United States had reached another historic high in the number incarcerated, with 2.2 million behind bars. Seven million are either in prison, on probation, or on parole.[1] Serious questions should be raised about this buildup. Rates of violent crime were falling even before the incarceration boom got underway, suggesting that there is little relationship between the two. Most of the growth in imprisonment is for nonviolent crime, particularly drug crime. The preponderance of those incarcerated are poor and minority citizens, a pattern that tends to be treated as unfortunate but morally irrelevant in the pursuit of public security. A more democratic perspective would see imprisonment of so many of our most vulnerable citizens as a symptom of more serious social disequilibria in the availability of education, housing, health care, and economic opportunity (see, e.g., Davis 2005).

New prisons are being built every year, creating new constituencies for incarceration. More than half of current prisons were built within the last twenty years (Mauer 2006b, 10–11, 12–13). Nearly one-third of the counties in the United States now have at least one prison—the number almost doubled in the past thirty years, from 592 in 1974 to 1,023 in 2000.

Imprisonment is popular in these communities. As a recent Urban Institute study of the prison-building boom explains: "In smaller communities, and particularly those with higher than average rates of unemployment, opening a new prison is believed to be an economically beneficial endeavor" (Lawrence and Travis 2004: 3). While the actual benefits of these institutions are contestable, it is clear that these communities benefit from state and federal funding formulae. Because the inmates are counted as residents of the counties in which they are incarcerated, they receive federal and state funding and greater political representation at the expense of the communities from where they prisoners came (Lawrence and Travis 2004). The imprisonment trend is a financial bonanza for what Reinarman and Levine have dubbed "the drug control complex—the many interlocking police, military, and drug enforcement agencies at all levels of the government" (1997, 329).

The signs of America's addiction to incarceration include not just the seemingly inexorable increases in the imprisoned population, but the relentless push for more imprisonment. Pro-imprisonment forces dominate Congress and the White House. The White House Office of National Drug Control Strategy continues to present statistics selectively chosen to suggest that the drug war is succeeding when it is not (Robinson 2005). Congress remains steadfast in promoting long prison terms, and has even adopted legislation to require Justice Department review of sentences that go below the federal Sentencing Guidelines.

The Bureau of Justice Statistics reports that federal drug control spending rose by over 50 percent between 1996 and 2005, with $12.6 billion requested for 2005 (Bureau of Justice Statistics 2005). This has required some adjusting of priorities. Marijuana arrests, for example, are dramatically up at both the state and federal levels, even as some states are rethinking the wisdom of criminal penalties for possession of small amounts of the drug.

Powerful forces are obviously at work to justify the seemingly endless war on drugs. David Garland blames hypocritical politicians seeking to stem public outrage over intractable social problems associated with late modernity:

> The war on drugs was the American state's attempt to "just say no." Disregarding evidence that the levels of drug use were already in decline, that drug use is not responsive to criminal penalties, that criminalization brings its own pathologies (notably street violence and disrespect for the authorities), and that declaring a war against drugs is, in effect, to declare a war against minorities, the US government proceeded to declare such

a war and to persist in pursuing it, despite every indication of its failure. (2001, 132)

The problem goes deeper. Moral entrepreneurs inside and outside of government have played up the dangers of drugs for at least a century, tapping American racism to amplify their message. The mass media have cooperated in the effort (see, e.g., Beckett and Sasson 2000, xii, 169–70; Cavender 2004). Drug abuse has been amazingly transformed from the relatively private activity it was before the twentieth century to the fearful source of violence and social disintegration that we understand it to be now. Hard evidence of the extent of the danger posed by drugs has never been necessary, nor has it been necessary to explain why some drugs are dangerous and others are not. The dangers of certain substances, not just to individuals but to society at large, long ago became common sense to Americans.

This book emphasizes the role of societal racism in the development of punitive attitudes toward drug use and in maintaining public support for harsh criminal controls. Racism makes it easy to construct a frightening image of the racial "other" as out of control, violent, and sexually predatory. The images became less explicit after the 1960s, but the theme of racial danger persists. Critical race theory, which posits the enduring significance of race, finds much support in this history (see, e.g., Yosso and Solorzano 2005; and, more generally, Romero and Margolis 2005; Winant 2004).

The prevailing ideology of color blindness protects officials from having to acknowledge and deal with the blatant racial and class inequalities in the punishment system. As David Cole notes, our system "affirmatively depends on inequality," in maintaining one costly system that offers the full panoply of rights protections, while the other, much cheaper version, offers rough justice featuring unchecked police and prosecutorial discretion to quickly move arrestees toward imprisonment (1999, 5). Race helps mark people for one system or the other. How this works in practice is normally kept in the shadows by plea bargaining, which now constitutes between 94.6 percent and 97 percent of all dispositions in the federal system, and probably more in the states. Drug offenses are the crime category most likely to be handled with pleas (U.S. Sentencing Commission 2004b, 22, 26).

The incarceration addiction periodically needs a new drug threat to justify the enormous costs it imposes on society. Methamphetamine has emerged to play this role. In terms highly reminiscent of those used to describe crack cocaine two decades ago, Attorney General Alberto Gonzales (2005) describes this new threat:

I believe it bears repeating that meth is a unique and deadly threat to our Nation. It is highly addictive. It is easy and cheap to produce. And as many in this room know, it destroys lives far beyond those of just the addicts and users. . . . Meth requires pressure at every stage, and it demands the concerted effort of every level of government to stop it. . . . I have directed the United States Attorney's Offices to make the prosecution of the meth cooks and distributors—especially those who are repeat offenders—a high priority. This means U.S. Attorneys will be going into federal court, seeking stiff sentences for major players in the meth trade.

Once again, the government is ignoring the facts: that methamphetamine is among the least used drugs, affecting only 0.2 percent of the population; that use rates have remained stable since 1999 and declined among high school youth; and that treatment is effective against addiction (King 2006, 2 3). And once again, government is relying on incentives to stir police interest in enforcement: a "Meth/Drug Hot Spots" program offering $385.6 million for eradication of labs, with much of it earmarked for certain locales (King 2006, 14–15).

The mass media have also proven ready, once again, to uncritically broadcast the government's message. In a critical review of news coverage, Jack Shafer notes that *Newsweek*, which two decades ago had been aggressive in reporting the crack "epidemic," recently ran a cover story on the current meth "epidemic," giving it "most dangerous drug" status. He also cites stories describing "meth babies" on CBS News and CNN and in the *Chicago Tribune*, *New York Times*, *Los Angeles Times*, *Sunday Oklahoman*, and Minneapolis-St. Paul *Star Tribune*. Newspapers, including the venerable *New York Times*, still quote law-enforcement officials rather than medical experts in describing the dangers of such drugs (Shafer 2005; King 2006).

There are nevertheless signs that something may have been learned from past experience. The "meth baby" stories provoked an immediate critical reaction from drug researchers. When the House Judiciary Committee proposed a Methamphetamine Epidemic Elimination Act that set a mandatory ten-year term for possession of 5 grams of meth, it died after Democrats subjected the proponents to sharp questioning. It can be counted as a victory of sorts that meth has not yet been associated with any particular racial or ethnic minority.

Drug-war rhetoric seems to be losing its force with the American public, in tandem with declining interest in street crime. Michael Jacobson (2006), a researcher with the Vera Institute of Justice, describes a drop since the 1990s in public concern about crime that is evident in Gallup and other polling data. Congress has responded, in a small way, to long-standing criticism of the crack laws by creating a "safety valve" that shortens crack penalties for some first offenders. Recently it approved legislation that allows some students to regain eligibility for federal financial aid after a drug conviction, softening a program that had already disqualified 175,000 from student aid. Congress has also funded programs to assist in prisoner reentry. The 100:1 crack/powder sentencing disparity is also likely to be reduced with the ascension of a Democratically controlled Congress in January 2007.[2]

Changes are also occurring at the state level, where politicians seek to be "smart" on crime, rather than simply "tough." In 2002, twenty-five states reduced funding for prisons, and in 2003, seventeen states either closed prisons or delayed construction of new prisons (Jacobson 2006, 280). Mandatory-minimum sentences may once again be going out of fashion (Mauer 2006; Butterfield 2003). At its 2006 annual convention, the U.S. Conference of Mayors passed a resolution condemning mandatory minimum sentences, with an explicit reference to the twentieth anniversary of the federal mandatory minimums in crack cases. Drug courts and other forms of diversion from prison are becoming more numerous because they promise cost savings and a more humane approach to drug control. Felony disenfranchisement laws are being reformed in some states, and over half are engaged in sentencing reform, generally to lighten sentences. Even the death penalty is under serious attack because of its financial and human costs and because of increasing doubts about the validity of some convictions.

These changes are occurring under bipartisan leadership and sometimes with financial support from the federal government (Mauer 2006, 210–15). The U.S. Sentencing Commission, for example, held another set of hearings on crack cocaine sentences on November 14, 2006, in which the sentiment for reform was overwhelming from judges, interest groups, and even the deputy drug czar under the first Bush administration (*Mercury News* 2006). Marc Mauer, a longtime advocate of sentencing reform, notes "the beginnings of a new dialogue on crime and punishment" brought about by the decline in crime, by fiscal crises at the state level, and by the increasingly obvious failures of the war on drugs. He notes the willingness of leaders in the American Bar Association and of Supreme Court Justice Anthony Kennedy to criticize the incarceration approach. Restorative-justice advocates are finding a hearing in the present debate about punishment and its alternatives (see, e.g., Braithwaite 2000, 97). Trial judges are also speaking out, expressing their disagreement with the no-longer-mandatory Guidelines and fashioning their own drug-sentencing criteria (e.g., *United States v. Otis Fisher*, S3 CR 1501 (SAS) (S.D.N.Y. October 11, 2005); and see *USA Today* 2006; Mauer 2006).[3]

These are promising developments, but it is noteworthy that much of this nascent reform movement is centered on the state level and is driven by fiscal necessity. The federal government, which is better insulated from financial shortfalls than the states, has shown less inclination to soften its commitment to the incarceration approach. Its prison system continues to grow, and so does the overall size of the prison population, up 2.6 percent between 2004 and 2005, with a 50 percent increase since 1991 when crime rates began to fall.

The war on drugs is likely to remain invulnerable to thoroughgoing reform until people seriously begin to discuss its purpose and its racial and class impact. Reading race and class out of the reform effort, or downplaying their significance, only weakens the potential movement for reform. There are small signs of a growing willingness to focus more explicitly on race, such as the formation of a coalition of African American professional organizations dedicated to drug-law reform and public-health alternatives (National African American Drug Policy Coalition 2004). A key journal in the field, *Drugs & Society*, sports a new name: *Journal of Ethnicity in Substance Abuse*. More significant has been the recent and growing movement to encourage legislatures to produce racial-impact assessments. This movement would be much stronger, of course, if the Supreme Court would declare such assessments a legislative responsibility on constitutional grounds.

The absence of any tradition or norm requiring legislators to take responsibility for the laws they produce is a serious weakness in a racially and ethnically diverse nation with a troubling history of officially mandated and condoned racism. The majority's power to turn legislators out of office is really no protection at all for oppressed minorities. Democratic norms would be better protected if statutes were thought of as works in progress, inevitably incomplete at the time of adoption. Lawmakers should be obliged to follow the process of implementation, taking responsibility to ensure that their statutory purposes are achieved, including their responsibility to justice.

The current color-blind approach to public policy is a major obstacle to any movement to require more responsible behavior from legislators. Color blindness trivializes racism and obliterates institutional and psychological connections to the past. The war on crack cocaine is a good example of this blocking action because its terrible toll on impoverished minority communities is quite obvious, and so is the rootedness of drug policy in white racial and class anxieties.

Rethinking the incarceration approach to drugs and to other anxiety-provoking behavior will also require Americans to realize that we cannot easily free ourselves from our past and our unconscious and semiconscious fears and prejudices. Nor can we continue to think that we control institutions in some simple fashion, when in fact institutions shape our very sense of ourselves and tell us who we are (see, e.g., Douglas 1986). Institutions, after all, maintain the current approach to drugs, and to crime more generally. They will fight any significant change of direction. It is indeed unfortunate that the Supreme Court has refused to take on some of the burden of shifting priorities. In its dogged adherence to color blindness, it allows public officials to dodge their constitutional responsibilities to equal protection of the law.

It will take a broad political movement that draws strength from race and class consciousness to make significant changes in the criminalized order of the day. Glaring injustice and anxiety-driven policymaking have enormous staying power, particularly when buttressed by a large, well-funded police apparatus and prison system. There is no better example of the problem than our misguided war on drugs.

notes

Introduction

1. *United States v. Clary*, 846 F. Supp. 768 (E.D. Mo. 1994).

2. The idea of an "other America" comes from a classic analysis of an earlier era: Michael Harrington's searing portrayal of isolation and neglect of poor minority communities in the midst of affluence in *The Other America* (New York: Scribner, 1962). This book, which proposed that poverty could be eliminated, helped Presidents Kennedy and Johnson decide to initiate a series of reforms that came to be labeled the War on Poverty. More recently, sociologist Elijah Anderson has explored how these economically neglected and racially segregated neighborhoods survive: *Code of the Street: Decency, Violence, and the Moral Life of the Inner City* (New York: Norton, 1999), and *Streetwise: Race, Class, and Change in an Urban Community* (Chicago: University of Chicago Press, 1990).

3. This data is drawn from findings in several reports summarized in the *New York Times* on March 20, 2006: "Plight Deepens for Black Men, Studies Warn," pp. A1, A18. The cited studies are Ronald B. Mincy, "Black Males Left Behind" (Washington, DC: Urban Institute Press, 2006); Harry Holzer, Peter Edelman, and Paul Offner, "Reconnecting Disadvantaged Young Men" (Washington, DC: Urban Institute Press, 2006); Gary Orfield, "Dropouts in America" (Cambridge, MA: Harvard Education Press, 2004); and Bruce Western, *Punishment and Inequality in America* (New York: Russell Sage Foundation, 2006). The percentage of Hispanic youth who drop out of school are as high or higher than for Blacks, but the rates of unemployment and crime are much less, according to these reports.

4. These statistics are based on a report by the United States Sentencing Commission: 2003 *Sourcebook of Federal Sentencing Statistics,* Table 34, p. 29 (2005), and a report by the federal Substance Abuse and Mental Health Services Administration: *National Household Survey on Drug Use and Health,* 2005.

5. Paul Butler (2003) takes up the possibility that government could usefully seek more racial diversity in the criminal justice process and in prisons. To draw more attention to the racial injustices in the system and to unconscious racism in criminal justice decision making, he recommends "that African-Americans be arrested, tried, and sentenced for drug crimes only in proportion to their actual commission of those crimes" and that a goal be to have "a prison population that more accurately reflects the racial diversity of America" (374).

Chapter One

1. 846 F. Supp. 768 (E.D. Mo. 1994).

2. Only one state court of last resort, the Minnesota Supreme Court, ruled against large sentencing disparities for powder and crack cocaine. It did so on state constitutional grounds. See *State v. Russell*, 477 N.W.2d 886 (Minn. 1991).

3. 998 F.2d 634 (8th Cir. 1993)

4. Id. at 635 n.2.

5. 846 F. Supp. at 796. Chapter 6 looks at the arguments that Judge Cahill developed in greater detail and finds strong support for them in the scientific literature.

6. 846 F. Supp. at 785.

7. Id:

8. Id. at 779.

9. *United States v. Clary*, 34 F.3d 709 (8th Cir. 1994).

10. Id. at 713.

11. The debate took place on October 11, 2000. ("Mr. Bush: I can't imagine what it would be like to be singled out because of race and stopped and harassed. That's just flat wrong. And that's not what America's all about. . . . Mr. Gore: I . . . hate this practice also.")

12. Discrimination by ethnicity in the development of the law on drugs can be analyzed with the same analytical approach discussed here. The desirability of a synthetic approach is usefully discussed in Cornell and Hartmann 2004.

Chapter Two

1. He nevertheless estimates that about 500,000 people were convicted during Prohibition under state statutes, paying fines of more than $75 million (1932, 46).

2. See the discussion in chapter 1 in the section titled "The Racial Impact of the War on Drugs."

3. Forty-one people died on New Year's Day 1927 in New York's Bellevue Hospital, apparently from a single batch of grain alcohol disguised as liquor. The wars over turf among bootlegging gangs were also frequently lethal. Gangs in New York killed more than a thousand people between 1920 and 1930 (Pegram 1998, 174). Their leaders were becoming celebrities at the same time that gang warfare was becoming more violent.

Chapter Three

1. Drug scholars Craig Reinarman and Harry G. Levine (1997, 321–33) coined this useful term, which is discussed at more length in the previous chapter.

2. Although it did not become well known as a pain reliever until the nineteenth century, its lineage is much longer. Martin Booth suggests that even Neanderthal man may have used it (1996, 15).

3. David Cortwright, a well-respected historian of opiate regulation, suggests that there were never more than 313,000 addicts in the United States before 1914. Promoters of Prohibition, such as Hamilton Wright, put the number much higher, but Cortwright suggests that they bent the facts. This misinformation nevertheless had a profound effect on opinion leaders. It gave the impression that the problem of addiction was growing, when in fact it was declining (2001, 33).

4. Riis later introduced Roosevelt to nocturnal walks about the city, and the men became friends. Frances Perkins was also impressed by this book, claiming that it had

inspired her to adopt a life in social work. See Donald Bigelow's introduction to the 1957 edition.

5. *Ex parte Yung Jon*, 28 F. 308, 312 (D. Or. 1886).

6. These efforts began in 1880, with a series of bills to increase the duty on imported smoking opium and a tax on domestic manufacture. Later there were bills to forbid opium smoking in the District of Columbia and U.S. territories, none of which succeeded (Cortwright 2001, chap. 2). The U.S. Congress was persuaded to impose a tax on opium and morphine in 1890, under pressure from California, but it was ineffective in reducing drug smuggling. Congress was not particularly interested in opium, which it regarded as a regional policing problem that the federal government had no authority to interfere with.

7. Cortwright refers to the Harrison Act as "a classic piece of progressive legislation" in which "reform effort (restrict the sale of narcotics) met business self-interest (rationalize the narcotic market) to produce a compromise measure. Large pharmaceutical firms were perfectly willing to see small-time unregistered peddlers prosecuted; enlightened and professionalized pharmacists agreed to restrict sale to those possessing a prescription; and the nostrum makers could go on merchandizing their wares, provided they contained no more than the allowable amounts of narcotics" (2001, 103).

8. The tone and content of these articles stands in striking contrast to medical literature of an earlier period that focuses on the tragic circumstances of youth drawn in by patent medicines or doctors' prescriptions. See, e.g., a 1903 address before the Pittsburg Academy of Medicine by Dr. Thomas Simonton, who discussed the greediness of pharmacies that supply young addicts and the need for legislative controls. Simonton had little to say about Blacks. He noted in passing that "the colored race is at the present day by far the greatest consumer of cocaine," but also noted that Blacks are less susceptible to "cocainmania" than whites (1903, 556–60).

9. Consider, for example, a 1919 report conducted by a committee appointed by the secretary of the Treasury that divided addicts into those from "the underworld," who acquired the drug habit from associates, white slavers, or prostitutes, and "the addict of good social standing," who became addicted through a physician, self-medication, or, in rare cases, "as a social diversion." The medically addicted were sick, deserving of a physician's care, and the rest were "criminal drug addicts whose addiction, in its inception and in its continuance, is due to vice, vicious environment and criminal associations." These "voluntary" addicts, considered by some researchers to be the greater number, belonged in prison (quoted in Terry and Pellens 1928/1970, 120, 130). The tendency to associate drugs with mental illness may be at least partly explained by the fact that experts of the day tended to study addiction by interviewing prisoners and inmates in mental institutions (Cortwright 2001, 137–38; see also Musto 1973, 248–50; Helmer 1975).

10. The drafters were acutely aware of the possibility that the law might be declared unconstitutional as a violation of the principle of federalism that put criminal law enforcement in state hands. This remained a concern even as late as 1937, when the Treasury Department chose to seek a separate law, rather than amend the Harrison Act, to prohibit marijuana (Musto 1973, 247).

11. 254 U.S. 189 (1916).

12. In 1922 the Court went further in *United States v. Behrman*, 258 U.S. 280 (1922), to outlaw prescription of narcotics to an addict, even if it was the physician's belief that the prescription would help the person regain his or her health.

13. For example, from the *New York Times*: "The poisonous weed which maddens the senses and emaciates the body of the user, is being sold more or less openly in pool halls and beer gardens throughout the West and Southwest and, according to some authorities, it is being peddled to school children. The Federal government is powerless to stop the traffic, officials of the Narcotic Bureau say, because marijuana was left out of the Harrison Act under which the bureau gets its authority to stop the traffic in opium and its derivatives" (1934a).

14. See, e.g., the front-page story on December 9, 1934. The *Times* continued to follow this story, reporting on the role of the Bureau of Narcotics in the breakup of "a plot to make high school students slaves to narcotics" (1934f), the discovery of a "mail order dope-racket" (1934g), and the Bureau's investigation of marijuana trading at Army camps (1935). Commissioner Anslinger's name appears prominently in all of these stories.

15. The problem of distortion by government and the media has received critical attention with respect to the alleged methamphetamine epidemic. For a thoughtful discussion see Ryan S. King, "The Next Big Thing? Methamphetamine in the United States," The Sentencing Project, 2006.

16. This respite, an exception that proves the general rule, is discussed in the chapter that follows.

Chapter Four

1. Public Law 91-513, *U.S. Statutes at Large* 84 (1970): 1236.
2. Public Law 98-473, *U.S. Statutes at Large* 98 (1984): 1987.
3. Anti-Drug Abuse Act, Public Law 99-570, *U.S. Statutes at Large* 100 (1986): 3207.
4. Ibid.
5. Public Law 100-690, *U.S. Statutes at Large* 102 (1988): 4181.
6. *Congressional Record* 132 (September 24, 1986): S 13741.
7. Ibid.
8. *Congressional Record* 132 (September 11, 1986): H 6679.
9. See, e.g., Representative Hanson's testimony, *Congressional Record* 132 (August 13, 1986): H 6224.
10. Blythe 1986, quoted in *Congressional Record* 132 (April 22, 1986): S 4668.
11. *Congressional Record* 132 (July 29, 1986): S 9788.
12. *Congressional Record* 132 (September 26, 1986): S 13741.
13. *Congressional Record* 132 (September 26, 1986): S 13741.
14. *Congressional Record* 132 (June 17, 1986): S 7636.
15. The material quoted below comes from two sources: (1) A series of articles entitled "Cocaine Rocks: The New Epidemic" in the *Palm Beach Post & Evening Times*, authored by journalist Paul Blythe and introduced into the record by Senator Chiles (*Congressional Record* 132 [April 22, 1986]: S 4668); and (2) two long pieces by Peter McKillop entitled "Crack and Crime" and "An Inferno of Craving, Dealing and Despair" that Senator Hawkins introduced from the June 16, 1986, edition of *Newsweek* (*Congressional Record* 132 [June 9, 1986]: S 7123).
16. Media scholars have developed an analytical tool that is useful in this context. Qualitative discourse analysis, sometimes known as ethnographic content analysis, is an approach to textual analysis designed by media scholar David Altheide and widely used by others. It is designed to discover and clarify themes, rather than to test specific hypotheses, on the theory that those who write the news and create other information for public

consumption convey this information by creating conceptual frames that give the news direction and significance, providing preordained meaning for what would otherwise be a confusing welter of daily stimuli (Altheide 2004, 325).

17. Eric Sterling, a close observer of this process from his vantage point as assistant counsel to the House Judiciary Committee, reports: "As flawed as the work of the Subcommittee on Crime in developing the mandatory minimum sentences, however, it was much more deliberative than the overall Congressional environment in which the anti-drug legislation was being considered in August, September and October of 1986" (Sterling 1995, 410).

18. *Congressional Record* 134 (October 14, 1988): S 16036.

19. Out of 23 members at this time, 10 voted in favor of PL 100-690, 6 were opposed, and 7 did not vote. Three out of four of the newest members voted in favor.

20. *Congressional Record* 116 (February 3, 1970): H 2338.

21. *Congressional Record* 116 (October 20, 1970): S 13676.

Chapter Five

1. Public Law 99-570, *U.S. Statutes at Large* 100 (1986): 3207.

2. Public Law 100-690, *U.S. Statutes at Large* 102 (1988): 4485.

3. Blumenson and Nilsen note that forfeiture provisions encourage very aggressive enforcement of drug laws, but do not necessarily result in prosecutable arrests. Eighty percent of drug seizures are unaccompanied by any prosecution (1998).

4. *United States v. Clary,* 846 F. Supp. 768 (E.D. Mo. 1994).

5. Public Law 98-473, *U.S. Statutes at Large* 98 (1984): 1987.

6. Senate Judiciary Committee, *Federal Sentencing Guidelines: Hearings before the Senate Judiciary Committee*, testimony of William Mercer, 108th Cong., 2d sess., July 12, 2004 (Washington, DC: Government Printing Office, 2004).

7. *Mistretta v. United States,* 488 U.S. 361, 415, 427 (1989) (Scalia, J., dissenting).

8. *Congressional Record* 132 (September 30, 1986): S 14301.

9. Public Law 84-728, *U.S. Statutes at Large* 70 (1956): 567.

10. Public Law 91-513, *U.S. Statutes at Large* 84 (1970): 1236.

11. 488 U.S. 361 (1989). See also *Chapman v. United States,* 500 U.S. 453 (1991), holding that the mandatory-minimum statute was not unconstitutionally vague.

12. John Martin, a judge from the U.S. District Court for the Southern District of New York, for example, cited the Sentencing Guidelines as one reason for his 2003 resignation (Berman 2003). Judge J. Lawrence Irving, a Reagan appointee, retired with a searing critique of the guidelines: "If I remain on the bench, I have no choice but to follow the law. I just can't, in good conscience, continue to do this." "Criticizing Sentencing Rules, US Judge Resigns," *New York Times*, September 30, 1990, section 1, at 2.

13. In 2003, Congress made these downward departures more difficult when it adopted the Feeney Amendment to the Prosecutorial Remedies and Other Tools to End the Exploitation of Children Today (PROTECT) Act of 2003, Public Law 108-21, § 401, *U.S. Statutes at Large* 117 (2003): 650. Then, in a series of cases that culminated in a 2005 decision, *United States v. Booker*, 543 U.S. 220 (2005), the Supreme Court ruled that mandatory sentencing rules violate the Sixth Amendment guarantee to a jury trial. Sentences for crimes involving crack cocaine are not likely to be much affected by this decision because the mandatory minimums arise out of congressional legislation. The only impact is on Commission rules to handle cases not covered by the mandatory minimums.

14. Interview with Michael Gelacek, August 1996, Syracuse, NY.

15. *Federal Register* 60 (May 10, 1995): 25074. This vote occurred on May 1, 1995. Congress rejected this recommendation in Public Law 104-38, *U.S. Statutes at Large* 109 (1995): 334. It sent the matter back to the Commission.

16. Telephone interview with Paul Hofer, March 1999.

17. Disapproval of Certain Sentencing Guidelines Amendments, 104th Cong., 1st sess., 1995, H. Rep. 272.

18. Telephone interview with Commissioner John Conyers, June 5, 2003.

19. *Congressional Record* 141 (October 18, 1995): H 10264.

20. Ibid., H 10273.

21. Ibid., H 10269.

22. Ibid., H: 10262; and see McCollum at H 10264 and Bryant at H 10266.

23. Ibid., H 10277 (statement of Rep. Waters). The colloquy is quoted in Taifa 1998, 202.

24. *Congressional Record* 141 (October 18, 1995): H 10211.

25. See, e.g., Representative Jim Moran (D-Va.), ibid., H 10258.

26. Ibid., H 10263.

27. Ibid., H 10266.

28. Ibid., H 10265.

29. Ibid., H 10271.

30. See, e.g., Reps. Bryant and Schiff, ibid., H 10267.

31. Ibid., H 10275.

32. *Congressional Quarterly*, October 21, 1995, 3212.

33. Expressing the Resolve of Congress to Take an Active Role in Eliminating Racism, H.R. Res. 138, 105th Cong., 1st sess. (April 30, 1997).

34. Amendment 2879 to Disapprove of Amendments to the Federal Sentencing Guidelines, S. 1254, 104th Cong., 1st sess. (September 29, 1995).

35. Judge Richard Conaboy, telephone interview with author, May 22, 1999.

36. Interview, October 1997, Syracuse, NY.

37. The letter is reprinted in the *Federal Sentencing Reporter* 10 (4) (1998): 192–93. It is summarized in Wren 1997.

38. Letter to Hon. Diana Murphy, Chair, U.S. Sentencing Commission, from Barry Boss, Co-Chair, Practitioners' Advisory Group, May 17, 2002, reprinted in the *Federal Sentencing Reporter* 14 (no. 3–4) (2001–2002): 228–30.

39. Statement of Hon. Diana Murphy, Chair, U.S. Sentencing Commission, before the Senate Subcommittee on Crime and Drugs, May 22, 2002, citing *Report to Congress: Cocaine and Federal Sentencing Policy*, May 2002, 193.

40. 543 U.S. 160 (2005).

41. Letter from U.S. Sentencing Commission to Chairman Coble and Ranking Member Scott, April 19, 2005. The letter was in response to H.R. 1528, a bill that would increase penalties for underage drug offenders.

Chapter Six

1. *State v. Russell*, 477 N.W.2d 886 (Minn. 1991), a case decided by the supreme court of Minnesota that held more severe penalties in crack cases to be a violation of the state's constitution. The invalidated law, it should be noted, was much more draconian than the federal legislation. Possession of 3 grams of crack could carry a penalty of twenty years

in prison, while the same amount of powder could bring up to five years. The trial court found that 97 percent of those convicted for possessing crack were Black, while nearly 80 percent of those convicted of powder were white. The state supreme court upheld a lower court decision that there was no real distinction between the dangers posed by the two drugs.

2. 488 U.S. 361 (1989). John Mistretta, under indictment for a cocaine sale, claimed that Congress's decision to create an administrative body to set sentences violated the separation-of-powers principle and delegated excessive authority to an administrative body. The Court decided against Mistretta in an 8 to 1 decision, Justice Scalia dissenting. For the majority, Congress was well within its powers, and the delegation made sense in view of the complexity of the sentencing problem: "Developing proportionate penalties for hundreds of different crimes by a virtually limitless array of offenders is precisely the sort of intricate, labor-intensive task for which delegation to an expert body is especially appropriate." 488 U.S. at 379.

3. 347 U.S. 483 (1954).

4. See, e.g., Janice Deaton Hogan's briefs for the NACDL in *United States v. Reese*: in the district court, Crim. No. 92-234-LFO and U.S. Dist. Ct. No. CR-93-0817, and in the Ninth Circuit, USCA No. 94-50-206; and the NACDL *amicus* brief in *United States v. Walls*: in the U.S. District Court for the District of Columbia, Crim. No. 92-234-LFO (decision in *Walls*, 841 F. Supp. 24 (D.D.C. 1994)).

5. House Select Committee on Narcotics Abuse and Control, *The Federal Drug Strategy: What Does It Mean for Black America? Hearings before the Select Committee on Narcotics Abuse and Control*, statement of William J. Bennett, 101st Cong., 1st sess., September 15, 1989 (Washington, DC: Government Printing Office, 1989).

6. Ibid.

7. Ibid.

8. House Select Committee on Narcotics Abuse and Control, *The Federal Drug Strategy: What Does It Mean for Black America? Hearings Before the Select Committee on Narcotics Abuse and Control*, statement of Randolph Stone, 101st Cong., 1st sess., September 15, 1989 (Washington, DC: Government Printing Office, 1989).

9. Ibid.

10. *United States v. Clary*, 846 F. Supp. 768 (E.D. Mo. 1994).

11. 454 U.S. 370 (1982).

12. 501 U.S. 957 (1991).

13. 981 F.2d 92, 94 (3d Cir. 1992).

14. 481 U.S. 279 (1987).

15. 481 U.S. at 298 (emphasis added).

16. 34 F.3d 709, 714 (8th Cir. 1994).

17. U.S. Sup. Ct., No. 96-1492, *cert. denied*, 117 S. Ct. 3687 (1997).

18. 517 U.S. 456 (1996).

19. 48 F.3d 1508 (9th Cir. 1995).

20. Ibid., 1522 (Rymer et al. dissenting).

21. 517 U.S. at 457.

22. Ibid., 469. Rehnquist's reasoning was circular. He used statistics of the U.S. Sentencing Commission to argue that crack defendants are overwhelmingly Black. The litigation, however, was an effort to explain this pattern. Only Justice Stevens dissented, arguing that the trial judge had not abused her discretion in granting the defendant's

discovery motion because "judicial vigilance" is necessary in drug prosecutions: "The extraordinary severity of the imposed penalties and the troubling racial patterns of enforcement give rise to a special concern about the fairness of charging practices for crack offenses." 517 U.S. at 480.

23. October 11, 1995, memo addressed to "Persons Interested in Crack Cocaine Sentencing," no page number, on file with the National Association of Criminal Defense Lawyers, Washington, DC.

24. Judge Harold Greene has been most consistent in criticizing Congress and the Sentencing Commission for the Guidelines and mandatory minimums. He was one of the judges who declared the Guidelines unconstitutional before the Supreme Court had upheld them in *Mistretta*. A few years later, in *United States v. Bethancurt*, 692 F. Supp. 1427 (D.D.C. 1988), he criticized Congress for the shift in sentencing authority from judges to prosecutors.

25. The authors of the letter to Judge Weinstein were Bob Michel, Newt Gingrich, Dick Armey, Henry Hyde, Bill McCollum, Tom DeLay, Duncan Hunter, and Bill Paxton. Letter to Hon. Jack B. Weinstein, April 26, 1993.

26. As Cover noted with some exasperation, other choices were available to them besides reluctant acceptance of an unjust law: Judges could have disregarded the law in favor of conscience, they could have resigned, or they could have evaded the full effect of legal rules without challenging the law directly.

27. 7 F.3d 1506 (10th Cir. 1993), *cert. denied*, 510 U.S. 1030 (1994).

28. 7 F.3d at 1510.

29. 27 F.3d 671 (D.C. Cir.), *cert. denied*, 513 U.S. 1050 (1994).

30. 27 F.3d at 679.

31. 64 F.3d 1427 (9th Cir. 1995).

32. Ibid., 1432.

33. 985 F.2d 65 (2d Cir. 1993).

34. Ibid., 70.

35. 29 F.3d 733 (1st Cir. 1994).

36. Ibid., 741.

37. 878 F. Supp. 170 (D. Minn. 1991).

38. 864 F. Supp. 1303 (N.D. Ga. 1994).

39. Ibid., 1409.

40. 841 F. Supp. 24 (D.D.C. 1994).

41. 370 U.S. 153 (1964).

42. 857 F. Supp. 105 (D.D.C. 1994).

43. Ibid., 111–12.

44. 817 F. Supp. 176 (D.D.C. 1993).

45. See, e.g., *United States v. Buchanon*, 909 F. Supp. 99 (N.D.N.Y. 1995): "Defendant derives this novel argument from *US v. Davis*.... After careful deliberation, the Court declines to follow *Davis*." Ibid., 100.

46. *United States v. Lattimore* is the exception. Senior Judge Bright, dissenting from the court of appeals decision, found Judge Rosenbaum's arguments persuasive and suggested that the racially disparate impact of the Sentencing Guidelines should be considered as a mitigating factor in crack cases.

47. *United States v. Carolene Products*, 304 U.S. 144, 152 (1938).

48. 347 U.S. 483 (1954).

49. Public Law 88-352, *U.S. Statutes at Large* 78 (1964): 241.

50. See Gerstmann 1999. Dean Christopher Edley has argued similarly that the Court has "sucked much of the life from *Brown*" in favor of an anti-classification principle that can prevent affirmative action efforts. A. Wade Smith Memorial Lecture, April 19, 2005, Arizona State University.

51. 401 U.S. 424 (1971).

52. 426 U.S. 229 (1976).

53. Ibid., 242.

54. Since the *Davis* case, these statutory-based cases have become an important source of protections for plaintiffs complaining of race, sex, and now age discrimination from employers. A recent case announced that deliberate discrimination is not necessary in cases brought under the federal Age Discrimination in Employment Act (ADEA), Public Law 90-202, *U.S. Statutes at Large* 81 (1967): 602. It is enough to show harm because of a policy that went beyond "reasonable" business considerations. *Smith v. City of Jackson, Mississippi*, 544 U.S. 228 (2005), *affirming* 351 F.3d 183 (5th Cir. 2003).

55. 426 U.S. at 242.

56. Ibid.

57. 163 U.S. 537 (1896).

58. Public Law 90-202, *U.S. Statutes at Large* 81 (1967): 602.

59. *Syvock v. Milwaukee Boiler Manufacturing Co.*, 665 F.2d 149, 155 (7th Cir. 1981), quoting volume 113 of the *Congressional Record* at pp. 34, 742.

Epilogue

1. Bureau of Justice Statistics, U.S. Department of Justice, "Prisoners in 2005," http://www.ojp.usdoj.gov/bjs/abstract/p05.htm.

2. Members of Congress critical of the mandatory minimums have taken chairships of the Judiciary Committee in each chamber. Senator Jeff Sessions chairs the Senate Judiciary Committee, and Representative John Conyers Jr. chairs the House committee.

3. The issue of whether federal district judges are still obligated to follow the Guidelines in sentencing crack defendants, however, has divided the federal circuits and is currently under appeal in the U.S. Supreme Court in *Claiborne v. United States*, No. 06-5618, on writ of certiorari from the U.S. Court of Appeals for the Eighth Circuit.

references

Altheide, David L. (2002). *Creating Fear: News and the Construction of Crisis.* New York: Aldine de Gruyter.

———. (2004). "Ethnographic Content Analysis." In *Encyclopedia of Social Science Research Methods,* ed. Michael S. Lewis-Beck, Alan Bryman, and Tim Futing Liao, 325–26. New York: Russell Sage Foundation.

American Bar Association. (2003). *Justice Kennedy Commission Recommendations.* October. http://www.abanet.org/medic/jkcrecs.html.

———. (1999). *Code of the Street: Decency, Violence, and the Moral Life of the Inner City.* New York: Norton.

Andreae, Percy. (1915). *The Prohibition Movement in Its Broader Bearings upon Our Social, Commercial, and Religious Liberties.* Chicago: Mendelsohn.

Anslinger, H. J. (1937a). Statement on HR 6385. House of Representatives, Committee on Ways and Means. 75th Cong., 1st sess., April 27–30 and May 4.

———. (1937b). Statement on HR 6906. U.S Senate, Subcommittee of the Committee on Finance. 75th Cong., 1st sess., July 12.

———. (1951). *U.S. News and World Report.* June 29, 18–19.

Anslinger, H. J., and Courtnery Ryley Cooper. (1937). "Marijuana: Assassin of Youth." *American Magazine,* July. Reprinted in *The American Drug Scene: An Anthology,* 2nd ed., ed. James A. Inciardi and Karen McElrath. Los Angeles: Roxbury.

Anslinger, H. J., and Will Oursler. (1961). *The Murderers: The Story of the Narcotic Gangs.* New York: Farrar, Straus, and Cudahy.

Anslinger, H. J., and William F. Tompkins. (1953). *The Traffic in Narcotics.* New York: Funk and Wagnalls.

Asbury, Herbert. (1950). *The Great Illusion: An Informal History of Prohibition.* Garden City, NY: Doubleday.

Bailey, Pearce. (1916). "The Heroin Habit." *New Republic,* April 22, 314–16.

Baker, Ray Stannard. (1904/1973). *Following the Color Line: An Account of Negro Citizenship in the American Democracy.* Repr. Williamstown, MA: Corner House Publishers.

Banaji, M. R., and A. G. Greenwald. (1995). "Implicit Social Cognition: Attitudes, Self-Esteem, and Stereotypes." *Psychological Review* 102 (1): 4–27.

Baum, Dan. (1996). *Smoke and Mirrors: The War on Drugs and the Politics of Failure.* Boston: Little, Brown.

Becker, Howard S. (1973). *Outsiders: Studies in the Sociology of Deviance.* New York: Free Press.

Beckett, Katherine. (1997). *Making Crime Pay: Law and Order in Contemporary Politics.* New York: Oxford University Press.

Beckett, Katherine, Kris Nyrop, and Lori Pfingst. (2006). "Race, Drugs, and Policing: Understanding Disparities in Drug Delivery Arrests." *Criminology* 44 (1): 105–38.

Beckett, Katherine, Kris Nyrop, Lori Pfingst, and Melissa Bowen. (2005). "Drug Use, Drug Arrests, and the Question of Race: Lessons from Seattle." *Social Problems* 52 (3): 419–41.

Beckett, Katherine, and Theodore Sasson. (1997). "The Media and the Construction of the Drug Crisis in America." In *The New War on Drugs: Symbolic Politics and Criminal Justice Policy,* ed. Eric L. Jensen and Jerg Gerber, 25–43. Cincinnati: Anderson.

———. (2000). The Politics of Injustice: Crime and Punishment in America. Thousand Oaks, CA: Pine Forge.

Behr, Edward. (1997). *Prohibition: Thirteen Years That Changed America.* New York: Arcade.

Belenko, Steven R. (1993). *Crack and the Evolution of Anti-Drug Policy.* Westport, CT: Greenwood Press.

Bell, Daniel. (1960). *The End of Ideology.* Glencoe, IL: Free Press of Glencoe.

Bell, Derrick. (1995). "Racial Realism—After We're Gone: Prudent Speculations on America in a Post-Racial Epoch." In *Critical Race Theory: The Cutting Edge,* ed. Richard Delgado, 2–8. Philadelphia: Temple University Press.

Bergman, Carol. (1998). "The Politics of Federal Sentencing Reform." *Federal Sentencing Reporter* 10 (4): 196–99.

Berman, Zachary L. (2003). "Judge Martin Leaves Bench Critical of Sentencing Rules." *New York Law Journal* 230: 1.

Berridge, Virginia. (1977). "Fenland Opium Eating in the Nineteenth Century." *British Journal of Addiction* 72: 275–84.

Blakeslee, Nate. (2005). *Tulia: Race, Cocaine, and Corruption in a Small Texas Town.* New York: Public Affairs Books.

Blume, John H., Theodore Eisenberg, and Sheri Lynn Johnson. (1998). "Post-*McCleskey* Discrimination Claims in Capital Cases." *Cornell Law Review* 83: 1771–1810.

Blumenson, Eric, and Eva Nilsen. (1998). "Policing for Profit: The Drug War's Hidden Economic Agenda." *University of Chicago Law Review* 65 (Winter): 35–114.

Blumstein, Alfred. (1993). "Racial Disproportionality of U.S. Prison Populations Revisited." *University of Colorado Law Review* 64: 743–60.

Blythe, Paul. (1986). "Cocaine Rocks: The New Epidemic." A series of articles by Paul Blythe in the *Palm Beach Post & Evening Times.* Reprinted in *Congressional Record* 132 (April 22, 1986): S 4668.

Bobo, Lawrence D. (2004). "Inequalities That Endure? Racial Ideology, American Politics, and the Peculiar Role of the Social Sciences." In *The Changing Terrain of Race and Ethnicity,* ed. Maria Krysan and Amanda Lewis, 13–42. New York: Russell Sage Foundation.

Bobo, Lawrence D., and Ryan A. Smith. (1998). "From Jim Crow Racism to Laissez-Faire Racism: The Transformation of Racial Attitudes." In *Beyond Pluralism: The*

Conception of Groups and Identities in America, ed. Wendy F. Katkin, Ned Landsman, and Andrea Tyree, 182–220. Urbana: University of Illinois Press.

Bonilla-Silva, Eduardo. (1996). "Rethinking Racism: Toward a Structural Interpretation." *American Sociological Review* 62: 465–80.

Bonnie, Richard J., and Charles H. Whitebread II. (1974). *The Marihuana Conviction: History of Marihuana Prohibition in the United States.* Charlottesville: University Press of Virginia.

Booth, Martin. (1996). *Opium, A History.* London: Simon and Schuster.

Bordin, Ruth. (1990). *Women and Temperance: The Quest for Power and Liberty, 1873–1900.* New Brunswick, NJ: Rutgers University Press.

Bourgois, Philippe. (1995). *In Search of Respect: Selling Crack in El Barrio.* Cambridge: Cambridge University Press.

Braithwaite, John. (2000). "Republican Theory and Crime Control." In *Social Dynamics of Crime and Control: New Theories for a World in Transition*, ed. Susanne Karstedt and Kai-D Bussmann, 85–103. Portland, OR: Hart.

Breyer, Stephen. (1988). "The Federal Sentencing Guidelines and the Key Compromises Upon Which They Rest." *Hofstra Law Review* 17: 1–50.

Bromwich, Michael R. (1999). "Put a Stop to Savage Sentencing." *Washington Post*, November 2, A23.

Brook, Timothy, and Bob Tadashi Wakabayashi. (2000). *Opium Regimes: China, Britain, and Japan, 1839–1952.* Berkeley: University of California Press.

Brown, Kevin. (2005). *Race, Law, and Education in the Post-desegregation Era: Four Perspectives on Desegregation and Re-segregation.* Durham, NC: Carolina Academic Press.

Brown, Michael K., Martin Carnoy, Elliott Currie, Troy Duster, David B. Oppenheimer, Marjorie M. Shulty, and David Wellman. (2003). *Whitewashing Race: The Myth of a Society.* Berkeley: University of California Press.

Brummett, Pamela, Robert Edgar, Neil Hackett, George Gensbuy, Alastair Taylor, Nels Bailkey, Clyde Lewis, and Thomas Wallbank. (1999). *Civilizations Past and Present.* New York: Longman.

Bureau of Justice Statistics. (2005). "Prisoners in 2005." http://www.ojp.usdoj.gov/bjs/abstract/p05.htm.

Burke, Kenneth. (1989). *On Symbols and Society.* Ed. and with an introduction by Joseph Gusfield. Chicago: University of Chicago Press.

Butler, Paul. (2003). "Affirmative Action and the Criminal Law." In *Crime Control and Social Justice: The Delicate Balance*, ed. Darnell F. Hawkins, Samuel L. Meyers Jr., and Randolph N. Stone, 373–414. Westport, CT: Greenwood Press.

Butterfield, Fox. (2003). "With Cash Tight, States Reassess Long Jail Terms." *New York Times*, November 10, A1, A16.

Cabranes, Jose. (1992). "The Federal Sentencing Guidelines: A Dismal Failure." Speech delivered to the University of Chicago Law School, January 15.

Calavita, Kitty. (2000). "The Paradoxes of Race, Class, Identity, and 'Passing': Enforcing the Chinese Exclusion Acts, 1882–1910." *Law & Social Inquiry* 25 (1): 1–40.

_____. (2006). "Collisions at the Intersection of Gender, Race, and Class: Enforcing the Chinese Exclusion Laws." *Law & Society Review* 40 (2): 249–82.

Carmody, Chris. (1993). "Revolt to Sentencing Is Gaining Momentum." *National Law Journal*, May 17, 10.

Cavender, Gray. (2004). "Media and Crime Policy: A Reconsideration of David Garland's
    The Culture of Control." Punishment and Society 6: 335–48.
Chambliss, William J. (1995). "Crime Control and Ethnic Minorities: Legitimizing Racial
    Oppression by Creating Moral Panics." In *Ethnicity, Race, and Crime: Perspectives
    across Time and Place*, ed. Darnell F. Hawkins, 235–58. Albany: State University Press
    of New York.
———. (1999). *Power, Politics, and Crime.* Boulder, CO: Westview Press.
———. (2003). "Drug War Politics: Racism, Corruption, and Alienation." In *Crime Control
    and Social Justice: The Delicate Balance*, ed. Darnell F. Hawkins, Samuel L. Meyers Jr.,
    and Randolph N. Stone, 295–318. Westport, CT: Greenwood Press.
Chilton, Roland. (2001). "Viable Policy: The Impact of Federal Funding and the Need for
    Independent Research Agendas—The American Society of Criminology 2000 Presi-
    dential Address." *Criminology* 39 (1): 1–8.
Chiricos, Ted, Kelly Welch, and Marc Gertz. (2004). "Racial Typification of Crime and
    Support for Punitive Measures." *Criminology* 42: 359–89.
Cohen, Stanley. (1972). *Folk Devils and Moral Panics: The Creation of the Mods and
    Rockers.* London: MacGibbon and Kee.
———. (1980). *Folk Devils and Moral Panics: The Creation of the Mods and Rockers*, with
    new introduction. London: Martin Robertson.
———. (1987). *Folk Devils and Moral Panics: The Creation of the Mods and Rockers.* 2nd
    ed. London: Basil Blackwell.
———. (2002). *Folk Devils and Moral Panics: The Creation of the Mods and Rockers.* 3rd
    ed. New York: Routledge.
Cole, David. (2000). *No Equal Justice: Race and Class in the American Criminal Justice
    System.* New York: New Press.
Cornell, Stephen, and Douglas Hartmann. (2004). "Conceptual Confusions and Divides:
    Race, Ethnicity, and the Study of Immigration." In *Not Just Black and White: Histori-
    cal and Contemporary Perspectives on Immigration, Race, and Ethnicity in the United
    States*, ed. Nancy Foner and George M. Fredrickson, 23–41. New York: Russell Sage
    Foundation.
Corning, Leonard. (1908). "The Growing Menace of the Use of Cocaine." *New York
    Times*, August 2, Magazine section, pt. 5.
Cortwright, David T. (2001). *Dark Paradise: A History of Opiate Addiction in America.*
    Cambridge, MA: Harvard University Press.
Cover, Robert M. (1975). *Justice Accused: Antislavery and the Judicial Process.* New Ha-
    ven, CT: Yale University Press.
Crowe, Charles. (1968). "Racial Violence and Social Reform—Origins of the Atlanta Riot
    of 1906." *Journal of Negro History* 53: 234–56.
Curtin, John T. (1997). "Why a Federal Judge Concludes Drug Legalization Is the Way to
    Go." *Buffalo News*, March 2, at 3.
Dabney, Virginius. (1949). *Dry Messiah: The Life of Bishop Cannon.* New York: Knopf.
Davis, Angela Y. (2005). *Abolition Democracy: Beyond Empire, Prisons, and Torture.* New
    York: Seven Stories Press.
De Genova, Nicholas. (2005). *Working the Boundaries: Race, Space, and "Illegality" in
    Mexican Chicago.* Durham, NC: Duke University Press.
Denzlinger, Jerry D., and David E. Miller. (1991). "The Federal Probation Officer: Life
    Before and After Guideline Sentencing." *Federal Probation* 55 (4): 49–53.

De Quincey, Thomas. (1898). *The Opium-Eater and Essays*. London: Ward, Lock.

Devine, Patricia G. (1989). "Stereotype and Prejudice: Their Automatic Controlled Components." *Journal of Personality and Social Psychology* 56: 5–18.

Devine, Patricia G., E. G. Plant, D. M. Amodio, E. Harmon-Jones, and S. L. Vance. (2002). "The Regulation of Explicit and Implicit Race Bias: The Role of Motivations to Respond Without Prejudice. *Journal of Personality and Social Psychology* 82: 835–48.

Dewoy, Ann. (1995). "Clinton Retains Tough Law on Crack Cocaine: Panel's Call to End Disparity in Drug Sentencing Is Rejected." *Washington Post*, October 31.

Dittmer, John. (1977). *Black Georgia in the Progressive Era, 1900–20*. Urbana: University of Illinois Press.

Donziger, Steven R., ed. (1996). *The Real War on Crime: The Report of the National Criminal Justice Commission*. New York: HarperCollins.

Douglas, Mary. (1986). *How Institutions Think*. Syracuse, NY: Syracuse University Press.

Dovidio, John F., Nancy Evans, and Richard B. Tyler. (1986). "Racial Stereotypes: The Contents of Their Cognitive Representations." *Journal of Experimental Social Psychology* 22: 22–37.

Dovidio, John F., and S. L. Gaertner. (2000). "Aversive Racism and Selection Decisions: 1989 and 1999." *Psychological Science* 11: 315–19.

Duster, Troy. (1970). *The Legislation of Morality*. New York: Free Press.

_____. (1997). "Pattern, Purpose, and Race in the Drug War: The Crisis of Credibility in Criminal Justice." In *Crack in America: Demon Drugs and Social Justice*, ed. Craig Reinarman and Harry G. Levine, 260–87. Berkeley: University of California Press.

Eagly, Alice, and Shelly Chaiken. (1998). *The Psychology of Attitudes*. Fort Worth, TX: Harcourt Brace Jovanovich.

Edelman, Murray (1988). *Constructing the Political Spectacle*. Chicago: University of Chicago Press.

Elliot, James. (1881). "The Opium Traffic." *British Medical Journal* 2: 29–31.

Edsall, Thomas Byrne, and Mary D. Edsall. (1991). *Chain Reaction: The Impact of Race, Rights, and Taxes on American Politics*. New York: Norton.

Elwood, William N. (1994). *Rhetoric in the War on Drugs: The Triumphs and Tragedies of Public Relations*. Westport, CT: Praeger.

Erickson, Patricia G., and Jennifer Butters. (1998). The Emerging Harm Reduction Movement: The De-Escalation of the War on Drugs?" In *The New War on Drugs: Symbolic Politics and Criminal Justice Policy*, ed. Eric L. Jensen and Jurg Gerber, 177–196. Cincinnati: Anderson.

Everett, Ronald S. (1998). "The Evolution of the federal Sentencing Guidelines for Crack Cocaine: Social Construction and Social Control." In *The New War on Drugs: Symbolic Politics and Criminal Justice Policy*, ed. Eric L. Jensen and Jurg Gerber, 91–106. Cincinnati: Anderson.

Federal Judicial Center. (1996). *Federal Judicial Center Survey*. http://www.sentencing .org1judge.html.

Fiske, Susan T., and Shelley E. Taylor. (1991). *Social Cognition*. New York: McGraw Hill.

Flaherty, Mary Pat, and Joan Biskupic. (1996a). "Prosecutors Can Stack the Deck: Sentencing Powers Shift from Judges." *Washington Post*, October 2, 1, A12, A13.

_____. (1996b). "Rules Often Impose Toughest Penalties on Poor, Minorities." *Washington Post*, October 9, A26.

Fletcher, George P. (1988). *The Crime of Self Defense: Bernard Goetz and the Law on Trial.* Chicago: University of Chicago Press.

Fossier, A. E. (1931). "The Marijuana Menace." *New Orleans Medical and Surgical Journal* 84 (4): 247–50.

Foxcraft, Frank. (1908). "Prohibition in the South." *Atlantic Monthly*, May, 627–34.

Frankel, Marvin E. (1973). *Criminal Sentences: Law without Order.* New York: Hill and Wang.

Franklin, Jimmie Lewis. (1971). *Born Sober: Prohibition in Oklahoma, 1907–1959.* Norman: University of Oklahoma Press.

Franklin, John Hope, and Alfred A. Moss Jr. (1988). *From Slavery to Freedom: A History of Negro Americans.* 6th ed. New York: Knopf.

Freed, Daniel J. (1992). "Federal Sentencing in the Wake of Guidelines: Unacceptable Limits on the Discretion of Sentences." *Yale Law Journal* 101: 1681–1754.

Frymer, Paul. (2005). "Racism Revised: Courts, Labor Law, and the Institutional Construction of Racial Animus." *American Political Science Review* 99 (3): 373–87.

Gallup Institute. (1986). "Most Important Problem." Gallup Report No. 252: 27–29.

Garland, David. (2001). *The Culture of Control: Crime and Social Order in Contemporary Society.* Chicago: University of Chicago Press.

George Bush Presidential Library and Museum. (1989). "Address to the Nation on the National Drug Control Strategy." September 5. http://bushlibrary.tamu.edu/research/papers/1989/89090502.html.

Gerber, Rudolph J. (2004). *Legalizing Marijuana: Drug Policy Reform and Prohibition Politics.* Westport, CT: Praeger.

Gerstmann, Evan. (1999). *The Constitutional Underclass: Gays, Lesbians, and the Future of Class-Based Equal Protection.* Chicago: University of Chicago Press.

Gest, Ted. (2001). *Crime and Politics: Big Government's Erratic Campaign for Law and Order.* New York: Oxford University Press.

Gilens, Marin. (1999). *Why Americans Hate Welfare.* Chicago: University of Chicago Press.

Goffman, Erving. (1974). *Frame Analysis.* New York: Harper & Row.

Golub, Andrew Lang, and Bruce D. Johnson. (1997). *Crack's Decline: Some Surprises Across U.S. Cities.* National Institute of Justice, NCJ 165707, July 1997: Research in Brief. http://www.ncjrs.gov/pdffiles/165707.pdf.

Gonzales, Alberto. (2005). "Prepared Remarks of Attorney General Alberto Gonzales." Press conference, Nashville, Tennessee, August 18. http://www.usdoj.gov/ag/speeches/2005/081805agmethamphetamine.htm.

Goode, Erich. (1990). "The American Drug Panic." *International Journal of Addictions* 25: 1083–98.

Goode, Erich, and Nachman Ben-Yehuda. (1994a). "Moral Panics: Culture, Politics, and Social Construction." *Annual Review of Sociology* 20: 149–71.

———. (1994b). *Moral Panics: The Social Construction of Deviance.* Cambridge, MA: Blackwell.

Gordon, Diana R. (1994). *Return of the Dangerous Classes: Drug Prohibition and Policy Politics.* New York: Norton.

Gordon, Ernest. (1943). *The Wrecking of the Eighteenth Amendment.* Francestown, NH: Alcohol Information Press.

Grantham, Dewey W. (1983). *Southern Progressivism: The Reconciliation of Progress and Tradition.* Knoxville: University of Tennessee Press.

Graves, John Temple. (1908). "The Fight Against Alcohol: Third Article—Georgia Pioneers the Prohibition Crusade." *Cosmopolitan* 45: 83–90.

Gray, Mike. (2000). *Drug Crazy: How We Got into This Mess and How We Can Get Out.* New York: Routledge.

Greenberg, David F. (2003). "'Justice' and Criminal Justice." In *Crime Control and Social Justice: The Delicate Balance,* ed. Darnell F. Hawkins, Samuel L. Meyers Jr., and Randolph N. Stone, 319–54. Westport, CT: Greenwood Press.

Greenberg, David F., and Valerie West. (2001). "State Prison Populations and Their Growth, 1971–91." *Criminology* 39 (3): 615–54.

Guinier, Lani, and Gerald Torres. (2002). *The Miner's Canary: Enlisting Race, Resisting Power, Transforming Democracy.* Cambridge, MA: Harvard University Press.

Gusfield, Joseph. (1986). *Symbolic Crusade: Status Politics and the American Temperance Movement.* 2nd ed. Urbana: University of Illinois Press.

Hagan, John. (1995). "Rethinking Crime Theory and Policy: The New Sociology of Crime and Disrepute." In *Crime and Public Policy: Putting Theory to Work,* ed. Hugh D. Barlow, 29–42. Boulder, CO: Westview Press.

Hanes, W. Travis, III, and Frank Sanello. (2002). *Opium Wars: The Addiction of One Empire and the Corruption of Another.* Naperville, IL: Sourcebooks.   .

Harcourt, Bernard E. (2003). "From the Ne'er-Do-Well to the Criminal History Category: The Refinement of the Actuarial Model in Criminal Law." *Law and Contemporary Problems* 66: 99–151.

Hartley, Roger E., and Lisa A. Holmes. (2002). "The Increasing Senate Scrutiny of Lower Federal Court Nominees." *Political Science Quarterly* 117 (2): 259–78.

Hawdon, James E. (1996). "Cycles of Deviance: Structural Change, Moral Boundaries, and Drug Use, 1880–1990." *Sociological Spectrum* 16: 183–207.

_____. (2001). "The Role of Presidential Rhetoric in the Creation of a Moral Panic: Reagan, Bush, and the War on Drugs." *Deviant Behavior* 22 (September): 419–45.

Hawk, Kathleen M. (1996). "Interview: Bureau of Prisons Director Kathleen Hawk Values Judges' Contributions." *The Third Branch.* Washington, DC: Government Printing Office.

Hawkins, Darnell F., ed. (1995). *Ethnicity, Race, and Crime: Perspectives across Time and Place.* Albany: State University of New York Press.

_____. (2003). "On the Horns of a Dilemma: Criminal Wrongs, Civil Rights, and the Administration of Justice in African-American Communities." In *Crime Control and Social Justice: The Delicate Balance,* ed. Darnell F. Hawkins, Samuel L. Meyers Jr., and Randolph N. Stone, 431–58. Westport, CT: Greenwood Press.

Helmer, John. (1975). *Drugs and Minority Oppression.* New York: Seabury.

Higginbotham, Leon A. (1996). *Shades of Freedom: Racial Politics and Presumptions of the American Legal Process.* New York: Oxford University Press.

Inciardi, James A. (1992). *The War on Drugs II: The Continuing Epic of Heroin, Cocaine, Crack, Crime, and Public Policy.* Mountain View, CA: Mayfield.

Irwin, Will. (1908). "More about 'Nigger Gin.'" *Collier's Weekly* 41: 28–30.

Isikoff, Michael. (1995). "Crack, Coke, and Race." *Newsweek,* November 6.

Jacobs, Bruce. (1999). *Dealing Crack: The Social World of Streetcorner Selling.* Boston: Northeastern University Press.

Jacobs, David, and Jason Carmichael. (2002). "The Political Sociology of the Death Penalty: A Pooled Time Series Analysis." *American Sociological Review* 67: 109–31.

Jacobson, Matthew Frye. (1998). *Whiteness of a Different Color: European Immigrants and the Alchemy of Race.* Cambridge, MA: Harvard University Press.

Jacobson, Michael. (2006). "Reversing the Punitive Turn: The Limits and Promise of Current Research." *Criminology and Public Policy* 5 (2): 277–84.

Jaffe, Jerome H. (2002). "One Bite of the Apple: Establishing the Special Action Office for Drug Abuse Prevention." In *One Hundred Years of Heroin*, ed. David Musto, with the assistance of Pamela Korsmeyer and Thomas W. Maulucci Jr., 43–53. Westport, CT: Auburn House.

Jensen, Eric L., and Jurg Gerber. (1998). "The Social Construction of Drug Problems: An Historical Overview." In *The New War on Drugs: Symbolic Politics and Criminal Justice Policy*, ed. Eric L. Jensen and Jurg Gerber, 1–24. Cincinnati: Anderson.

Jensen, Eric L., Jurg Gerber, and Ginna Babcock. (1991). "The New War on Drugs: Grass Roots Movement or Political Construction?" *Journal of Drug Issues* 21: 651–67.

Johnson, John M. (1995). "In Dispraise of Justice." *Symbolic Interaction* 18 (2): 191–205.

Johnson, Kerin. "Rioting Inmates Locked Away." (1995). *USA Today*, October 23.

Johnson, Thomas J., and Wayne Wanta, with Timothy Boudreau, Janet Blank-Libra, Killian Schaffer, and Sally Turner. (1996). "Influence Dealers: A Path Analysis Model of Agenda Building During Richard Nixon's War on Drugs." *Journalism and Mass Communication Quarterly* 73: 181–94.

Kansal, Tushar, and Marc Mauer. (2005). *Racial Disparity in Sentencing: A Review of the Literature.* Washington, DC: Sentencing Project.

Katzenbach Commission. (1967). *The Challenge of Crime in a Free Society.* Report of President Johnson's Commission on Crime. Washington, DC: Government Printing Office.

Katznelson, Ira. (2005). *When Affirmative Action Was White: An Untold History of Racial Inequality in Twentieth-Century America.* New York: Norton.

Kaufman, Stuart B., Peter Albert, and Grace Palladino, eds. (1996). *An Expanding Movement at the Turn of the Century, 1898–1902.* Vol. 5 of *The Samuel Gompers Papers.* Urbana: University of Illinois.

Kautt, Paula. (2001–2). "Differential Usage of Guideline Standards by Defendant Race and Gender in Federal Drug Sentences: Fact or Fiction?" *Federal Sentencing Reporter* 14 (3–4): 159–64.

Kennedy, Randall. (1997). *Race, Crime, and the Law.* New York: Pantheon.

Kerr, K. Austin. (1973). *The Politics of Moral Behavior: Prohibition and Drug Abuse.* Reading, MA: Addison-Wesley.

Kinder, Donald R., and Lynn M. Sanders. (1996). *Divided by Color: Racial Politics and Democratic Ideals.* Chicago: University of Chicago Press.

King, Ryan S. (2006). *The Next Big Thing? Methamphetamine in the United States.* Washington, DC: Sentencing Project.

King, Ryan S., and Marc Mauer. (2002). *Distorted Priorities: Drug Offenders in State Prisons.* Washington, DC: Sentencing Project.

———. (2005). *The War on Marijuana: The Transformation of the War on Drugs in the 1990s.* Washington, DC: Sentencing Project.

———. (2006). "Statement on Domestic Criminal Justice Issues in the United States and the International Covenant on Civil and Political Rights." March 17. http://www.sentencingproject.org/pdfs/iccpr-statement.pdf.

Kleber, Herbert D. (2002). "Methadone: The Drug, the Treatment, the Controversy." In *One Hundred Years of Heroin*, ed. David F. Musto, with the assistance of Pamela Korsmeyer and Thomas W. Maulucci Jr., 149–58. Westport, CT: Auburn House.

Krieger, Linda Hamilton. (1995). "The Content of Our Categories: A Cognitive Bias Approach to Discrimination and Equal Employment Opportunity." *Stanford Law Review* 47: 1161–1248.

Krieger, Linda Hamilton, and Susan Fiske. (2006). "Behavioral Realism in Employment Discrimination Law." *University of California at Los Angeles Law Review* 94: 997–1062.

Kyvig, David. (2000). *Repealing National Prohibition.* 2nd ed. Kent, OH: Kent State University Press.

Lampman, Rex H. (1924). "Heroin Heroes: An Interview with Capt. Richmond Pearson Hobson." *Saturday Evening Post,* September 20, 41–42.

Lauderdale, Pat, and James Inverarity. (1984). "Rationalizaiton of Economy and Bureaucracy: The Regulation of Opiates." *Journal of Drug Issues* 14: 567–78.

Lawrence, Sarah, and Jeremy Travis. (2004). *The New Landscape of Imprisonment: Mapping America's Prison Expansion.* Washington, DC: Urban Institute. http://www.urban.org/url.cfm?ID=410994.

Lieberman, Robert C. (2002). "Ideas, Institutions, and Political Order: Explaining Political Change." *American Political Science Review* 96: 697–712.

Literary Digest. (1914). "This Drug-Endangered Nation." March 28, 687–88.

López, Ian F. Haney. (1996). *White by Law: The Legal Construction of Race.* New York: New York Times.

Lusane, Clarence. (1991). *Pipe Dream Blues: Racism and the War on Drugs.* Boston: South End Press.

Lynch, Mona. (2002). "Pedophiles and Cyber-predators as Contaminating Forces: The Language of Disgust, Pollution, and Boundary Invasions in Federal Debates on Sex Offender Legislation." *Law & Social Inquiry* 27: 529–66.

Manski, Charles F., John V. Pepper, and Carol V. Petrie, eds. (2001). *Informing America's Policy on Illegal Drugs.* Washington, DC: National Academy Press.

Manza, Jeff, and Christopher Uggen. (2006). *Locked Out: Felon Disenfranchisement and American Democracy.* New York: Oxford University Press.

Mattingly, Carol. (1998). *Well-Tempered Women: Nineteenth Century Temperance Rhetoric.* Carbondale: Southern Illinois University Press.

Mauer, Marc. (2004). "Race, Class, and the Development of Criminal Justice Policy." *Review of Policy Research* 21: 79–92.

———. (2006). "Incarceration Nation." December 11. http://www.tompaine.com/articles/2006/12/11/incarceration_nation.php.

Mauer, Marc, and Meda Chesney-Lind. (2002). *Invisible Punishment: The Collateral Consequences of Mass Imprisonment.* New York: New Press.

McKelway, A. J. (1907). "State Prohibition in Georgia and the South." *Outlook,* August 31, 947–49.

McKillop, Peter. (1986). "Crack and Crime" and "An Inferno of Craving, Dealing and Despair." *Newsweek,* June 16. Reprinted in *Congressional Record* 132 (June 9, 1986): S 7123.

McWilliams, John C. (in press). *From Demon Rum to Crack Cocaine: A Social History of Drugs, Race, Class, and Control.* Unpublished manuscript.

Meares, Tracey L., and Dan M. Kahan. (1999). *Urgent Times: Policing and Rights in Inner-City Communities.* Boston: Beacon Press.

Meierhoefer, Barbara. (1992a). *The General Effect of Mandatory Minimum Prison Terms: A Longitudinal Study.* Washington, DC: Federal Judicial Center.

_____. (1992b). "The Role of Offense and Offender Characteristics in Federal Sentencing." *Southern California Law Review* 66: 367–97.

_____. (1999). "The Severity of Drug Sentences: A Result of Purpose or Chance?" *Federal Sentencing Reporter* 12 (1): 34–36.

Mendelberg, Tali. (2001). *The Race Card: Campaign Strategy, Implicit Messages, and the Norm of Equality*. Princeton, NJ: Princeton University Press.

Mercury News. (2006). "Crack Cocaine Sentencing Guidelines Need Changes." November 16. http://www.mercurynews.com/mld/mercurynews/news/opinion/16025819.htm.

Mettler, Suzanne. (2005). *Soldiers to Citizens: The G.I. Bill and the Making of the Greatest Generation*. New York: Oxford University Press.

Miller, Jerome G. (1996). *Search and Destroy: African American Males in the Criminal Justice System*. Cambridge: Cambridge University Press.

Miller, Lisa L., and James Eisenstein. (2005). "The Federal/State Criminal Prosecution Nexus: A Case Study in Cooperation and Discretion." *Law & Social Inquiry* 30 (2): 239–68.

Mills, Charles W. (1997). *The Racial Contract*. Ithaca, NY: Cornell University Press.

Mirandé, Alfredo. (1987). *Gringo Justice*. Notre Dame, IN: University of Notre Dame Press.

Mohamed, Rafik, and Erik Fritsvold. (2006). "Damn, It Feels Good to be a Gansta: The Social Organization of the Illicit Drug Trade Servicing a Private College Campus." *Deviant Behavior* 27: 97–125.

Monahan, M. (1909). *A Text-Book of True Temperance*. Ed. and comp. M. Monahan. New York: U.S. Brewers' Association.

Morgan, H. Wayne. (1981). *Drugs in America: A Social History, 1800–1880*. Syracuse, NY: Syracuse University Press.

Morris, Edmund. (2002). *Theodore Rex*. New York: Modern Library.

Moses, Jonathan M. "Many Judges Skirt Sentencing Guidelines." (1993). *Wall Street Journal*, May 7, B12.

Musto, David. (1973). *The American Disease: Origins of Narcotic Control*. New Haven, CT: Yale University Press.

_____. (1992). "Patterns in U.S. Drug Abuse and Response." In *Drug Policy in the Americas*, ed. Peter H. Smith, 29–44. Boulder, CO: Westview Press.

_____. (1999). *The American Disease: Origins of Narcotic Control*. 3rd ed. New York: Oxford University Press.

_____. (2002). "The History of Legislative Control over Opium, Cocaine, and Their Derivatives." Schaffer Library of Drug Policy. October 4. http://www.druglibrary.org/schaffer/History/ophs.htm.

_____, ed., with the assistance of Pamela Korsmeyer and Thomas W. Maulucci Jr. (2002). *One Hundred Years of Heroin*. Westport, CT: Auburn House.

Musto, David, and Pamela Korsmeyer. (2002). *The Quest for Drug Control: Politics and Federal Policy in a Period of Increasing Substance Abuse, 1963–1981*. New Haven, CT: Yale University Press.

National African American Drug Policy Coalition. (2004). "African American Professional Organizations Launch Historic Collaboration to Change Drug Policies." Press release, October 20.

National Association for the Advancement of Colored People. (2005). *Voter Reenfranchisement*. http://www.naacp.org/programs/vote/vote_reenfranchisement.html.

Neubeck, Kenneth J., and Noel A. Cazenave. (2001). *Welfare Racism: Playing the Race Card Against America's Poor.* New York: Routledge.

New York Times. (1905). "Negro Cocaine Evil." March 20, 14.

New York Times. (1934a). "Use of Marijuana Spreading in West: Children Said to Buy It." September 16.

New York Times. (1934b). "Narcotic Cigarettes Seized as 3 Are Held." October 8.

New York Times. (1934c). "Narcotic 'Garden' Found In Brooklyn: 1,000 Cigarettes Seized." October 18.

New York Times. (1934d). "Narcotic Bonfire Routs Officials." October 19.

New York Times. (1934e). "Brooklyn and Baghdad." October 20.

New York Times. (1934f). "Nation-wide Raids Jail 560 in Federal Narcotic Drive: 15 Arrested in New York." December 9.

New York Times. (1934g). "Narcotic Seizures Go On, Reach 765: Addicts Kindly Treated." December 10.

New York Times. (1934h). "Narcotic Arrests Are Raised to 793." December 11.

New York Times. (1944). "Marijuana Camp Sales Fought." February 5.

Ngai, Mai. (2004). *Impossible Subjects: Illegal Aliens and the Making of Modern America.* Princeton, NJ: Princeton University Press.

Nolan, James L., Jr. (2001). *Reinventing Justice: The American Drug Court Movement.* Princeton, NJ: Princeton University Press.

Oakley, Imogen B. (1973). "The Prohibition Law and the Political Machine." In *The Politics of Moral Behavior*, ed. K. Austin Kerr. Reading, MA: Addison Wesley.

Office of National Drug Control Policy. (2003). "Cocaine: November 2003." http://www.whitehousedrugpolicy.gov/publications/factsht/cocaine/.

O'Kane, James M. (1992). *The Crooked Ladder: Gangsters, Ethnicity, and the American Dream.* New Brunswick, NJ: Transaction.

Omi, Michael, and Howard Winant. (1994). *Racial Formation in the United States.* 2nd ed. New York: Routledge.

O'Neill, Thomas J. (1981). "The Language of Equality in a Constitutional Order." *American Political Science Review* 75 (3): 626–35.

O'Neill, Timothy J. (2003). Review of *Diversity in America. Law and Politics Book Review* 13 (8). http://www.bsos.umd.edu/gvpt/lpbr/subpages/reviews/Schuck03.htm.

"Opium throughout History." (1998). *Frontline.* PBS Online. http://www.pbs.org/wgbh/pages/frontline/shows/heroin/etc/history.html.

Orcutt, J. D., and J. B. Turner. (1993). "Shocking Numbers and Graphic Accounts: Quantified Images of Drug Problems in the Print Media." *Social Problems* 40: 190–206.

Orrin, Karen, and Stephen Skowronek. (1994). "Beyond the Iconography of Order: Notes for a New Institutionalism." In *Dynamics of American Politics: Approaches and Interpretations*, ed. Lawrence C. Dodd and Calvin Jilson, 311–30. Boulder, CO: Westview Press.

Ownby, Ted. (1990). *Subduing Satan: Religion, Recreation, and Manhood in the Rural South, 1865–1920.* Chapel Hill: University of North Carolina Press.

Panunzio, Constantine. (1934). "The Foreign Born's Reaction to Prohibition." *Sociology and Social Research* 18: 223–28.

Parker, Alison M. (1997). *Purifying America: Women, Cultural Reform, and Pro-Censorship Activism, 1873–1933.* Urbana: University of Illinois Press.

Patton, Simon E. (1891). "The Economic Basis of Prohibition." *Annals of the American Academy of Political and Social Science* 2: 59–68.

Pearson, C. C., and J. Edwin Hendricks. (1967). *Liquor and Anti-Liquor in Virginia, 1619–1919.* Durham, NC: Duke University Press.

Pegram, Thomas R. (1997). "Temperance Politics and Regional Political Culture: The Anti-Saloon League in Maryland and the South, 1907–1915." *Journal of Southern History* 63: 57–90.

———. (1998). *Battling Demon Rum: The Struggle for a Dry America, 1800–1933.* Chicago: Ivan R. Dee, 1998.

Perdue, C. W., and M. B. Gurtman. (1990). "Evidence for the Automaticity of Ageism." *Journal of Experimental Social Psychology* 26: 199–216.

Perry, Michael J. (1999). *We the People: The Fourteenth Amendment and the Supreme Court.* New York: Oxford University Press.

Practical Druggist and Review of Reviews. (1897). "The Cocaine Habit." March, 36.

Pratt, John. (2007). *Penal Populism.* New York: Routledge.

Reeves, Jimmie L., and Richard Campbell. (1994). *Cracked Coverage: Television News, the Anti-Cocaine Crusade, and the Reagan Legacy.* Durham, NC: Duke University Press.

Reiman, Jeffrey H. (1995). *The Rich Get Richer and the Poor Get Prison.* 2nd ed. Boston: Allyn and Bacon.

Reinarman, Craig, and Ceres Duskin. (2002). "The Culture's Drug Addict Imagery." In *Deviance: The Interactionist Perspective*, 8th ed., ed. Earl Rubington and Martin S. Weinberg, 32–41. Boston: Allyn and Bacon.

Reinarman, Craig, and Harry G. Levine. (1988). "The Politics of America's Latest Drug Scare." In *Freedom at Risk: Secrecy, Censorship, and Repression in the 1980s*, ed. Richard O. Curry, 251–58. Philadelphia: Temple University Press.

———. (1989). "Crack in Context: Politics and Media in the Making of a Drug Scare." *Contemporary Drug Problems* 16 (4): 535–77.

———. (1995). "The Crack Attack: America's Latest Drug Scare, 1986–92." In *Images of Issues: Typifying Contemporary Social Problems*, 2nd ed., ed. Joel Best, 147–86. New York: Aldine de Gruyter.

———, eds. (1997). *Crack in America: Demon Drugs and Social Justice.* Berkeley: University of California Press.

Report to Accompany S. 2388. (1937). 75th Cong., 1st sess., July 6. S. Rep. 883.

Riis, Jacob A. (1890/1957). *How the Other Half Lives: Studies among the Tenements of New York.* Repr. New York: Sagamore Press.

Robinson, Matthew B. (2005). "Drug War Lies 2005: White House Shenanigans in the 2005 National Drug Control Strategy." Paper presented to the annual meeting of the American Society of Criminology, Toronto, Canada, November 16.

Romero, Mary. (2005). "Review Essay: Brown Is Beautiful." *Law & Society Review* 39 (1): 11.

Romero, Mary, and Eric Margolis, eds. (2005). *The Blackwell Companion to Social Inequalities.* Malden, MA: Blackwell.

Ross, Thomas. (1996). *Just Stories: How the Law Embodies Racism and Bias.* Boston: Beacon Press.

Rush, James R. (1990). *Opium to Java: Revenue Farming and Chinese Enterprise in Colonial Indonesia, 1860–1910.* Ithaca, NY: Cornell University Press.

Ryan, Kevin F. (1998). "Globalizing the Problem: The United States and International Drug Control." In *The New War on Drugs: Symbolic Politics and Criminal Justice Policy*, ed. Eric L. Jensen and Jurg Gerber, 141–56. Cincinnati: Anderson.

Sandmeyer, Elmer Clarence. (1939). *The Anti-Chinese Movement in California*. Illinois Studies in the Social Sciences, vol. 24, no. 3. Urbana: University of Illinois Press.

Schaffer Library of Drug Policy. (1995). "DOJ Press Release: The Nation's Prison Population Grew Almost 9% Last Year." August 9. www.druglibrary.org/Schaffer/GovPubs/dojprl.htm.

Scherer, Nancy. (2005). *Scoring Points: Politicians, Activists, and the Lower Federal Court Appointment Process*. Stanford, CA: Stanford University Press.

Schlosser, Eric. (2003). *Reefer Madness: Sex, Drugs, and Cheap Labor in the American Black Market*. Boston: Houghton Mifflin.

Schneider, Anne, and Helen Ingram. (1993). "Social Construction of Target Populations: Implications for Politics and Policy." *American Political Science Review* 87 (2): 334–47.

Schuck, Peter H. (2003). *Diversity in America: Keeping Government at a Safe Distance*. Cambridge, MA: Harvard University Press.

Schwarzer, William W. (1992). "Sentencing Guidelines and Mandatory Minimums: Mixing Apples and Oranges." *Southern California Law Review* 66: 405–11.

Scully, Judith A. M. (2002). "Killing the Black Community: A Commentary on the United States War on Drugs." In *Policing the National Body*, ed. Jael Silliman and Anannya Bhattacharjee, 55–80. Cambridge, MA: South End Press.

Sears, David O., John J. Hetts, Jim Sidanius, and Lawrence Bobo. (2000). "Race in American Politics." In *Racialized Politics: The Debate about Racism in America*, ed. James Sidanius, 1–43. Chicago: University of Chicago Press.

Second Presidential Debate. (2000). October 11. Transcript available at http://www.pbs.org/newshour/bb/election/2000debates/2ndebate3.html.

Sellers, James. (1943). *The Prohibition Movement in Alabama*, 1702–1943. James Sprint Studies in History and Political Science, vol. 26. Chapel Hill: University of North Carolina Press.

Sentencing Project. (2004). "The Federal Prison Population: A Statistical Analysis." http://www.sentencingproject.org/pdfs/federalprison.pdf.

Shafer, Jack. (2005). "Crack Then. Meth Now: What the Press *Didn't* Learn from the Last Drug Panic." http://www.slate.com/toolbar.aspx?action=print&id=2124885.

Shoemaker, Pamela, Wayne Wanta, and Dawn Leggett. (1989). "Drug Coverage and Public Opinion, 1972–1986." In *Communication Campaigns about Drugs: Government, Media, and the Public*, Pamela Shoemaker, 67–80. Hillsdale, NJ: Erlbaum.

Simon, Jonathan. (1997). "Governing through Crime." In *The Crime Conundrum: Essays on Criminal Justice*, ed. Lawrence Friedman and George Fisher, 171–90. Boulder, CO: Westview.

———. (2007). *Governing through Crime: How the War on Crime Transformed American Democracy and Created a Culture of Fear*. New York: Oxford University Press.

Simonton, Thomas G. (1903). "The Increase of the Use of Cocaine among the Laity in Pittsburg." *Philadelphia Medical Journal* 11: 556–60.

Slosson, Preston William. (1935). *The Great Crusade and After, 1914–1928*. New York: Macmillan.

Smith, Elliot R. (1998). "Mental Representation and Memory." In *The Handbook of Social Psychology*, 4th ed., ed. Daniel T. Gilbert, Susan T. Fiske, and Gardner Lindzey, 1: 391–445. New York: McGraw Hill.

Smith, Rogers. (1997). *Civic Ideals: Conflicting Visions of Citizenship in U.S. History*. New Haven, CT: Yale University Press.

_____. (1999). "Historical Institutionalism and Public Law." *Law and Courts: Newsletter of the Law and Courts Section of the American Political Science Association* 9 (1): 5–7.

_____. (2004). "The Puzzling Place of Race in American Political Science." *PS,* January, 41–45.

Spillaine, Joseph. (2000). *Cocaine: From Medical Marvel to Modern Menace in the United States,* 1884–1920. Baltimore: Johns Hopkins University Press.

Spohn, Cassia C., and Jeffrey W. Spears. (2003). "Sentencing of Drug Offenders in Three Cities: Does Race/Ethnicity Make a Difference?" In *Crime Control and Social Justice: The Delicate Balance,* ed. Darnell F. Hawkins, Samuel L. Meyers Jr., and Randolph N. Stone, 197–232. Westport, CT: Greenwood Press.

Steiner, Benjamin. (2001). "The Consciousness of Crime and Punishment: Reflections on Identity Politics and Law Making in the War on Drugs." *Studies in Law, Politics, and Society* 23: 187–214.

Stelle, Charles C. (1981). *Americans and the China Opium Trade in the Nineteenth Century.* New York: Arno Press.

Sterling, Eric E. (1995). "The Sentencing Boomerang: Drug Prohibition Politics and Reform." *Villanova Law Review* 40: 383–427.

_____. (2005). "Uniform Sentencing or Effective Sentencing: How Should Federal Sentencing Be Fixed?" Op ed submission to the *Greensboro News-Record* circulated by the Open Society Institute on March 29.

Stith, Kate, and Jose A. Cabranes. (1998). *Fear of Judging: Sentencing Guidelines in the Federal Courts.* Chicago: University of Chicago Press.

Stith, Kate, and Steve Koh. (1993). "The Politics of Sentencing Reform: The Legislative History of the Federal Sentencing Guidelines." *Wake Forest Law Review* 28: 223–90.

Stone, Geoffrey R. (2004). *Perilous Times: Free Speech in Wartime.* New York: Norton.

Substance Abuse and Mental Health Services Administration. (1999). *National Household Survey on Drug Abuse.* Washington, DC: U.S. Department of Health and Human Services.

Sutherland, Edwin H. (1939). *Principles of Criminology.* Philadelphia: Lippincott.

Sutherland, Edwin H., and Donald R. Cressey. (1974). *Criminology.* 9th ed. Philadelphia: Lippencott.

Szalavitz, Maia. (1999). "Cracked Up." Salon.com, May 11.

Taifa, Nkechi. (1998). "Reflections from the Front Lines." *Federal Sentencing Reporter* 10 (January/February): 200–3.

Tajfel, H., and A. Wilkes. (1963). "Classification and Quantitative Judgment," *British Journal of Psychology* 54: 101–18.

Taylor, Stuart, Jr. (1990). "Ten Years for Two Ounces." *American Lawyer.* 65–66.

Terry, Charles E., and Mildred Pellens. (1928/1970). *The Opium Problem.* Repr. Montclair, NJ: Patterson Smith.

Timberlake, James H. (1963). *Prohibition and the Progressive Movement,* 1900–1920. New York: Atheneum.

Time. (1955). "Investigations: Dope from Red China." March 21, 35–36.

Tonry, Michael. (1995). *Malign Neglect—Race, Crime, and Punishment in America.* New York: Oxford University Press.

_____. (2004). *Thinking about Crime: Sense and Sensibility in American Penal Culture.* New York: Oxford University Press.

Tonry, Michael, and Kathleen Hatlestad, eds. (1997). *Sentencing Reform in Overcrowded Times: A Comparative Perspective.* New York: Oxford University Press.

Travis, Jeremy. (2005). *But They All Come Back: Facing the Challenges of Prisoner Reentry.* Washington, DC: Urban Institute Press.

Treaster, Joseph B. (1993). "Two Federal Judges, in Protest, Refuse to Accept Drug Cases." *New York Times,* April 17, Metro section, 1.

Tyrrell, Ian. (1991). *Woman's World/Woman's Empire: The Woman's Christian Temperance Union in International Perspective,* 1880–1930. Chapel Hill: University of North Carolina Press.

Uelmen, Gerald F. (1992). "Federal Sentencing Guidelines: A Cure Worse Than the Disease." *American Criminal Law Review* 29: 899–905.

Unrau, William. (1996). *White Man's Wicked Water: The Alcohol Trade and Prohibition in Indian Country,* 1802–92. Lawrence: University of Kansas Press.

USA Today. (2006). "Crack Convicts Getting Less Prison Time." January 13.

U.S. Department of Health and Human Services. Substance Abuse and Mental Health Services Administration (SAMHSA). (2006). *National Survey on Drug Use and Health.* http://www.oas.samhsa.gov/nhsda.htm.

U.S. General Accounting Office. (2002). "Strategic Objective: An Effective System of Justice." http://www.gao.gov/atext/strobj15.txt.

U.S. News and World Report. (1959). "Another Problem for the Big Cities: A Federal Official and a District Attorney Report on Narcotics." April 6, 74–80.

U.S. Sentencing Commission. (1991a). *Mandatory Minimum Penalties in the Federal Criminal Justice System.* Special Report to Congress, as directed by Section 1703 of Public Law 101-647. August. Washington, DC: U.S. Sentencing Commission.

_____. (1991b). *The Federal Sentencing Guidelines: A Report on the Operation of the Guidelines System and Short-Term Impacts on Disparity in Sentencing, Use of Incarceration, and Prosecutorial Discretion and Plea Bargaining.* Washington, DC: Government Printing Office.

_____. (1995a). *Update on the Activities of the U.S. Sentencing Commission.* September. Washington, DC: U.S. Sentencing Commission.

_____. (1995b). *Cocaine and Federal Sentencing Policy.* Special Report to Congress, as directed by Section 280006 of Public Law 103-322. February. Washington, DC: U.S. Sentencing Commission.

_____. (1997). *Cocaine and Federal Sentencing Policy.* Special Report to Congress, as directed by Section 2 of Public Law 104-38. April. Washington, DC: U.S. Sentencing Commission.

_____. (2002). *Report to the Congress: Cocaine and Federal Sentencing Policy.* Washington, DC: Government Printing Office. http://www.ussc.gov/r_congress/02crack/2002crackrpt.htm.

_____. (2003). *Fifteen Years of Guideline Sentencing.* Washington, DC: Government Printing Office.

_____. (2004a). *Fifteen Years of Guideline Sentencing.* Washington, DC: Government Printing Office. Available at http://www.ussc.gov/15 year/15year.htm.

_____. (2004b). 2003 *Sourcebook of Federal Sentencing Statistics.* Washington, DC: Government Printing Office.

Walker, Samuel, Cassia Spohn, and Miriam DeLone (2004). *The Color of Justice: Race, Ethnicity, and Crime in America.* 3rd ed. Belmont, CA: Wadsworth.

Walton, Hanes. (1970). "Another Force for Disfranchisement: Blacks and the Prohibitionists in Tennessee." *Journal of Human Relations* 18: 728–38.

Walton, Hanes, and James Taylor. (1971). "Blacks and the Southern Prohibition Movement." *Phylon* 32: 247–59.

Wang, Lu-in (2006). *Discrimination by Default: How Racism Becomes Routine.* New York:
New York University Press.

Warburton, Clark. (1932). *Economic Results of Prohibition.* New York: Columbia University Press.

Wegner, D. M., and R. M. Wenzlaff. (1996). "Mental Control." In *Social Psychology: Handbook of Basic Mechanisms and Processes,* ed. E. T. Higgins and A. Kruglanski, 466–92.
New York: Guilford.

Weich, Ronald, and Carlos Angulo (2000). "Racial Disparities in the American Criminal
Justice System." In *Justice on Trial: Racial Disparities in the American Criminal Justice
System,* 185–218. Report prepared for the Leadership Conference on Civil Rights and
the Leadership Conference Education Fund.

Western, Bruce. (2006). *Punishment and Inequality in America.* New York: Russell Sage
Foundation.

Wexler, Kathryn. (1995). "Charges of Racially Selective Prosecution Rise in Crack Cocaine Cases." *Washington Post,* August 21.

White, John E. (1908). "Prohibition: The New Task and Opportunity of the South." *South
Atlantic Quarterly* 7: 130–42.

Wilkins, William. (1991). "The United States Sentencing Commission: Its Many Missions."
Federal Probation 55 (4): 26–30.

Williams, Edward Huntington. (1914a). "The Drug-Habit Menace in the South." *Medical
Recorder* 85: 247–49.

———. (1914b). "Negro Cocaine Fiends Are a New Southern Menace: Murder and Insanity Increasing Among Lower Class Blacks Because They Have Taken to 'Sniffing'
Since Deprived of Whisky by Prohibition." *New York Times,* February 8, 12.

Williams, Henry Smith. (1938). *Drug Addicts Are Human Beings: The Story of Our Billion-
Dollar Drug Racket.* Washington, DC: Shaw.

Williams, Linda Faye. (2003). *The Constraint of Race: The Legacies of White Skin Privilege
in America.* University Park: Pennsylvania State University Press.

Willrich, Michael. (2003). *City of Courts: Socializing Justice in Progressive Era Chicago.*
New York: Cambridge University Press.

Wills, E. B., and P. K. Stockton. (1881). *Debates and Proceedings of the Constitutional
Convention of the State of California, Convened at the City of Sacramento, September
28, 1878.* Sacramento: State Office.

Winant, Howard. (1998). "Racism Today: Continuity and Change in the Post-Civil Rights
Era." *Ethnic and Racial Studies* 21 (4): 755–66.

———. (2004). *The New Politics of Race.* Minneapolis: University of Minnesota Press.

Windlesham, Lord. (1998). *Politics, Punishment, and Populism.* New York: Oxford University Press.

Wren, Christopher. (1997). Reno and Top Drug Official Urge Smaller Gap in Cocaine Sentences." *New York Times,* July 22, 1, A12.

Wright, Hamilton. (1910). *Report on the International Opium Commission and on the
Opium Problem as Seen Within the United States and Its Possessions.* 61st Cong., 2d
sess., February 21. S. Doc. 377.

Yosso, Tara J., and Daniel G. Solorzano. (2005). "Conceptualizing a Critical Race Theory in Sociology." In *The Blackwell Companion to Social Inequalities*, ed. Mary Romero and Eric Margolis, 117–46. Malden, MA: Blackwell.

Zatz, Marjorie S. (2000). "The Convergence of Race, Ethnicity, Gender, and Class on Court Decision Making: Looking Toward the 21st Century." In *Policies, Processes, and Decisions of the Criminal Justice System*, vol. 3. Washington, DC: National Institute of Justice.

Zatz, Marjorie S., and Richard P. Krecker Jr. (2003). "Anti-Gang Initiatives as Racialized Policy." In *Crime Control and Social Justice: The Delicate Balance*, ed. Darnell F. Hawkins, Samuel L. Meyers Jr., and Randolph N. Stone, 173–96. Westport, CT: Greenwood Press.

Zimring, Franklin E. and Gordon Hawkins. (1992). *The Search for Rational Drug Control*. Cambridge: Cambridge University Press.

index

abolitionists, 51

Adams, Samuel Hopkins, 67

addict(s), types of, 171n9

addiction: as disease, 79; as vice, 79; opiate, "the soldier's disease," 66

affirmative action, 6

African Americans, 1, 6, 10, 16, 17, 25, 82–84, 86–88, 91–92, 98, 100–102; alcohol use and stereotypes, 38, 40–41, 45, 48–58, 61–63; "Black Codes," 154; cocaine use, 74–78; crack cocaine and, 104, 106–7, 109–10, 113–14; death penalty disparities, 116, 146; heroin addiction, 94–96; imprisonment, rates of, 2, 14, 27, 32, 34, 102, 109–19, 120–21, 127–28, 130; joblessness, 3; marijuana use, 18; sentencing disparities, 23–24, 34, 141–61; voting rights, loss of, 20–21, 54–57, 61

Age Discrimination in Employment Act (ADEA), 159–60, 177n54

Agent Orange trial, 149

Agnew, Spiro, 97, 101

Alabama Baptist, 56

Albert, Peter, 70

alcohol, 12, 36–62, 97, 101; beer, 37, 44, 48; cider, hard, 37; rum, 37; whisky, 37, 74, 137; wine, 37, 44, 48, 65, 66, 137

Altheide, David, 29, 172–73n16 (chap. 4)

American Bar Association, 59, 94, 166

American Civil Liberties Union, 97

American Federation of Labor, 70

American Legion, 59

American Medical Association, 86, 94

American Pharmaceutical Association, 75

American Society of Criminology, 28

Amodio, D. M., 158

Anderson, Elijah, 169n2

Anderson, Richard, 150

Andreae, Percy, 46

Anslinger, Harry, 81, 83–88, 91, 93–94, 103

Anti-Chinese Union, 69

Anti-Drug Abuse Act (1986), 13, 92, 109, 111–15, 116, 120–24

Anti-Drug Abuse Act (1988), 13, 92, 109, 115, 120–24

Anti-Saloon League, 38, 40–42, 46, 47, 57

anti-Semitism, 47

anti-slavery movement, 39

Armey, Dick, 149, 176n25

Armstrong v. United States, 159

Bailey, Pearce, 78

Baker, Ray Stannard, 55

Banaji, M. R., 27, 157

Barker, Joan Marshall, 40

Barr, Burton, 132

Basic Liberation of Smokers and Sympathizers of Marijuana (BLOSSOM), 97

Baum, Dan, 98

Bayer Pharmaceutical Company, 66

Becker, Howard S., 31, 34

Beckett, Katherine, 3, 4, 6, 7, 18, 35, 89, 103, 104, 106, 107, 117, 164

Behr, Edward, 61

Belenko, Steven R., 19, 103, 104

Bell, Derrick, 9

Bennett, William J., 105, 143–44, 175n5

Ben-Yehuda, Nachman, 8, 117

Dutch: opium policy in Indonesia, 75; sailors, 68

Eagly, Alice, 157
Ecstasy, 19
Edelman, Murray, 31, 32, 117
Edelman, Peter, 169n3
Edley, Christopher, 177n50
Edsall, Mary D., 104
Edsall, Thomas Byrne, 104
Edwards v. United States, 147
Eighteenth Amendment, 37, 43, 48, 59–60
Eighth Amendment, 145, 147, 153
Eisenberg, Theodore, 156
Eisenstein, James, 30
Elliot, James, 65
Elwood, William N., 104, 108
Equal Economic Opportunity Commission (EEOC), 159
"equal protection under the law." *See* Fourteenth Amendment
Erickson, Patricia, 4
ethnic vice industries, 19–20, 45, 119
Evangelicals. *See* religious groups
Evans, Daniel J., 111
Evans, Nancy, 157
Everett, Ronald S., 110

Fattah, Chaka, 133
FBI (Federal Bureau of Investigation), 99, 103
Federal Bureau of Internal Revenue (U.S. Treasury Department). *See* Bureau of Internal Revenue
Federal Bureau of Investigation, 99, 103
Federal Bureau of Narcotics. *See* Bureau of Narcotics
Federal Judicial Center, 126, 127
Fifteenth Amendment, 55
Fiske, Susan, 27, 156, 158
Flaherty, Mary Pat, 124, 142, 145
Flake, Jeff, 133
Fletcher, George P., 21
Food and Drug Administration, U.S., 99
Foreign Relations Committee, U.S., 76
Forrester, J. Owen, 152, 153
Fossier, A. E., 82
Fourteenth Amendment: "equal protection under the law," 23–26, 145–46, 148, 153–55,168; "due process," 147
Foxcraft, Frank, 41
Frank, Barney, 111, 133, 134

Frankel, Marvin, 122
Franklin, John Hope, 55
Freed, Daniel, 145
Freud, Sigmund, 66
Fritsvold, Erik, 6
Frymer, Paul, 10, 11, 34, 134, 142
Fugitive Slave Law, 142, 150

Gaertner, S. L., 157
Garland, David, 93, 163
Garrison, William Lloyd, 51
Gelacak, Michael, 136–37, 174n14
General Federation of Women's Clubs, 47
Gerber, Jurg, 98, 105, 108
Gerber, Rudolph J., 96, 99
Gerstmann, Evan, 154, 177n50
Gertz, Marc, 102
Gest, Ted, 119
Gilens, Marin, 8
Gingrich, Newt, 149, 176n25
Goddard, James, 99
Goffman, Erving, 31
Golub, Andrew Lang, 17
Gompers, Samuel, 70
Goode, Erich, 8, 108, 117, 118
Good Templars, 52
Gonzales, Alberto, 164
Gordon, Diana R., 3, 89, 105
Gordon, Ernest, 47
Gore, Al, 33, 170n2
Grantham, Dewey, 41–42, 48, 54
Grassley, Charles, 142
Graves, John Temple, 53–54
Gray, Mike, 86
Great Britain, 55, 72–73; and opiate addiction, 94; youth disturbances, 117
Greenberg, David, 7, 102
Greene, Harold, 149, 153, 176n24
Greenwald, A. G., 27, 157
Griffith, D. W., 56
Griggs v. Duke Power Company, 154
Guinier, Lani, 9, 14, 27, 143
Gurtman, M. B., 157
Gusfield, Joseph, 45–46

Hagan, John, 19, 93, 119
Handbook of Social Psychology (Gilbert, Fiske, and Lindzey), 157
Hanes, W. Travis, III, 73
Harcourt, Bernard E., 128
Harmelin v. Michigan, 145–46